Rosemarie Jarski is as British as Greg Rusedski. She lives in Britain with a British Bulldog named Adolf. The happiest moment of her life was when she finally twigged the rules of the game, Mornington Crescent. The ringtone on her mobile is 'Always Look on the Bright Side of Life'.

For Henry: Great, British, and a Wit

GREAT BRITISH WIT

ROSEMARIE JARSKI

EBURY
PRESS

9 10

Copyright © 2005 Rosemarie Jarski

First published 2005 by Ebury Press,
an imprint of Random House,
20 Vauxhall Bridge Road, London SW1V 2SA

Random House Australia (Pty) Limited
20 Alfred Street, Milsons Point, Sydney, New South Wales 2061, Australia

Random House New Zealand Limited
18 Poland Road, Glenfield, Auckland 10, New Zealand

Random House South Africa (Pty) Limited
Isle of Houghton, Corner of Boundary Road & Carse O'Gowrie,
Houghton 2198, South Africa

The Random House Group Limited Reg. No. 954009

www.randomhouse.co.uk

Printed and bound in the UK by CPI Mackays, Chatham ME5 8TD

A CIP catalogue record for this book is available from the British Library

Cover design by Keenan
Union flag cover image © Getty Images
Winston Churchill cover image © Corbis
Interior design by seagulls

ISBN 9780091906313

CONTENTS

SCIENCE AND TECHNOLOGY

BODY, MIND AND SOUL

INTRODUCTION

—Where would we be without a sense of humour?
—Germany.

Well, I guess Willy Rushton's un-PC joke has set the tone. But you wouldn't have laughed if there wasn't a kernel of truth in it. The fact is, we British are defined by our sense of humour as much as the Germans are defined by their lack of one. To be British is to be a comedian waiting to be discovered.

In Britain, we place a premium on mirth. Victoria Wood said: 'To be able to make people laugh is the nicest thing you can do for somebody – apart from a blowjob.' We are willing to overlook serious faults in a person if they can tickle our funny bone. The late Alan Clark was a cad, an adulterer, a multi-millionaire, a Tory minister and a toff but he was redeemed by the brilliance of his wit. (Julie Burchill said she loved listening to the audio tape of his diaries because his voice struck her as 'half George Sanders and half Scar from *The Lion King*'.) If only Hitler had had a few good one-liners up his sleeve, the course of history might have been so different. 'It's ze vay I tell zem.'

Humour is one of only three things we take seriously in this country (the other two being football and IKEA). We're not hugely miffed when our politicians let us down – after all they are only running the country – but if someone's witticism flops or their punch line fails to connect, they are shown no mercy. To really offend the British, don't criticise our driving, or our intelligence, or our bedroom abilities, accuse us, instead, of having no sense of humour, and there'll be pistols at dawn, guaranteed. Only in the English language is it an insult to accuse somebody of trying to be funny.

Humour is the *lingua franca,* the *modus operandi* and the *raison d'être* for all communication in this green and pleasant land. In every walk of life – from sink estate to stately pile – the antic spirit rules. 'For what do we live,' asked Jane Austen, 'but to make sport for our neighbours and laugh at them in our turn?'

The British are, by nature, a reserved and easily embarrassed people, so humour is the oil that lubricates the social wheels and keeps the motor running. We crack a joke to break the ice or to darn a hole in a conversation. We also use wit to woo. Not so much 'Come up and see me sometime', as 'Come up and see me, *make me smile'*. In the Lonely Hearts columns, GSOH (Good Sense of Humour) trumps OHAC (Own House and Car) and even TLC (Tender Loving Care) as the most desirable quality in a potential partner – so I'm told.

Humour is also a coping mechanism in times of trouble – like when it turns out that the person you meet through the Lonely Hearts columns does *not* have a GSOH or OHAC or even any TLC but is, in fact, a prize SOB – not that that's ever happened to me, of course not, no, really, never.

Our use of humour as a safety valve was brought home to me for real last year while I was on a Mediterranean cruise. An outbreak of food poisoning (I blame the crab salad) confined practically half the ship to the sick bay. As well as Brits, there were Italians, Germans, French and Americans. Now, sickness has a way of bringing out a person's true character, but I was unprepared for how readily we all reverted to national stereotypes: The Italians prayed, the Germans organised, the French grizzled, the Americans threatened to sue, and the Brits – well, between bouts of projectile vomiting and violent stomach cramps, we joshed, we joked, we giggled, we guffawed; we sang rousing choruses of our unofficial national anthem, 'Always Look on the Bright Side of Life' – all to the dismay and bafflement of our fellow passengers. But we were just doing what came naturally. I made friends for life during that vomit-fest and look back on it as the highlight of my holiday (though I still can't look a crab straight in the eye).

The graver the situation, the keener our sense of humour. Englishman, John McCarthy, and Irishman, Brian Keenan, were held hostage together in Beirut for more than four years. Not a barrel of laughs, you'd have thought. Yet both men attest to how vital humour was to their survival. In his moving account of his incarceration, *An Evil Cradling,* Keenan describes how McCarthy would do impressions of the guards 'with a precision and zaniness that reduced their brutality to insignificance'. Their humour, says

Keenan, was not heroism; rather, it was a shield held up against the horror, and a way to wrest back a degree of control. Though totally different personalities, the two men bonded through humour and forged a strong and lasting friendship. Similarly, during World War II, shared laughter pulled people together and helped us through Our Darkest Hour.

So much for its value and benefits, but just what *is* British Humour? Many scholarly works have been written on the subject, but I confess I haven't read any of them. What's the point? How can you anatomise a beast as diverse as British Humour? It's Oscar Wilde and Tommy Cooper; *Pride and Prejudice* and *Carry on Camping*; Samuel Johnson and Monty Python; *Private Eye* and *Viz*; an epigram and a raspberry. British Humour is silly, sardonic, nasty, naughty, wry, surreal and nutty. (Did I just inadvertently name the Seven Dwarfs?)

The hallmark of British humour is irony. Slit the vein of a Brit and stand well back if you don't want to get your Jimmy Choos spattered with the stuff. Not that it is necessary to have read a single page of Jane Austen to be ironic: in Britain, it's as instinctive as binge drinking. So, what is irony? Let *Blackadder*'s answer to Einstein, the all-knowing Baldrick, enlighten you: 'Irony is like goldy and bronzy only it's made out of iron.' So now you know.

Understatement is a species of irony and Brits aren't bad at that either. A vintage cartoon depicts two Englishmen who have just conquered the Matterhorn, regarding the view from the top. 'Not bad,' says one. 'No,' says the other, 'but you needn't rave about it like a love-struck poet!'

Understatement can also mean underreacting. 'The English have an extraordinary ability for flying into a great calm,' Alexander Woollcott quipped. The famous British stiff upper lip has lately begun to wobble (witness the very public display of grief after the death of Diana, Princess of Wales) but it has not wilted yet. We'd still sooner die than make a scene: 'I always thought the worst thing about drowning was having to call "Help!" You must look such a fool. It's put me against drowning,' said Basil Boothroyd. We still prefer to play down our achievements: 'It's only jumping into a sandpit,' said world triple jump champion, Jonathan Edwards. And we still tend to make light of serious matters: When George Carman Q.C. was diagnosed with the prostate cancer that would kill him, he announced that he was 'having a little local difficulty'. Our determination to treat serious matters trivially and trivial matters seriously is one British tradition it would be tragic to lose. As G.K. Chesterton reminds us: 'Angels can fly because they take things lightly.' That goes for Angles too.

Our phlegmatic attitude to life does not mean that our humour is tame. On the contrary. Like the Ice Queen, there is a sliver of ice in the heart of the best British wits. 'If you can't annoy someone, there's little point in writing,' said Kingsley Amis, who daily dipped his quill in vinegar: 'The museum was full of imitations of Henry Moore and, worse still, Henry Moore himself.' Except when we're driving and some f****** b****** cuts us up, the British eschew vulgar abuse in favour of the witty insult, gift-wrapped in an elegant turn of phrase (and all the more lethal for that). The cutting comment, the wicked gibe, the waspish retort are used in a variety of ways: to fend off a verbal attack, to put someone in their place and, sometimes, just for the sheer hell of it... British wit is a blood sport more ruthless than fox-hunting.

So, what is the prey that British wits, with their trusty hounds of humour and irony baying at their feet, pursue remorselessly to the death? As Brando said in *The Wild One*, 'What've you got?' The pompous, the pious, the pretentious – that'll do for starters. Michael Bentine said the aim of 'The Goons' was 'to show that sacred cows all have hooves of clay'. John Osborne spoke of his 'beholden duty to kick against the pricks'. Malcolm Muggeridge referred to 'the gargoyle grinning beneath the steeple'. British wit is very often a salute to Authority – of the two-fingered variety. Other quarries include snobs, pseuds, bores, clever dicks (unless they wear their learning lightly à la Stephen Fry), political correctness, oh, and let's not forget one of our favourite whipping boys, 'Johnny Foreigner'.

The PC-police have done their darnedest to convince us that foreigners aren't funny, but they may as well tell us that the Pope is Muslim or Tony Blair a socialist. Anyone who doubts the funniness of foreigners need only be reminded of two words: 'The French'. Taking 'le michel' out of *les Français* is part of our heritage, our patriotic duty, and, when we're not busy buying up their farmhouses or getting sloshed on their Beaujolais, it's an obligation we carry out *très bien*. In fact, there's only one group of people we poke fun at more than our Gallic neighbours...no, not the Germans, but ourselves.

Self-mockery is at the heart of British humour. As one of the lesser known of the Beatitudes says, 'Blessed is the person who knows how to laugh at himself, for he will never cease to be amused.' Barbara Cartland, perhaps our most celebrated novelist after Jeffrey Archer, said: 'I don't mind journalists going on about my pills and my pink frocks and sending me up teasingly because nobody sends up Barbara Cartland better than I do myself.' There is an element of 'laugh at ourselves before anyone else can', but it cuts deeper than that: to laugh at ourselves is to see ourselves through someone else's eyes, to acknowledge that we are not perfect, and might even be wrong. Tolerance, fair play and common sense – three qualities for which our nation is renowned – are all born of this ability.

The British gift for humorous self-denigration is one we share with only two other societies: the Jews and the Poles. Both the Jewish and Polish peoples have a history of oppression so, for them, self-deprecation is a form of self-defence. The curious thing about the British is that we made fun of ourselves from a position of power. Even when the Empire was at its height, we made jokes at our own expense, smugly secure in our own superiority.

Sometimes, it's only when we rub up against other cultures that we realise how different our sense of humour is. Hop across The Channel and tune into French, Spanish or German TV on a Saturday night and it's clear that European humour hasn't evolved beyond the banana-skin stage. After the single currency, you dread to think what Brussels might have lined up next. The single humour: 'Euro-Humour'. That's one referendum guaranteed to have us breaking down the doors of the polling stations to vote in.

Across The Pond, you may imagine it's a different ballgame; after all, we share a common language and we're saturated by American culture. Don't be fooled. Anyone who has spent time in America knows that British and American laff-traks aren't actually in synch at all. John Cleese, now resident in Santa Barbara, tells how, when he was due to have a hip-replacement operation, he announced to his American pals that instead of titanium, his new hip would be 'all-wood, the finest, agèd oak, polished with beeswax'. 'And they all believed me,' said Cleese, 'but none of my Brit friends did.'

The American mindset – literal, sentimental, and hellbent on happy endings, doesn't sit comfortably with a British temperament soaked in cynicism and marinated in bile. It's one reason why British sitcoms rarely 'translate' across the Atlantic. When a US version of the classic sitcom, *Porridge*, was mooted, the American producer wanted the location changed to Florida so that when the prisoners looked out of the window they would see palm trees and sunshine. In the words of Norman Stanley Fletcher: 'Naff orf!' And can you imagine an American version of Monty Python's Dead Parrot sketch: '…It's not pining, it's passed on. This parrot is no more. This is an ex-parrot – no, wait, it's moving! Why, it's alive! Gee, I guess it was only napping!' (cue: group hug).

What also distinguishes British humour from its foreign counterparts is how pervasive it is. Humour is not something we add on to our lives; it *is* our take on life. Which begs the question, what shapes our sense of humour? Are we born with it? Is it something in the water? Is it the climate? Could it be the geography of being an island race?

Certainly, the English language has a profound effect on how we laugh. We take it for granted, but without it, the only British humour we'd be left with would be Charlie Chaplin, Mr Bean and Sooty. The English language is rich and versatile, brimming with opportunities for playfulness and mischief in sound and sense. We have been blessed with wordsmiths able to convert this excellent raw material into comic gold.

The English language allows us to indulge our national passion for wordplay, and of all the delights, our favourite has to be innuendo. 'The great thing about a *double entendre* is that it can only mean one thing,' said Ronnie Barker. There's Kenneth Williams in *Round the Horne*, the entire genre of 'Carry On' films, and who can forget Mrs Slocombe's pussy? Julian Clary and Graham Norton have built their careers on it (innuendo not Mrs Slocombe's pussy). But, for my money, the prize for the filthiest (and therefore the funniest) practitioner goes to Humphrey Lyttelton. Each week, as host of BBC Radio's *I'm Sorry I Haven't a Clue*, Humph introduces the scorer, 'the lovely Samantha', in a litany of innuendo so lewd it would bring a blush to the cheeks of Graham Norton. Try this for size (no, that wasn't it): 'Samantha is an expert cook and is often to be seen at the nearby inn, enjoying some of the local pork in cider.' Humph's butter-wouldn't-melt delivery of such lines serves only to heighten their suggestiveness, but most credit must go to the writer, Iain Pattinson, who invents the riot of rudery.

I'm Sorry I Haven't a Clue epitomises a very British brand of humour which revels in silliness for its own sake. The 'antidote to panel games' makes no concessions to any influences beyond these shores. The purity of its pottiness, the undiluted essence of Britishness it embodies and celebrates, make it beloved by Brits – and impenetrable to non-Brits. Listeners are made to feel that we belong to an exclusive club, in on all the in-jokes that have accumulated over the 30-odd years the show has been running. Of course, part of the pleasure of an in-joke is the knowledge that others are excluded from that pleasure – a point neatly illustrated by this plaintive plea posted on the BBC's online message-board: 'I listen to *I'm Sorry I Haven't a Clue*, but Mornington Crescent was already established by the time I became a regular. There was never an item, 'New Listeners Start Here' or something like that. Although I know the London tube quite well, I couldn't fathom the game, the aim or the sense. Should I be asking for an explanation in a brown envelope? My first sin is that I live in Brussels.'

That all lines lead to Mornington Crescent is the first lesson anyone who is serious about understanding British humour needs to learn. Forget Norman Tebbit's 'cricket test'; if there has to be a test for British loyalty and citizenship, it ought to be this: 'What are the rules of Mornington Crescent?' Anyone who comes within a gnat's crotchet of explaining them correctly is clearly one of us and should be welcomed to these shores with open arms and a burst on the swanny kazoo.

Whether our chuckle muscle is more highly developed than the rest of the world's, I could not possibly comment; it wouldn't be British to blow our own swanny kazoo. That said, I couldn't imagine any book called 'Wit' offering an embarrassment of comic riches equal to one prefixed by the word 'British'. ('The English know how to boast modestly,' wrote George Mikes.) You could fill volume after volume without ever missing Groucho, Woody or Dorothy (who they?)

Welcome to *Great British Wit*. The brief was simple: to amass the greatest collection of British wit and humour ever. No pressure then. At the risk of upsetting the sort of people who complain when the Union flag is flown upside down, I should warn you that in this book 'British' has been used in the loosest possible sense of the word. It would have been churlish to gather a bouquet of the rose, the thistle and the daffodil, and leave out the shamrock – and the green carnation.

The quotations chosen are as varied as British Humour itself. Expect to find something old, something new, something barbed, and something blue. Like the best disabled toilet or tart's knickers, the book has been arranged for easy access. Whatever your cup of tea – be it sex, vicars, cricket, class or the amber nectar itself, you are signposted swiftly to your chosen subject for instant light relief.

Non-Brits who stumble across this volume en route to Madame Tussaud's may be surprised to find no category for 'British Eccentrics' since they are considered to be as much a part of the fabric of British society as Beefeaters and Lager Louts. The reason for their absence is simple: I didn't find any. Which could either mean that there are *no* eccentrics in our isles or else we are *all* eccentrics…

As a Brit, I'm too close to the subject to make a judgement on that. 'No fish ever defined water,' said Marshall McLuhan. With this in mind, a section of the book has been given over to the ethnically-disadvantaged, i.e. non-Brits, to shine a more dispassionate light on we soggy islanders. A word of warning: not all are Anglophiles, so don't expect a love-in.

So, what does it all add up to? First and foremost, a hilarious romp through the annals of British comedy from Chaucer to 'Chubby' Brown. But, also, if you care to look closer, a portrait of a nation. 'Nothing shows a man's character more than what he laughs at,' wrote Goethe. Draw your own conclusions, but for what they're worth, I'll leave you with a few random thoughts that struck me about what it means to be British: we value friendship over romantic love; we prefer the cloud to the silver lining; we may no longer rule the waves but we love to waive the rules; our greatest fear is boredom; we are staunch defenders of freedom, stalwart upholders of justice, mad as hatters, daft as brushes, nutty as fruitcakes and when it comes down to it, I wouldn't want to be anything else, not for all the tea in China.

Put the kettle on and carry on laughing.

GREAT
BRITAIN

GREAT BRITAIN AND THE BRITISH

Britain, Britain, Britain…it's been called 'Heaven on Earth' and it's easy to see why – Ribena is plentiful, shoe laces are available in different lengths, and there's a new Fred Bassett cartoon strip in the *Daily Mail* every day. But let's not forget the people of Britain for it is they what make it good and nice. Yippety doo-dah! **TOM BAKER, NARRATOR,** *LITTLE BRITAIN*

We are a small country with a large sense of its own importance.

DAVID WALLIAMS

We may be a small country but we are a nation of Shakespeare, Churchill, the Beatles, Sean Connery, Harry Potter, David Beckham's right foot…David Beckham's left foot, come to that. **RICHARD CURTIS**

The glories of Britain were the plays of Shakespeare, the presumption of innocence, the herbaceous border and the great British breakfast. Now, Shakespeare is sidelined as a Dead White Male, and two of the other three have lost out to an age of David Blunkett and muesli.

JOHN MORTIMER

Cool Britannia? What, I should like to know, is so great about being cool, anyway? …Uncool people never hurt anybody – all they do is collect stamps, read science-fiction books and stand on the end of railway platforms staring at trains. **BEN ELTON**

USA: Britney Spears; *The Matrix*; *Harry Potter*
Canada: *Finding Nemo*; Paris Hilton; Inuyasha
Australia: *Australian Idol*; Britney Spears; Christina Aguilera
Great Britain: Prince Charles; *EastEnders*; Winnie the Pooh

MOST POPULAR INTERNET SEARCHES, 2003

There are only three things against living in Britain: the place, the climate and the people.   **JIMMY EDWARDS**

Sheep with a nasty side.   **CYRIL CONNOLLY**

Now that the BBC has enjoyed such success with *100 Great Britons*, the obvious sequel is *100 Worst Britons*. A fascination of the new series would be the not inconsiderable number of names that fall within both lists.   **JOHN GODFREY**

I find the word 'Brit', a recent, and I suspect, Irish coinage, objectionable, as it lumps us with the Scots and Welsh, with a suggestion of football hooliganism thrown in.   **PAUL JOHNSON**

ENGLAND AND THE ENGLISH

We are English, that is one good fact.   **OLIVER CROMWELL**

I get down on my knees every night and thank God for making me English.   **LT. COL. ALFRED DANIEL WINTLE**

Not to be English was for my family so terrible a handicap as almost to place the sufferer in the permanent invalid class.   **OSBERT LANCASTER**

There are hardly two things more peculiarly English than Welsh rarebit and Irish stew.   **G.K. CHESTERTON**

Nobody can be truly English until he can say 'really' in 17 different ways.   **PAUL JOHNSON**

The world is a place on which England is found.   **G.K. CHESTERTON**

Warm beer, invincible green suburbs, dog lovers.

JOHN MAJOR

So little, England. Little music. Little art. Timid. Tasteful. Nice.

ALAN BENNETT

I shall tell you what is so good about England: it is the only country in the world that isn't semi-detached. **CAPTAIN PEACOCK,** *ARE YOU BEING SERVED?*

England is like an old gentleman who married late in life, and married his cook. **SYLVIA TOWNSEND WARNER**

A family with the wrong members in control – that, perhaps, is as near as one can come to describing England in a phrase. **GEORGE ORWELL**

In England, we have come to rely upon a comfortable time-lag of 50 years or a century intervening between the perception that something ought to be done and a serious attempt to do it. **H.G. WELLS**

We English have been in a muddle for so long that most of us now regard it as our normal environment. **ERIC LINKLATER**

This country cherishes the belief that the sounding alarm is only the dinner gong signalling second helpings. **JOHN PEYTON**

The only possible way there'd be an uprising in this country would be if they banned car boot sales and caravanning. **VICTORIA WOOD**

—What is the population England?
—Thirty millions, mostly fools. **THOMAS CARLYLE**

This once glorious land of Henry The Eighth and West Ham United.

ALF GARNETT, *THE THOUGHTS OF CHAIRMAN ALF*

The funniest thing of all is that even if you love England and belong to it, you still can't make head or tail of it. **G.K. CHESTERTON**

LONDON

Your question for £10: What is the capital of England? Is it: a) London b) Somewhere else c) Somewhere else entirely d) A worm.

FRENCH AND SAUNDERS

Welcome to London's litter-filled West End – sorry, that should be *glitter*-filled West End. There's a missing 'g', as in the phrase, 'Arnold Schwarzenegger's a bit ropey.' **STEPHEN FRY**

Definition of a Londoner: one who has never been to Madame Tussaud's.

CRAIG WILLIS

I am a true Cockney: I was born in Cadogan Gardens. **BETTY KENWARD**

People think Islington is all canapés with Tony and Cherie. But we have council estates the size of the Gobi Desert. **TONY PARSONS**

I have nothing against Hampstead; I used to live there myself in the days when I was an intellectual. I gave that up when I became Leader of the House. **NORMAN ST JOHN-STEVAS**

Crowds without company, and dissipation without pleasure. **EDWARD GIBBON**

When a man is tired of London, he is tired of life; for there is in London all that life can afford. **SAMUEL JOHNSON**

PLACES

Did you hear Fred West's house is up for sale? What a horrible place that would be to live...Gloucester. FRANK SKINNER

He chose to live in Manchester, a wholly incomprehensible choice for any free man to make. MR JUSTICE MELFORD STEVENSON

I've never seen such a place for wanton women as Northampton. GEORGE BORROW

The spa town of Cheltenham first found favour during the Regency period, largely due to the patronage of the Duke of Wellington, who popularised his eponymous footwear here, Lord Sandwich who brought the leading convenience food item that bears his name and Viscount Picnic, who introduced the two. Their alfresco social gatherings were invariably also graced by Alfred Thermos, third Earl of Bovril, and Sir Jonathan-James Wasp. HUMPHREY LYTTELTON

Very flat, Norfolk. NOËL COWARD, *PRIVATE LIVES*

East Angular – that's abroad innit? JADE GOODY, *BIG BROTHER*

We also saw Haworth, which surpassed even my appetite for gloomy churchyards. Glutted, is the only word for it. SYLVIA TOWNSEND WARNER

Chester is the historic Cheshire city whose good people once returned Gyles Brandreth as an MP. And who can blame them? HUMPHREY LYTTELTON

I always feel like I want to gather up all the locals in Chinatown and go, 'Guys, in what way is this a town? At best, what you've got here is a novelty street.' RICKY GERVAIS

I'm enjoying being in Blackpool. You know what I did this afternoon?
I had a blow on the front. **JULIAN CLARY**

What is about Blackpool, this jewelled magnet, that draws the Barnsley
jet-set back year after year? It is the death wish. **SPIKE MILLIGAN**

Wensleydale lies between Tuesleydale and Thursleydale. **ARTHUR SMITH**

Founded on textiles, until 1969 Leeds had the world's oldest surviving
woollen mill. Then someone pulled at a loose thread and the whole
building unravelled. **HUMPHREY LYTTELTON**

Henley is a supermodel constituency – and like all supermodels it looks
lovely on the postcards but when you get up close and personal it's smug,
selfish, demanding and vain. **A.A. GILL**

Henley is the Venice of the South. **BORIS JOHNSON**

Bexhill-on-Sea is a peck on the cheek; Hastings is a big lolloping tongue
down the throat. **JO BRAND**

I had a walk around Bradford this afternoon and I have to say, I like the
place. I mean, it's not often that I feel fashionable. **FRANK SKINNER**

The show *Goodnight, Vienna* was being staged in Lewisham. On the third
night the play's author, Eric Maschmitz, asked the doorman how the
show was going. The doorman replied: 'About as well as *Goodnight,
Lewisham* would do in Vienna.' **MILLICENT LOW**

I never had lunch in Brighton without wanting to take a woman to bed in the afternoon.
JOHN OSBORNE

Bournemouth is one of the few English towns that one can safely call 'her'.

SIR JOHN BETJEMAN

Brighton is a town that looks as if it has been out on the tiles all night... It looks like it's permanently helping the police with its enquiries.

KEITH WATERHOUSE

Brighton Downs is a country so truly desolate that if one had a mind to hang oneself for desperation at having to live there, it would be difficult to find a tree on which to fasten the rope.

SAMUEL JOHNSON

In Cornwall it's Saturday before you realise it's Thursday.   WILFRED PICKLES

My apologies to the citizens of Chipping Sodbury for calling their town Chipping Sudbury last week. Fact is almost always stranger than fiction.

STEPHEN GLOVER

One has no great hopes from Birmingham. I always say there is something direful in the sound.   JANE AUSTEN

If you live in Birmingham, then being awake is not necessarily a desirable state.

TONY WILSON

I see you come from Slough. It is a terrible place. You can go back there.

MR JUSTICE MELFORD STEVENSON TO A MAN ACQUITTED OF RAPE

I spent a year in Prestatyn one Sunday.

CHRIS LOCKE

Bugger Bognor.

KING GEORGE V

THE NORTH/ SOUTH DIVIDE

London is the financial capital. Wigan is the pie capital. **SUE NELSON**

I don't speak French. I don't speak English. I am from Yorkshire.

GEOFFREY BOYCOTT

Seb Coe is a Yorkshireman, which means that he's a complete bastard and will do well in politics. **DALEY THOMPSON**

Northerners are far too busy breeding pigeons, eating deep-fried chip butties and executing drive-by shootings on Moss Side to dally over the new Sebastian Faulks. **HILDY JOHNSON**

—You should see Newcastle, sir.
—I once knew a girl in Burton-on-Trent, Lewis. Further north than that I have no desire to go. **SGT LEWIS AND INSPECTOR MORSE,** *THE LAST ENEMY*

Islington is about as far as you can get from London without needing yellow-fever jabs. **A.A. GILL**

A woman goes into a hairdresser's in Newcastle and says, 'Can I have a perm, please?' And the hairdresser goes, 'I wandered lonely as a cloud…' **TED ROBBINS**

Don Warrington has to go to Newcastle for Christmas. I say I like Newcastle. 'Why? It's all vomit and love-bites.' **ALAN BENNETT**

The word 'gay' in Newcastle means 'owns a coat'. **JIMMY CARR**

Newcastle people are so hard they hold in their piss until they go on holiday. **SEAN LOCK**

My first impulse when I hear a strange noise in my house in the middle of the night is to go to the top of the stairs and shout down, 'Go back to Liverpool!' **JACK DEE**

People from Liverpool tend to think people from Manchester are a bunch of cunts. And people from Manchester tend to think people from Liverpool are a bunch of cunts. When will they realise... **JIMMY CARR**

Northerners don't live in the north, because the north already lives in them. Penny Lane is in their ears and in their eyes. **NANCY BANKS-SMITH**

It's silly to make generalisations but if you talk to anyone in the south for longer than five minutes they will try to sell you fruit. **PAUL MERTON**

People in the North die of ignorance and crisps. **EDWINA CURRIE**

IRELAND AND THE IRISH

An Irishman goes into a fish-and-chip shop, says, 'Fish and chips twice.' The guy says, 'I heard you the first time.' **SPIKE MILLIGAN**

Ah, Ireland... That damnable, delightful country, where everything that is right is the opposite of what it ought to be. **BENJAMIN DISRAELI**

Ireland, the *Big Issue* seller of Europe. **A.A. GILL**

The Irish people do not gladly suffer common sense. **OLIVER ST. JOHN GOGARTY**

Other people have a nationality. The Irish and the Jews have a psychosis. **BRENDAN BEHAN**

The Irish climate is wonderful, but the weather ruins it. **TONY BUTLER**

An Irishman can be worried by the consciousness that there is nothing to worry about.   **AUSTIN O'MALLEY**

I've only been Irish since I moved to England last October. Back home, there didn't seem much point.   **DERMOT CARMODY**

Jesus must have been an Irishman. After all, He was unmarried, 32 years old, lived at home, and His mother thought He was God.   **SHANE CONNAUGHTON**

The Irish are a fighting race who never won a battle, a pious race excelling in blasphemy...have a harp for an emblem and no musicians... whose tongue is silver and whose heart is black.   **TOM PENHALIGON**

There are over 30 words in the Irish language which are equivalent to the Spanish, mañana. But somehow none of them conveys the same sense of urgency.   **PATRICK KAVANAGH**

Ireland has a great reputation as a literary nation. You walk into any pub in Dublin and it's full of writers and poets. In most other countries they're called drunks.   **ARDAL O'HANLON**

God created alcohol just to stop the Irish from ruling the world.

PATRICK MURRAY

Man Kept Arms Under Bed After Relative's Death   **HEADLINE, *THE IRISH TIMES***

If the English could only learn to believe in fairies, there wouldn't ever have been any Irish problem.   **W.B. YEATS**

Drink is the curse of this land. It makes you fight with your neighbour. It makes you shoot at your landlord. And it makes you miss him.

IRISH PROVERB

My only claim to originality among Irishmen is that I have never made a speech.

GEORGE MOORE

Ireland has the honour of being the only country which never persecuted the Jews...because she never let them in.

JAMES JOYCE

Did you hear about the Irish girl who went home and told her mother she was pregnant – and the mother said, 'Are you sure it's you?'

DENNIS TAYLOR

I don't tell Irish jokes any more. I told one at the club last night and an Irishman came after me with a razor. He would have used it too – if he could have found somewhere to plug it in.

TERRY HERBERT

Mrs Windsor can come and go in Northern Ireland as she wishes.

GERRY ADAMS

Born To Walk The Garvaghy Road – No Surrender.

SLOGAN ON IRISH BABY'S BIB

Such is the prevalence of organised crime in Northern Ireland that it is now known as 'Sicily without the sun'.

TONY THOMPSON

Gladstone spent his declining years trying to guess the answer to the Irish Question; unfortunately, whenever he was getting warm, the Irish secretly changed the Question.

W.C. SELLAR AND R. J. YEATMAN, 1066 AND ALL THAT

The only solution for dealing with the IRA is to kill 600 people in
one night.   **ALAN CLARK**

I never met anyone in Ireland who understands the Irish question,
except one Englishman who had only been there a week.   **KEITH FRASER**

If there were only three Irishmen left in the world you'd find two of
them in a corner talking about the other.   **BRENDAN BEHAN**

An Irish diver is on a wreck at the bottom of the sea. A voice from the
ship says, 'Are you down there, Mick?' 'Yes.' 'Come up right away!'
'Why?' 'The ship's sinking!'   **SPIKE MILLIGAN**

May the curse of Mary Malone and her nine blind illegitimate children
chase you so far over the hills of Damnation that the Lord himself
cannot find you with a telescope.   **IRISH CURSE**

SCOTLAND
AND THE SCOTS

I said, 'Haggis is mince in a sheep's stomach,' and he went, 'What?
They force-feed a sheep and then kill it?'   **RICKY GERVAIS**

The haggis – a mess of minced lights, livers, suet, oatmeal, onions,
and pepper, enclosed in a sheep's stomach – had a very sudden effect
upon mine.   **TOBIAS SMOLLETT**

The kilt is an unrivalled garment for fornication and diarrhoea.

JOHN MASTERS

Some people hate the English. I don't. They're just wankers. We, on the
other hand, are colonised by wankers. Can't even find a decent culture to
get colonised by. We're ruled by effete arseholes. **MARK RENTON,** *TRAINSPOTTING*

If Freud had worn a kilt in the prescribed Highland manner, he might have had a very different attitude to genitals.   **ANTHONY BURGESS**

There are two things a Highlander likes naked, and one is whisky.

OLD HIGHLAND SAYING

I have been trying all my life to like Scotchmen, and am obligated to desist from the experiment in despair.   **CHARLES LAMB**

The noblest prospect that a Scotsman ever sees is the high road that leads him to England.   **SAMUEL JOHNSON**

I look upon Scotland as an inferior sort of Switzerland.   **REVD SYDNEY SMITH**

White settlers.   **SCOTS TERM FOR ENGLISH LIVING IN SCOTLAND**

It is never difficult to distinguish between a Scotsman with a grievance and a ray of sunshine.   **P.G. WODEHOUSE**

Edinburgh is the loft extension of England.   **AL MURRAY**

WALES AND THE WELSH

Do you know what the most common crime is in Wales? Ram-raiding.

JIMMY CARR

Take my tip and stay out of Wales even if you are the Prince of it.

JEFFREY BERNARD

The purpose of the Welsh is to keep the English and the Irish apart.

M.K. BISSIMIRE

The Welsh are just Italians in the rain.   **NANCY BANKS-SMITH**

Eddy was a tremendously tolerant person, but he wouldn't put up with the Welsh. He always said, surely there's enough English to go round.

JOHN MORTIMER

R.S. Thomas is not noticeably Welsh, which is one comfort. **PHILIP LARKIN**

I once heard a Welsh sermon in which the word 'truth' was repeatedly uttered in English. Apparently there is no exact equivalent in Welsh.

GEOFFREY MADAN

When asked his opinion of Welsh nationalism, Mr Thomas replied in three words, two of which were 'Welsh nationalism'. **DYLAN THOMAS**

Environmentalists tell us that every day an area the size of Wales is destroyed. Why is it never Wales? **JIMMY CARR**

THE BRITISH EMPIRE

How is the Empire? **KING GEORGE V, LAST WORDS, 1936**

Once, when a British Prime Minister sneezed, men half a world away would blow their noses. Now when a British Prime Minister sneezes nobody else will even say, 'Bless You.' **BERNARD LEVIN**

In my childhood it was said by all: 'A child of ten can go on the road of a town playing with a golden ball in perfect safety under British rule.'

JANE MARSHALL

The British Empire was created by men who never drew a sober breath after the age of seven. **JOHN DOXAT**

We are the first race in the world, and the more of the world we inherit the better it is for the human race. **CECIL RHODES**

I think we may say we put India on the map. Hardly any of one's friends in England had ever even heard of India, before we went there, you know.

NANCY MITFORD

When we lived in India, my parents were oblivious to everything Indian except their servants.

RUMER GODDEN

I know why the sun never sets on the British Empire; God wouldn't trust an Englishman in the dark.

DUNCAN SPAETH

It's a well-known saying that the women lost us the Empire. It's true.

SIR DAVID LEAN

We didn't lose the Empire; it wasn't a pair of spectacles to lose. We simply handed it back.

PAMELA GLASER

Blimey, the countries we gave away an' only kept this little bit. What we should have done is kept all the rest, an' give away *England*. I mean, there's all yer wogs sitting out there in the sun by bloody oil wells, an' there's all us over here in the bleeding rain an' fog, an' snow, catching colds an' bronchitis.

ALF GARNETT, *THE THOUGHTS OF CHAIRMAN ALF*

We are to be understood as having given away the Empire and received, in return, the street-corner tandoori house.

JOHN LANCHESTER

I went to a restaurant the other day called 'A Taste of the Raj'. The waiter hit me with a stick and got me to build a complicated railway system.

HARRY HILL

The empires of the future are the empires of the mind.   **WINSTON CHURCHILL**

It is clear to me that the Empire ended in 1995 when the tourist attraction sign at Junction 3 on the M3, which used to say, 'Windsor Castle. Royalty and Empire', was changed to read, 'Windsor. Legoland'.

CHRISTOPHER HOLBOROW

LITTLE BRITAIN

'Who's 'im, Bill?' 'A stranger!' ''Eave 'arf a brick at 'im.'

PUNCH MAGAZINE, 1854

We don't bother the outside world, we don't want it bothering us.

EDWARD, *THE LEAGUE OF GENTLEMEN*

Britain, Britain, Britain. Everybody is welcome in Britain. We are open 'til six, Monday to Saturday. No foreign gentlemen, please.

TOM BAKER, NARRATOR, *LITTLE BRITAIN*

Oh! it's a snug little island,
A right little, tight little island.

THOMAS DIBDIN

All the people like us are We,
And everyone else is They.

RUDYARD KIPLING

I for one should love to have a real moat round my house, with a little drawbridge which could be let down when I really like the look of the visitor. I do not think I am a misanthrope. I am only an Englishman – that is, an islander.

G.K. CHESTERTON

PATRIOTISM

—But, James, I need you!
—So does England.

LOG CABIN GIRL AND JAMES BOND, *THE SPY WHO LOVED ME*

Love of one's country is not a cause. **LORD ANNAN**

Patriotism is your conviction that this country is superior to all other countries because you were born in it. **GEORGE BERNARD SHAW**

If I had to choose between betraying my country and betraying my friend, I hope I should have the guts to betray my country. **E.M. FORSTER**

A man may fight for many things: his country, his principles, his friends, the glistening tear on the cheek of a golden child. But personally I'd mud-wrestle my own mother for a ton of cash, an amusing clock and a sack of French porn. **EDMUND BLACKADDER,** *BLACKADDER III*

He was inordinately proud of England and he abused her incessantly. **H.G. WELLS**

Patriotism is the last refuge of a scoundrel. **SAMUEL JOHNSON**

Patriots always talk of dying for their country and never of killing for their country. **BERTRAND RUSSELL**

Patriotism is the willingness to kill and be killed for trivial reasons. **BERTRAND RUSSELL**

'My country, right or wrong' is a thing that no patriot would think of saying, except in a desperate case. It is like saying 'My mother, drunk or sober.' **G.K. CHESTERTON**

In left-wing circles it is always felt that there is something slightly disgraceful in being an Englishman, and that it is a duty to snigger at every English institution, from horse racing to suet puddings.

GEORGE ORWELL

I came in here in all good faith to help my country. I don't mind giving a reasonable amount of blood, but a pint...why, that's very nearly an armful. I'm sorry. I'm not walking around with an empty arm for anybody. **TONY HANCOCK,** *HANCOCK'S HALF HOUR*

Why are two Union Jacks like Margaret Thatcher's knickers? Because no power on earth can pull them down. **SPIKE MILLIGAN**

The idea that Englishmen might favour the cross of St George over the Union Flag will never catch on. Where's the fun in having a flag about which nobody can complain that it is being flown upside down? **MICHAEL BIRD**

Oh the things I do for England! **JAMES BOND**

NATIONALISM

A patriot is a man who loves his country; a nationalist is one who hates everybody else's. *THE LISTENER* **MAGAZINE**

It is not easy to see how the more extreme forms of nationalism can long survive when men have seen the Earth in its true perspective as a single small globe against the stars. **ARTHUR C. CLARKE**

Many people do take pride in being English, but the idea of discussing nationalism is, in polite circles, rather like talking about an embarrassing itch. **GAVIN ESLER**

I'm as British as the Union Jack and the Bangladeshi women in Tower Hamlets. **LADY GAVRON**

My policy is to be able to buy a ticket at Victoria Station and go anywhere I damn well please. **ERNEST BEVIN, 1951**

The English are the greatest nationalists in the world, but they're also the subtlest. They do it by convincing everyone that any other kind of nationalism is in bad taste.   **WINIFRED EWING**

What William Blake's *Jerusalem* is saying is, 'Wouldn't it be nice if Jesus lived in England'.   **REVD DONALD ALLISON, WHO DEEMED THE HYMN TOO NATIONALISTIC TO BE SUNG AT A WEDDING**

RACE AND RACISM

Robert Kilroy-Silk is not racist at all – he employs a black driver.
                                    HILARY HUNTER, SECRETARY TO ROBERT KILROY-SILK

The British National Party's Christmas bash turned out to be a fiasco when they mistakenly booked a black DJ. A BNP spokesman said: 'He sounded white on the phone.'   **DANIEL THOMAS, *THE DAILY MIRROR*, 2004**

Don't you just hate it when your granny knits you an embarrassing jumper for Christmas? My gran knitted me a red jumper that said 'Asylum Seekers Out' on it. I mean, just look at the colour.   **JIMMY CARR**

Ladies and gentlemen, let's have a big round of applause for the waiters. I've never seen staff work as hard. And they thought walking through the Channel Tunnel was hard...   **JACK DEE AT A DORCHESTER HOTEL FUNCTION**

I was walking past Buckingham Palace, and I noticed they've got a black guardsman there now. Just the one. But it shows how far we've come: a black guy standing outside the Queen's house with a loaded gun and he's not been arrested...   **LENNY HENRY**

It would have been great if Prince Charles had been told to marry someone black. Imagine what message that would have sent out.

                                    LADY GAVRON

When we win an Olympic medal, we're English; when we riot and throw petrol bombs, we're West Indian. **WINSTON PRICE**

I'm very secure with the fact that I'm not black. **BONO**

'England for the English', as we used to say about India.

AUDREY FFORBES-HAMILTON, *TO THE MANOR BORN*

I never deal with countries who have green in their flag or where people do not wear overcoats in winter. **BENJAMIN SLADE**

I do not prejudge. I have formed my dislikes on the basis of long experience. I tried explaining this once to James Baldwin, who complained to me that it was sheer race prejudice and homophobia which made people dislike him: 'No, James, it is not prejudice, it is actual experience of how awful you are.' **PAUL JOHNSON**

It's never bothered me, race. I don't care if people are navy blue so long as they don't spit up. There was a lot of that in Boulogne, I remember. I said to Marge, they can stick their bread, I couldn't live there.

KITTY, *VICTORIA WOOD*

The English – in England – are among the most tolerant bigots on earth.

STEPHEN BURGER

Tolerance is only another word for indifference. **W. SOMERSET MAUGHAM**

If, like me, you were born in England red-haired, left-handed and a Roman Catholic, there's nothing you don't know about prejudice. **PAUL JOHNSON**

The crunch time for tolerance in this country will be when gays and lesbians can openly admit they are Conservatives. **PHILIP LEVY**

I'm the first Afro-Saxon. **DEREK LAUD**

Derek Laud is the first black Master of Foxhounds in the New Forest. One day he's out hunting, looking splendid in his hunting pinks. And these antis are there, and they shout, 'What are you doing hunting with these people?' So Derek gives them this great smile and says, 'I am enjoying a good day's hunting, old boy.' 'Well a hundred years ago, they would have been hunting your ancestors,' they said. So Derek looks down imperiously from his mount, and says to them, 'A hundred years ago, my ancestors would have been eating you.' **GERALD HOWARTH**

As a black Briton, I suggest that books like *Little Black Sambo* not be burned, but rather put in a permanent exhibition along with some of the jokes from *The Comedians*. The exhibition could be titled 'Echoes of Britannia's Rule' – subtitled – 'Information That Made The British Think They Were Great.' **DOROTHY KUYA**

It is, of course, a particularly British characteristic to think that every man is the same under the skin, and that Eskimos are really only would-be old Etonians wearing fur coats. **JOHN HARVEY-JONES**

For me this is a vital litmus test: no intellectual society can flourish where a Jew feels even slightly uneasy. **PAUL JOHNSON**

I never heard Hitler mention the Jews; I know he didn't like them, that he murdered them…maybe instead they could have gone somewhere like Uganda – very empty and a lovely climate. **DIANA MOSLEY**

The TUC has brought out a Guide For The Use Of Inappropriate Language. Among the terms deemed unacceptable are 'spicks', 'dagos', 'Argies', 'krauts' and 'wops'. Wouldn't it just be easier to stop Prince Philip going out? **WILLIAM HAGUE, HAVE I GOT NEWS FOR YOU**

CHARACTER

CHARACTER – GENERAL

He was a characteristic British personality. He looked stolid. He said little, and what he said was obscure.

WINSTON CHURCHILL

What I say is this, if a fellow really likes potatoes, he must be a pretty decent sort of fellow.

A.A. MILNE

The Englishman is born and bred to think one thing and say the other instead.

***THE CONSULTANTS*, BBC RADIO 4**

The people of England are never so happy as when you tell them that they are ruined.

ARTHUR MURRAY

An Englishman's mind works best when it is almost too late.

LORD D'ABERNON

The British are the only people who like to be told how bad things are – who like to be told the worst.

WINSTON CHURCHILL

Remember the kettle, always up to its neck in hot water, yet it still sings.

ENGLISH SAYING

The English man-in-the-street is largely envious, vindictive and punitive. It is a mercy that there aren't more referendums in this country. They would be hanging children.

JEFFREY BERNARD

'Nothing surprises me nowadays,' said the Colonel, 'it merely disgusts me.'

J.B. MORTON

I am afraid of buffet lunches, Tories, striped suits, Greek food and proud virgins.

KENNETH TYNAN

He was always hovering somewhere, waiting to be offended. **PETER USTINOV**

Identity cards won't just give your name and address. They'll say: 'He's got a genetic heart defect, his sister's against GM crops and in 1997 he took a video late back to Blockbuster.' **JEREMY HARDY**

I am righteously indignant; *you* are annoyed; *he* is making a fuss about nothing. **NEW STATESMAN MAGAZINE**

That typically English characteristic for which there is no English name – esprit de corps. **FRANK EZRA ADCOCK**

I know myself to be capable of dealing with most of the stock situations or even the great moments of life – birth, marriage, death, the successful jumble sale, the garden fête spoilt by bad weather. **BARBARA PYM**

You must not miss Whitehall. At one end you will find a statue of one of our kings who was beheaded; at the other the monument to the man who did it. This is just an example of our attempts to be fair to everybody.

SIR EDWARD APPLETON ON CHARLES I AND CROMWELL

I-D cards are antipathetical to being an Englishman. I do not see why I need a card in order to breathe in my own country. **MATTHEW PARRIS**

—My most embarrassing moment was when my artificial leg fell off at the altar on my wedding day.
—How awful! Do you still have an artificial leg?

LISTENER AND SIMON FANSHAWE, *TALK RADIO*

Some of us are like wheelbarrows – only useful when pushed, and very easily upset. **JACK HERBERT**

It is not only in war and politics that the English favour the habit of muddling through. They do it in life, where it is even more dangerous. **SIR RICHARD LIVINGSTONE**

Do you have any idea what it's like being English? Being so correct all the time, being so stifled by this dread of doing the wrong thing, of saying to someone 'Are you married?' and hearing 'My wife left me this morning,' or saying, 'Do you have children?' and being told they all burned to death on Wednesday. You see, we're all terrified of embarrassment. **JOHN CLEESE AS ARCHIE LEACH, *A FISH CALLED WANDA***

Lord Glenconner was often embarrassed by his wife's exploits, and was once heard to answer the question, 'Are you related?' with the evasive if truthful reply, 'Only by marriage.' **HUGH MASSINGBERD**

I find the sex scene in *The Tall Guy* extraordinarily embarrassing, even though I wasn't in it. **ROWAN ATKINSON**

Watching sex on telly with Mum and Dad, that's embarrassing. I didn't even know they knew how to use the camcorder. **JIMMY CARR**

I am one of those unfortunates to whom death is less hideous than explanations. **WYNDHAM LEWIS**

When we find that we are not liked, we assert that we are not understood; when probably the dislike we have excited proceeds from our being too fully comprehended. **COUNTESS OF BLESSINGTON**

If egg is dripping on my face, I can scramble it and serve it up to my own advantage.   **RUSSELL HARTY**

In England you have to know people very intimately indeed before they tell you about the rust in their Volvo.   **ALAN COREN**

Most human beings have an absolute and infinite capacity for taking things for granted.   **ALDOUS HUXLEY**

My dear, there's nothing so ordinary as to try to be extraordinary.   NOËL COWARD

Sophistication is not an admired quality. Nobody likes it anywhere. In England at any rate.   **STEPHEN FRY**

Not often is it that you meet a man you can immediately trust. I can now add Doctors McNab and Collins to the list comprising the first Duke of Wellington, Mr Micawber, Rocky Graziano, Fred Winter, my brothers, my ex-wife Ashley and the breakfast television weather forecaster on BBC.   **JEFFREY BERNARD**

The English instinctively admire any man who has no talent and is modest about it.   **JAMES AGATE**

You have a magnificent chance, with all the advantages of wealth and position. Don't throw it away by any exhibition of talent.   **W. SOMERSET MAUGHAM**

The English never abolish anything. They put it in cold storage.   **ALFRED NORTH WHITEHEAD**

Perfection has one grave defect: it is apt to be dull.   **W. SOMERSET MAUGHAM**

Great events make me quiet and calm; it is only trifles that irritate
my nerves.   QUEEN VICTORIA

The degree of one's emotions varies inversely with one's knowledge of
the facts – the less you know the hotter you get.   BERTRAND RUSSELL

I dislike arguments of any kind. They are always vulgar, and often
convincing.   OSCAR WILDE

If I can put one touch of rosy sunset into the life of any man or woman,
I shall feel that I have worked with God.   G.K. CHESTERTON

You wouldn't notice another person if she was sitting on your face.
                                                          HOWARD JACOBSON

Nothing short of physical handicap has ever made anyone turn over a
new leaf.   KINGSLEY AMIS

ENGLISHMAN

Remember that you are an Englishman, and have consequently won
first prize in the lottery of life.   CECIL RHODES

He was born an Englishman and remained one for years.   BRENDAN BEHAN

He is a typical Englishman, always dull and usually violent.   OSCAR WILDE

The Englishman has all the qualities of a poker except its occasional
warmth.   DANIEL O'CONNELL

I am feeling a bit out of sympathy with England at present – God what a
hole, what a witless crapulous people, delivered over gagged and bound
to TV, motoring and Mackeson's stout!   PHILIP LARKIN

I like a man to be a clean, strong, upstanding Englishman who can look his gnu in the face and put an ounce of lead in it. **P.G. WODEHOUSE**

When God wants a hard thing done, he tells it to his Englishmen. **JOHN HARDING**

It is the perpetual boast of the Englishman that he never brags.

WYNDHAM LEWIS

Englishmen never will be slaves: they are free to do whatever the Government and public opinion allow them to do. **GEORGE BERNARD SHAW**

Curse the blasted jelly-boned swines, the slimy bell-wriggling invertebrates, the miserable sodding rotters, the flaming sods, the snivelling, dribbling, dithering, palsied pulseless lot that make up England today. They've got white of egg in their veins, and their spunk is that watery it's a marvel they can breed…Why, why, why was I born an Englishman! **D.H. LAWRENCE**

The way to tell an Englishman is by the quality of his drugs. **LORD HESKETH**

We were not fairly beaten, my lord. No Englishman is ever fairly beaten.

GEORGE BERNARD SHAW

Why do Englishmen like sitting on the fence so much? Because they enjoy the sensation. **DR DAVID STARKEY**

You can get any Englishman to do anything you want simply by whispering in his ear: 'I know your guilty secret.' **P.G. WODEHOUSE**

I've always said, if you want to outwit an Englishman, touch him when he doesn't want to be touched. **JULIAN BARNES**

Almost the only Englishmen left in the world today are Indians.
Who cares about the Boat Race outside Calcutta or Bombay? Where is
regimental silver polished as assiduously as in Indian Army messes?
If there are any Bertie Woosters still around, they are called, we may be
sure, Sen Gupta or Abdul Rahman. **MALCOLM MUGGERIDGE**

STIFF UPPER LIP

The English are very good at hiding emotions, but without suggesting
there is anything to hide. **DAVID HARE**

The average Englishman goes six months without crying depending on
football results. **FRANK SKINNER**

How did the Englishman get his stiff upper lip? He sucked a Viagra tablet
instead of swallowing it. **BILL MCCLINTOCK**

BORE

Well, you've joined me at a very exciting moment. These are
Mr Freeman's pants, which have just been bored right off him by the
British contestant in The Most Boring Man in the World Competition,
Edward Marle, who is Mr Droitwich. **PETER COOK**

Perhaps the world's second worst crime is boredom. The first is being
a bore. **SIR CECIL BEATON**

Bores can be divided into two classes; those who have their own
particular subject, and those who do not need a subject. **A.A. MILNE**

I am one of those unfortunate persons who inspires bores to the greatest
flights of art. **EDITH SITWELL**

At a dinner in America, I was seated next to a scientist who talked interminably on the subject of ants. 'They're such fascinating creatures,' he explained. 'They have their own highly organised system, with its own rulers and workers. They even have their own police force and army.' 'No navy?' I enquired.   **MRS PATRICK CAMPBELL**

So wearied was I by the long-winded account of his illness that I fell asleep, only to awake and hear myself say, 'And did you die?'   **ENID EVANS**

Coming away from dinner at a house noted for its dullness, Dumas père was asked by someone if he had not been dreadfully bored. 'I should have been,' he replied, 'if I hadn't been there.'   **E.V. LUCAS**

The English sent all their bores abroad and acquired an Empire as a result of it.   **EDWARD BOND**

...and thirteenthly...   **OXFORD DON, OVERHEARD**

Swinburne has now said not only all he has to say about everything, but all he has to say about nothing.   **A.E. HOUSMAN**

Is boredom anything less than the sense of one's own faculties slowly dying?   **JOHN BERGER**

It's so much easier to pray for a bore than to go and see one.   **C.S. LEWIS**

A yawn is a silent shout.   **G.K. CHESTERTON**

The great advantage of being in a rut is that when one is in a rut, one knows exactly where one is.   **ALAN BENNETT**

I do not object to people looking at their watches when I am speaking. But I strongly object when they start shaking them to make sure they are still going.   **LORD BIRKETT**

I knew it would be dull, but not so dull as this.   **LORD MELBOURNE**

The effect of boredom on a large scale in history is underestimated. It is a main cause of revolutions.   **DEAN INGE**

My Dinner With André is a film as boring as being alive.   **QUENTIN CRISP**

Went to see *Don't Look Now*. It was so boring I let my hand wander into the crotch of my companion and his only reaction was the line, 'Any diversion is welcome.'   **KENNETH WILLIAMS**

The boredom of Sunday afternoons, which drove De Quincey to opium, also gave birth to surrealism: hours propitious for making bombs.
                                                                                        CYRIL CONNOLLY

Sunday should be abolished except between consenting adults in private.
                                                                                        PENELOPE GILLIAT

Everyone is a bore to someone. That is unimportant. The thing to avoid is being a bore to oneself.   **GERALD BRENAN**

Any subject can be made interesting, and therefore any subject can be made boring.   **HILAIRE BELLOC**

Sir, you have but two topics, yourself and me. I am sick of both.
                                                                        DR JOHNSON TO JAMES BOSWELL

Somebody's boring me, I think it's me.   DYLAN THOMAS

When you're bored with yourself, marry, and be bored with
somebody else.   DAVID PRYCE-JONES

EGO AND MODESTY

'I' is the most popular letter in the alphabet.   OLIVER HERFORD

I am always pleased to see my friends, happy to be with my wife and
family, but the high-spot of every day is when I first catch a glimpse of
myself in the shaving mirror.   ROBERT MORLEY

I am not conceited. It is just that I have a fondness for the good things
in life and I happen to be one of them.   KENNETH WILLIAMS

A black hole of egotism.   NICHOLAS WAPSHOTT ON REX HARRISON

The mome rath isn't born that could outgrabe me.   NICOL WILLIAMSON

He fell in love with himself at first sight and it is a passion to which he
has always remained faithful. Self-love seems so often unrequited.
                                                      ANTHONY POWELL

To love oneself is the beginning of a lifelong romance.   OSCAR WILDE

Pavarotti is not vain, but conscious of being unique.   PETER USTINOV

Although he did not believe in God himself, he somehow gave the
impression that God believed in him.   CHAIM BERMANT

I've never any pity for conceited people because I think they carry their
comfort about with them.   GEORGE ELIOT

There, but for the grace of God, goes God.   **WINSTON CHURCHILL**

No one hears his own remarks as prose.   **W.H. AUDEN**

As God once said – and I think, rightly… **FIELD MARSHAL VISCOUNT MONTGOMERY**

No man thinks there is much ado about nothing when the ado is about himself.   **ANTHONY TROLLOPE**

I wrote a book called *Humility*. It was a pioneering work which has not, to my knowledge, been superseded.   **LORD LONGFORD**

I play the drums badly well.   **MATT LUCAS**

Boasting about modesty is typical of the English.   **GEORGE BERNARD SHAW**

Clement Attlee is a modest man who has much to be modest about.   **WINSTON CHURCHILL**

False modesty is something I abhor. I cannot tolerate civility unless one is actually paying for it.   **ROBERT MORLEY**

I know he is a truly great and good man, for he told me so himself.   **W.S. GILBERT, *H.M.S. PINAFORE***

The advantage of doing one's praising for oneself is that one can lay it on so thick and exactly in the right places.   **SAMUEL BUTLER**

If one hides one's talent under a bushel one must be careful to point out to everyone the exact bushel under which it is hidden.   **SAKI**

Eating words has never given me indigestion.

WINSTON CHURCHILL

As a child, I sneaked into the study of my grandfather, Winston Churchill, who was busy working on a speech. 'Grandpapa,' I said, 'is it true that you are the greatest man in the world?' 'Yes,' he snarled, 'now bugger off.'

NICHOLAS SOAMES

GENTLEMAN

When an Englishman is totally incapable of doing any work whatsoever, he describes himself on his income tax form as a 'gentleman.'

ROBERT LYND

A gentleman need not know Latin, but he should at least have forgotten it.

BRANDER MATTHEWS

A gentleman is a man who uses a butter knife when dining alone.

GERALD JENKINS

A gentleman is one who can fold a newspaper in a crowded train.

LEONORA CUNNINGHAM

I always think you can tell a gentleman by the way he honks his horn.

HYACINTH BUCKET, *KEEPING UP APPEARANCES*

He says, 'Kelly-Marie Tunstall, just because I have tattoos and a hairy navel button does not mean I do not have the instincts of an English gentleman.'

KELLY, *VICTORIA WOOD*

If I am a gentleman and you are a gentleman, who will milk the cow?

IRISH PROVERB

A gentleman is a patient wolf.

HENRIETTA TIARKS

A gentleman is always sick out of the window.

SADIE BARNETT

A gentleman is one who never swears at his wife while ladies are present.

PAUL QUINN

A gentleman never eats. He breakfasts, he lunches, he dines, but he *never* eats.

LORD FOTHERHAM

It's only if a man's a gentleman that he won't hesitate to do an ungentlemanly thing.

W. SOMERSET MAUGHAM

A gentleman never offends unintentionally.

OSCAR WILDE

Perfect soldier, perfect gentleman, never gave offence to anyone, not even the enemy.

A.J.P. TAYLOR

No real English gentleman, in his secret soul, was ever sorry for the death of a political economist.

WALTER BAGEHOT

Gentleman's wash: A hurried washing of the male genitals (usually in a pub toilet sink) in anticipation of forthcoming sex.

VIZ

The only infallible rule we know is that the man who is always talking about being a gentleman never is one.

R.S. SURTEES

The final test of a gentleman is his respect for those who can be of no possible service to him.

WILLIAM LYON PHELPS

Gentlemen do not throw wine at ladies. They pour it over them.

AUBERON WAUGH

CAD

He is every other inch a gentleman.

REBECCA WEST

A cad is one who does the crossword when you're out; shows his friends your letters; tells you whodunnit; calls breasts 'bristols' and is the one you want to go out with more than anyone in the world.

CATHARINE HUNT

A cad is the sort of chap who'll enjoy a lady's favours and then announce it to the world by posting off her knickers in a see-through envelope.

LIONEL MARSH

BLOODY-MINDEDNESS

Fat, lazy old cob required for fat, lazy old man who wishes to go hunting now that it is illegal.   ADVERTISEMENT, *NORTH DEVON JOURNAL*

I never allow myself to be photographed if I'm not smoking. It's a strict policy I initiated when it became politically correct not to smoke.

MAGGI HAMBLING

Vicky Pollard hates smoking except in places where it is prohibited.

TOM BAKER, NARRATOR, *LITTLE BRITAIN*

She fell down a lift shaft on Ascension Day – so perverse of her.

NOËL COWARD

We're against bureaucracy, hypocrisy and anything ending in 'y'.

JOHNNY ROTTEN

GRUMPINESS

—Oh, Jim, you have more faces than the town-hall clock.
—Yes, and every one of them is miserable.

BARBARA AND NANA ROYLE, *THE ROYLE FAMILY*

If you are foolish enough to be contented, don't show it, but grumble with the rest.

JEROME K. JEROME

Alan Sugar smiles as if there's a tax on it.

JOE JOSEPH

If not actually disgruntled, he was far from being gruntled.

P.G. WODEHOUSE

The fact that I am not a millionaire aristocrat with the sexual capacity of a rutting rhino is a constant niggle.

EDMUND BLACKADDER, *BLACKADDER III*

I have always been a grumbler. I am designed for the part – sagging face, weighty underlip, rumbling, resonant voice. Money couldn't buy a better grumbling outfit.

J.B. PRIESTLEY

So I went down to my local supermarket and said to the guy, 'I want to make a complaint. The vinegar's got lumps in it.' He said, 'Those are pickled onions.'

TIM VINE

Oh, these English are always complaining. You make one perfectly normal request at a normal volume and they pucker their rectums.

FRENCH AND SAUNDERS

Grumblers are at their best in restaurants. Within ten swift minutes a practised grumbler can take a dislike to the shape of his chair, the position of his table, the insolent way the waiter's looking at him, and the well-known fact that no foreigner can cook a simple dish without putting octopus tentacles in it.

ANGELA INCE

It is part of English hypocrisy – or English reserve – that, whilst we are fluent enough in grumbling about small inconveniences, we insist on making light of any great difficulties or griefs that may beset us.

SIR MAX BEERBOHM

LUCK

God not only plays dice. He also sometimes throws them where they
cannot be seen. **STEPHEN HAWKING**

Oh god, Fortune vomits on my eiderdown once more.
EDMUND BLACKADDER, *BLACKADDER III*

We suffer from bad luck in our family. My great granddad once came
third in a duel. **DAVE SPIKEY**

Having escaped the *Titanic,* he clambered aboard the *Marie Celeste.*
PETER SHARPE

I lift my eyes to the blue remembered hills, and they call back: 'Shove off.'
JOHN OSBORNE

God always has another custard pie up his sleeve. **LYNN REDGRAVE**

Some folk want their luck buttered. **THOMAS HARDY**

Bad luck was always as welcome as a sandy foreskin. **OLIVER REYNOLDS**

HAPPINESS

The British do not expect happiness. I had the impression, all the time
that I lived there, that they did not want to be happy; they want to
be right. **QUENTIN CRISP**

Suspicion of happiness is in our blood. **E.V. LUCAS**

I'm not happy. But I'm not unhappy about it. **ALAN BENNETT**

He's simply got the instinct for being unhappy highly developed.   **SAKI**

Men who are unhappy, like men who sleep badly, are always proud
of the fact.   **BERTRAND RUSSELL**

I was as happy as a king – indeed, a lot happier than most kings I
have met.   **HARRY LAUDER**

I'm as happy as a Frenchman who's invented a pair of self-removing trousers.   **PRINCE GEORGE,** *BLACKADDER III*

To be without some of the things you want is a vital part of happiness.   **BERTRAND RUSSELL**

I cannot help being happy. I've struggled against it but no good. There is,
I am well aware, no virtue whatever in this. It results from a combination
of heredity, health, good fortune and shallow intellect.   **ARTHUR MARSHALL**

A man likes not to be ignored even by a railway accident. A man with
a grievance is always happy.   **W.N.P. BARBELLION**

The secret of happiness is to find a congenial monotony.   **V.S. PRITCHETT**

Happiness is the sublime moment when you get out of your corsets
at night.   **JOYCE GRENFELL**

A large income is the best recipe for happiness I ever heard of.   **JANE AUSTEN**

The happiest part of a man's life is what he passes lying awake in bed in
the morning.   **SAMUEL JOHNSON**

Nothing sets a person up more than having something turn out just the way it's supposed to be, like falling into a Swiss snowdrift and seeing a big dog come up with a little cask of brandy round its neck.   **CLAUD COCKBURN**

If there were in the world today any large number of people who desired their own happiness more than they desired the unhappiness of others, we could have paradise in a few years.   **BERTRAND RUSSELL**

No man knows what true happiness is until he has a complete set of false teeth and has lost all interest in the opposite sex.   **LORD ROSEBERY**

The formula for complete happiness is to be very busy with the unimportant.   **A. EDWARD NEWTON**

Don't forget about what happened to the man who suddenly got everything he wanted. He lived happily ever after.   **ROALD DAHL**

SADNESS

My capacity for happiness you could fit into a matchbox – without taking out the matches.   **DOUGLAS ADAMS**

I was so upset that I cried all the way to the chip shop.   **JILTED JOHN**

A little misery wouldn't matter very much with her; it would go so well with the way she does her hair.   **SAKI**

Unhappiest moments? Take your pick from deaths and divorces to Gower being out for a duck or hearing Norman shout, 'Last orders, please.' Actually, he doesn't say it quite as politely as that.   **JEFFREY BERNARD**

The secret of being miserable is to have leisure to bother about whether you are happy or not.   **GEORGE BERNARD SHAW**

PRAISE

If you can't get compared to the Queen Mother, the Virgin Mary's the next best thing.   **ALAN BENNETT**

Flattery is like icing on a cake. You can never guess whether the foundation of this is seed, sponge or sultana.   **MARGOT ASQUITH**

Among the smaller duties of life, I hardly know any one more important than that of not praising when praise is not due.   **REVD SYDNEY SMITH**

When was there a prophet who found honour in his own country until he was very rich or very dead.   **REGINALD ARKELL**

What really flatters a man is that you think him worth flattering.

GEORGE BERNARD SHAW

AMBITION

I don't know what I want, but I want it NOW!   **VIVIAN STANSHALL**

Napoleon said, 'Every soldier carries a marshal's baton in his pack.' Yes, but don't let it stick out.   **DAVID OGILVY**

It's important in this world to be pushing, but it is fatal to seem so.

BENJAMIN JOWETT

An Englishman's real ambition is to get a railway compartment to himself.

IAN HAY

We are all in the gutter, but some of us are looking at the stars.

OSCAR WILDE

SUCCESS

Success is the ability to go from one failure to another with no loss of enthusiasm. **WINSTON CHURCHILL**

All the rudiments for success in life are to be found ironing trousers.

CHRIS EUBANK

Moderation is a fatal thing. Nothing succeeds like excess. **OSCAR WILDE**

Winning is everything. The only ones who remember when you come second are your wife and dog. **DAMON HILL**

If you can keep your head when all about are losing theirs, you'll be taller than anybody else. **TIM BROOKE-TAYLOR**

The penalty for success is to be bored by the people who used to snub you. **NANCY ASTOR**

I attribute my whole success in life to a rigid observance of the fundamental rule – never have yourself tattooed with any woman's name, not even her initials. **P.G. WODEHOUSE**

FAILURE AND THE UNDERDOG

In England, failure is all the rage. **QUENTIN CRISP**

What annoys me about Britain is the rugged will to lose. **WILLIAM CAMP**

My friends, as I have discovered myself, there are no disasters, only opportunities. And, indeed, opportunities for fresh disasters. **BORIS JOHNSON**

Somebody said that it couldn't be done –
But he, with a grin, replied
He'd not be the one to say it couldn't be done –
Leastways, not 'til he'd tried.
So he buckled right in, with a trace of a grin;
By golly, he went right to it.
He tackled The Thing That Couldn't Be Done
And he couldn't do it.   **ANON [READ ALOUD FOR BEST EFFECT]**

The British public has always had an unerring taste for ungifted amateurs.

JOHN OSBORNE

One British Olympic sports commentator described a UK runner who
was lagging far behind the field as 'coming in confidently and supremely
fit – a gallant sixteenth'.   **MICHAEL BENTINE**

If at first you don't succeed, failure might be your style.   **QUENTIN CRISP**

John Lydon (a.k.a Johnny Rotten of the Sex Pistols) has left *I'm a
Celebrity, Get Me Out of Here* early fearing he might actually win.

THE SUN NEWSPAPER

Part of me suspects I'm a loser and the other part thinks I'm God Almighty.

JOHN LENNON

You never find an Englishman among the underdogs – except in England
of course.   **EVELYN WAUGH**

There is nothing the British like more than a bloke who comes from
nowhere, makes it and then gets clobbered.

MELVYN BRAGG ABOUT RICHARD BURTON

VOICE AND ACCENT

It is impossible for an Englishman to open his mouth without making some other Englishman hate him or despise him.   **GEORGE BERNARD SHAW**

That voice! She sounds as if she thinks a crèche is something that happens on the M1.   **JEANANNE CROWLEY**

A voice that reminded one of a fat bishop blessing a butter-making competition.   **SAKI**

Humphrey Lyttelton's voice sounds like God looking for his spectacles.   **JASPER REES**

Sybil's laugh always reminds me of somebody machine-gunning a whale.   **BASIL FAWLTY,** *FAWLTY TOWERS*

The word papa gives a pretty form to the lips. Papa, potatoes, poultry, prunes and prisms are all good words for the lips.   **CHARLES DICKENS**

OPTIMISM AND PESSIMISM

The news is always bad, even when it sounds good.   **ALDOUS HUXLEY**

Eeyore without the *joie de vivre*.   **MIKE SELVEY**

He's as doomed as a virgin on a first date with Rod Stewart.   **OWEN NEWITT,** *THE VICAR OF DIBLEY*

Sometimes I wonder if we don't actually prefer things a little crap.   **BEN ELTON**

Oh, isn't life a terrible thing, thank God? DYLAN THOMAS

It's not the despair, Laura. I can take the despair. It's the hope.

JOHN CLEESE AS BRIAN STIMPSON, *CLOCKWISE*

Always look on the bright side of life. MONTY PYTHON

It is worth a thousand pounds a year to have the habit of looking on the bright side of things. DR SAMUEL JOHNSON

Benjamin Britten wanted all life to be in C Major. ANON

An optimist is someone who fills up his crossword puzzle in ink.

CLEMENT K. SHORTER

I am an optimist. It does not seem too much use being anything else.

WINSTON CHURCHILL

I'm an optimist, but I'm an optimist who carries a raincoat. HAROLD WILSON

The fluffy newborn chick of hope tumbles from the eggshell of life and splashes into the hot frying pan of doom. HUMPHREY LYTTELTON

—I'm afraid you've got a bad egg, Mr Jones!
—Oh no, my Lord, I assure you! Parts of it are excellent!

BISHOP AND CURATE, *PUNCH* MAGAZINE 1895

The answer to darkness is to turn on the light. LORD HAILSHAM

I would rather live in a workhouse with an optimist than a palace with a pessimist. CARDINAL HEENAN

VICE AND VIRTUE

Everybody was up to something, especially, of course, those who were
up to nothing. **NOËL COWARD**

I believe in getting into hot water. It keeps you clean. **G.K. CHESTERTON**

Vice is its own reward. **QUENTIN CRISP**

Do you know what '*le vice Anglais*' – the English vice – really is?
Not flagellation, not pederasty – whatever the French believe it to be.
It's our refusal to admit our emotions. We think they demean us.
TERENCE RATTIGAN

The English vice is not flagellation or homosexuality as continentals
sometimes suppose. It is whimsy. **A.N. WILSON**

One of the worst things that can happen in life is to win a bet on a horse
at an early age. **DANNY MCGOORTY**

We cannot go about, unfortunately, telling everybody about the
temptations we have resisted. As a result, people judge us exclusively
by the temptations to which we yield. **E.V. LUCAS**

He has all the virtues I dislike and none of the vices I admire.
WINSTON CHURCHILL

This scarlet woman. Was she scarlet all over, or was it just that her face
was red? **P.G. WODEHOUSE**

I hope you have not been leading a double life, pretending to be
wicked and being really good all the time. That would be hypocrisy.
OSCAR WILDE

It is queer how it is always one's virtues and not one's vices that precipitate one into disaster. **REBECCA WEST**

When people agree with me I always feel I must be wrong. **OSCAR WILDE**

Men do not suspect faults that they do not commit. **SAMUEL JOHNSON**

Not all the sins of my past life passed in front of me but as many as could find room in the queue. **BRENDAN BEHAN**

Everyone says forgiveness is a lovely idea, until they have something to forgive. **C.S. LEWIS**

Like a good many bad-tempered people, she was quick to forgive affronts, so that she could start giving and receiving them again.

PAMELA HANSFORD JOHNSON

Never trust a man who has not a single redeeming vice. **WINSTON CHURCHILL**

TRUTH

Men occasionally stumble over the truth, but most of them pick themselves up and hurry off as if nothing had happened.

WINSTON CHURCHILL

Something unpleasant is coming when men are anxious to tell the truth.

BENJAMIN DISRAELI

The great advantage about telling the truth is that nobody ever believes it.

DOROTHY L. SAYERS

Always tell the truth. You may make a hole in one when you're alone on the golf course some day. **BOB MONKHOUSE**

Truth for him was a moving target. He rarely pierced the outer ring.

HUGH CUDLIPP

It's discouraging to think how many people are shocked by honesty and how few by deceit.   **NOËL COWARD**

The best measure of a man's honesty isn't his income tax return. It's the zero adjust on his bathroom scale.   **ARTHUR C. CLARKE**

A little sincerity is a dangerous thing, and a great deal of it is absolutely fatal.   **OSCAR WILDE**

No good story is quite true.   **LESLIE STEPHEN**

LIES

I should think it hardly possible to state the opposite of the truth with more precision.   **WINSTON CHURCHILL**

Men were born to lie, and women to believe them.   **JOHN GAY**

Remember, if a man will twist his wife, he will twist anyone else.

NORRIS MCWHIRTER

I do not mind lying, but I hate inaccuracy.   **SAMUEL BUTLER**

It is sometimes necessary to lie damnably in the interests of the nation.

HILAIRE BELLOC

The lie is the basic building block of good manners. That may seem mildly shocking to a moralist – but then what isn't?   **QUENTIN CRISP**

In a controversy it is safest to assume that both sides are lying.   **ROBERT LYND**

The real trouble with liars is that there is never any guarantee against their occasionally telling the truth.   **KINGSLEY AMIS**

There are lies, damned lies, and statistics.   **BENJAMIN DISRAELI**

The only statistics you can trust are those you falsified yourself.

WINSTON CHURCHILL

MANNERS AND ETIQUETTE

Manners are the outward expression of expert interior decoration.

NOËL COWARD

Politeness is fictitious benevolence.   **SAMUEL JOHNSON**

He is the very pineapple of politeness!   **RICHARD BRINSLEY SHERIDAN**

The more the English dislike you, the more polite they are.

RABBI LIONEL BLUE

There was a young lady of Tottenham,
Who'd no manners or else she'd forgotten 'em.
At tea at the vicar's
She tore off her knickers,
Because, she explained, she felt 'ot in 'em.   **ANON**

Britain gave the world courtesy, table-manners and slavery.   **MARK STEELE**

Mrs Hinds explained to the Bench that although she did strike Mrs Card first she asked her to remove her glasses before doing so.

THE EAST ANGLIAN TIMES

There can be no defence like elaborate courtesy. **E.V. LUCAS**

His courtesy was somewhat extravagant. He would write and thank people who wrote to thank him for wedding presents and when he encountered anyone as punctilious as himself the correspondence ended only with death. **EVELYN WAUGH**

Manners are especially the need of the plain. The pretty can get away with anything. **EVELYN WAUGH**

In my day, there were things that were done, and things that were not done, and there was even a way of doing things that were not done. **PETER USTINOV**

Always behave as if nothing had happened, no matter what has happened. **ARNOLD BENNETT**

The trouble nowadays is that no one stares, however outrageous one's behaviour. **QUENTIN CRISP**

A kiss on the cheek is sufficient greeting. After all, we are not French generals. LADY DIANA COOPER

The distinction between asking 'How is your brother?' and saying 'I hope your brother is well', is laid down in a Manual of Etiquette (1860). **GEOFFREY MADAN**

The one social lapse for which there is no forgiveness is forgetting people's names – it makes them feel that they are small and unmemorable. **KATHARINE WHITEHORN**

I still like a man to open a door for me – even if he does let it swing back and hit me in the face.   **PAULINE DANIELS**

Ghosts, like ladies, never speak till spoke to.   **RICHARD HARRIS BARHAM**

It's impolite to have sex anywhere that is visible to the other people who aren't having sex.   **JENNY ECLAIR**

Try not to make a noise in the bathroom, dear.

HYACINTH BUCKET, *KEEPING UP APPEARANCES*

A large number of people are adamant that the toilet seat should be put down after use. Last year I was commissioned by a client to paint on the top of the seat the badge of Sunderland Football Club and on the underside Chelsea's. Her husband is a Sunderland supporter and I understand it has had excellent results.   **JAMES WILLIAMS**

If you stay in a house and you go to the bathroom and there is no toilet paper, you can always slide down the bannisters. Don't tell me you haven't done it.   **PAUL MERTON**

My tent's blown away. I knew I shouldn't have eaten those radishes.

CHARLIE MUGGINS, *CARRY ON CAMPING*

Would you mind not farting while I'm trying to save the world.

THE DOCTOR TO THE BRITISH CABINET, *DOCTOR WHO*

He found that a fork in his inexperienced hand was an instrument of chase rather than of capture.   **H.G. WELLS**

Air Tulip: a delightfully fragrant fart, as dropped by Lady Di or Grace Kelly. But not Jocky Wilson.
Butler's Revenge: A silent but deadly fart. **VIZ**

Public-school boys are bloody rude unless they make a decision to be charming. They tend to eat like pigs; it is those poised on social brinks who worry about table manners. **BEVIS HILLIER**

He gave me the sort of greeting a corpse would give to an undertaker.

STANLEY BALDWIN

I'm going to put the phone down on you, but very quietly and very politely.

ALAN BENNETT TO A JOURNALIST

Rudeness is annoying, but offended flouncing is worse, being so dreadfully conceited. **ALICE THOMAS ELLIS**

One can always be kind to people about whom one cares nothing.

OSCAR WILDE

Coleridge says that to bait a mouse-trap is as much as to say to the mouse, 'Come and have a piece of cheese,' and then, when it accepts the invitation, to do it to death is a betrayal of the laws of hospitality.

ROBERT LYND

The great secret is not having bad manners or good manners or having any other particular sort of manners, but having the same manner for all human souls; in short, behaving as if you were in Heaven, where there are no third class carriages and one soul is as good as another.

GEORGE BERNARD SHAW

HYGIENE

Oh! that halitosis. It's so thick – a greyhound couldn't jump it.

CECIL BEATON

Henry IV's feet and armpits enjoyed an international reputation.

ALDOUS HUXLEY

—Your hands are dirty.
—You should see my feet.

ACQUAINTANCE AND LADY MARY WORTLEY MONTAGU ARRIVING AT THE OPERA

My grandmother took a bath every year, whether she needed it or not.

BRENDAN BEHAN

QUEUE

Who so comth first to mill, first grynt. **GEOFFREY CHAUCER, THE CANTERBURY TALES**

Standing in line at the post office is a social experience for most people.
They actually want to meet the people in the queue.

DAVID MILLS, CHIEF EXECUTIVE OF ROYAL MAIL

IKEA is pronounced 'I Queue Here'. **GRAHAM WYNNE**

OOAQICI82QB4IP. **GRAFFITI IN A LADIES' TOILET**

During an outing on a safari trip to Africa with a group of fellow
British tourists, a friend of mine stopped for a pee. Having located a
suitable bush, she relieved herself, but was amazed on standing up
to find a queue of ladies behind her all waiting for the same bush.

CATHERINE BETTS

Never join a queue unless you know what's at the end of it. **GERALD CHALLIS**

I never queue. I wouldn't queue for a seat at the Last Supper, with the original cast.   **ROBERT HELPMAN**

PUNCTUALITY AND TIME

—Come with me when the fiery ball weighs heavy in the sky.
—About 7.00 then?   **TUBBS AND DAVID, *THE LEAGUE OF GENTLEMEN***

'Twenty-three and a quarter minutes past,' Uncle Matthew was saying furiously, 'in precisely six and three-quarter minutes the damned fella will be late.'   **NANCY MITFORD**

I always make a point of arriving later than expected in order to transform the anxiety of the chairman into extravagant relief and enthusiasm when I do appear.   **ROBERT MORLEY**

No wonder you're late. Why, this watch is exactly two days slow.
                           MAD HATTER, *ALICE'S ADVENTURES IN WONDERLAND*

In truth, people can generally make the time for what they choose to do; it is not really the time but the will that is lacking.   **SIR JOHN LUBBOCK**

I have never been able to take anything seriously after eleven o'clock in the morning.   **NOËL COWARD**

A French five minutes is ten minutes shorter than a Spanish five minutes, but slightly longer than an English five minutes which is usually ten minutes.   **GUY BELLAMY**

How long a minute is depends on which side of the bathroom door you're on.   **BOB MONKHOUSE**

I always arrive late at the office, but I make up for it by leaving early.

CHARLES LAMB

Punctuality is the virtue of the bored.

EVELYN WAUGH

Time is an illusion. Lunchtime doubly so.

DOUGLAS ADAMS

If I wrote about England I should call it 'What about Wednesday Week?' which is what English people say when they are making what they believe to be an urgent appointment.

CLAUD COCKBURN

SORRY

This is the only country in the world where you step on somebody's foot and he apologises.

KEITH WATERHOUSE

'What about apologising?' my tennis-partner went on. 'Shall we do it after every stroke, or at the end of each game, or when we say good-bye, or never? I get so tired of saying "Sorry".'

A.A. MILNE

They say 'sorry' is the hardest word but they're wrong. It's that Welsh name of a railway station.

HARRY SECOMBE

It's a good rule of life never to apologise. The right sort of people don't want apologies, and the wrong sort take a mean advantage of them.

P.G. WODEHOUSE

A stiff apology is a second insult. The injured party does not want to be compensated because he has been wronged; he wants to be healed because he has been hurt.

G.K. CHESTERTON

If you apologise for turning your back, the Chinese reply, 'A rose has no back.'

GEOFFREY MADAN

Say you're sorry. No one says you have to mean it. **JEFF GREEN**

MORALITY

I like the English. They have the most rigid code of immorality in the world. **MALCOLM BRADBURY**

Everything's got a moral, if only you can find it. **LEWIS CARROLL**

An Englishman thinks he is moral when he is only uncomfortable. **GEORGE BERNARD SHAW**

If you can't be a good example, then you'll just have to serve as a horrible warning. **CATHERINE AIRD**

There is nothing so bad or so good that you will not find an Englishman doing it; but you will never find an Englishman in the wrong. He does everything on principle. **GEORGE BERNARD SHAW**

Throwing acid is wrong. In some people's eyes. **JIMMY CARR**

A man who moralises is usually a hypocrite, and a woman who moralises is invariably plain. **OSCAR WILDE**

Like everyone who talks of ethics all day long, one could not trust Koestler half an hour with one's wife, one's best friend, one's manuscript or one's wine merchant. **CYRIL CONNOLLY**

Every saint has a bee in his halo. **E.V. LUCAS**

—What do you do with your moral impetus these days?
—I give it a little groundsel and feed it gently – it does all right.

DAVID FROST AND NOËL COWARD

You assume that Goodness, like Guinness, is good for people. That's never been proved.

ALAN MELVILLE

Decency must be an even more exhausting state to maintain than its opposite. Those who succeed seem to need a stupefying amount of sleep.

QUENTIN CRISP

What after all is a halo? It's only one more thing to keep clean.

CHRISTOPHER FRY

THE PECKING
ORDER – CLASS

CLASS – GENERAL

I am his Highness's dog at Kew;
Pray tell me, sir, whose dog are you?   **ALEXANDER POPE**

Sex you can get anywhere in the world. But class, I mean, real class,
you can get only in Britain.   **MALCOLM BRADBURY**

Everybody thinks himself well-bred.   **EARL OF SHAFTESBURY**

All men are born equal, but quite a few get over it.
                    LORD STORMONT MANCROFT

Put three Englishmen on a desert island and within an hour they'll have
invented a class system.   **ALAN AYCKBOURN**

What I want to know is: what is actually wrong with an elite,
for God's sake?   **PRINCE CHARLES**

Without class differences, England would cease to be the living theatre it is.
                    ANTHONY BURGESS

Model trains caused one's first awareness of class distinctions. The upper
class consisted of boys whose O gauge engines came from a miraculous
Holborn shop called Bassett-Lowke. The middle class consisted of boys
who possessed Hornby trains. The lower class was, I regret to say, any
train component that came from Gamages.   **ARTHUR MARSHALL**

I'm determined to travel through life either first class or third, but never
in second.   **NOËL COWARD**

If I had the choice between smoked salmon and tinned salmon, I'd have it
tinned. With vinegar.   **HAROLD WILSON**

Mankind is divisible into two classes: hosts and guests.

SIR MAX BEERBOHM

Striking stevedores in London's Victoria Dock yesterday rejected an appeal to unload 41 tons of melons going over-ripe in a British ship. The melon, they said, is not 'a working man's fruit'. **NEWS CHRONICLE**

I've changed. I no longer keep coal in the bath. I keep it in the bidet.

JOHN PRESCOTT

Only on the third class tourist class passengers' deck was it a sultry overcast morning, but then if you do things on the cheap you must expect these things. **SPIKE MILLIGAN**

Middle class girls get degrees. The working class get jobs. And the underclass get a baby as soon as they can. **TONY PARSONS**

I've met a better class of person in the gutter than I have in the drawing room. **JEFFREY BERNARD**

ROYALTY

Like tea, shepherd's pie, English country life, and much else in Great Britain, the Royal Family is not supposed to be glamorous, exciting, or chic. It is, above all, supposed to be English. **MICHAEL KORDA**

A family on the throne is an interesting idea. It brings down the pride of sovereignty to the level of petty life. **WALTER BAGEHOT**

The most loathsome family since the Mansons. **ANON**

Royalty is the gold teeth in a mouthful of decay. **JOHN OSBORNE**

The institution of monarchy is inherently silly. **LORD HATTERSLEY**

Once you touch the trappings of monarchy, like opening an Egyptian tomb, the inside is liable to crumble. **ANTHONY SAMPSON**

The monarchy is finished. It was finished a while ago, but they're still making the corpses dance. **SUE TOWNSEND**

The British monarchy is secure: what would the mass media do without it? **W.H. COUSINS**

We don't need the Royal Family but they're fun for tourists to look at. Anything hereditary is anachronistic and illogical; you wouldn't have a hereditary cricket team. **LADY GAVRON**

Britain, Britain, Britain. Land of tradition. Fish and fries. The changing of the garden. Trooping the coloureds.

TOM BAKER, NARRATOR, *LITTLE BRITAIN*

Ceremony is nothing more than middle-aged men dressing up like refugees from a pack of cards. PHILIP HOWARD

In America such a balance between grandeur and jollity would be impossible; in France or Italy hysterical; in Germany heavy-handed, and in Russia ominous. But in dear London it was lusty, charming, romantic, splendid and conducted without a false note.

NOËL COWARD ON THE WEDDING OF PRINCESS MARGARET AND ANTHONY ARMSTRONG-JONES

—You look awfully like the Queen.
—How frightfully reassuring. **PERSON IN CROWD AND QUEEN ELIZABETH II**

Oh, that reminds me, I must buy a stamp.

JIMMY TARBUCK, *ROYAL VARIETY PERFORMANCE*

The Queen arrived after a prodigious amount of the prancing about in fancy dress which the British call History. **MATTHEW PARRIS**

The Queen's wave: like the unscrewing of a chutney jar.

SARAH KENNEDY SHOW, RADIO 2

It was lovely to talk to the Queen, especially since I am a Windsor too.

BARBARA WINDSOR

I'm told it's not polite to turn your back on the Queen. I don't get that. She's very unlikely to nick anything. **HUGH DENNIS**

When Tommy Cooper was introduced to the Queen at the end of a Royal Variety Performance, he asked her, 'Do you like football, Ma,'am?' 'No,' came the reply. 'In that case,' said Tommy, 'can I have your tickets to the Cup Final?' **BOB MONKHOUSE**

I think I could say that Her Majesty prefers animals to human beings. For one thing, they don't talk so much. **SIR JOHN MILLER**

Buckingham Palace rejected a suggestion by Mrs Thatcher that a procedure be instituted to ensure she and the Queen never appear in public in similar or identical oufits with this terse reply: 'Her Majesty never notices what anyone wears.' **LAURA GREY**

In the Queen's Speech, Her Majesty has to read out this jargon, this pap, this pre-digested New Labour drivel, like someone who expects *foie gras* and lobster but has to eat Pot Noodle. **SIMON HOGGART**

Prince Philip has perfected the art of saying hello and goodbye in the
same handshake. **JENNIE BOND**

Watch out for the Queen's corgis. The little buggers nip. **WILLIAM WHITELAW**

Buckingham Palace isn't ours. It's just a tied cottage. **PRINCE PHILIP**

My one regret in life is that I have never climbed over a fence. **QUEEN MARY**

Prince Edward is one of the chief flag-bearers for the Republican cause.
WILL SELF

After a man dressed as Batman scaled the walls of the Palace, a spokesman
for Buckingham Palace says the security system works. Presumably in
much the same way as Prince Charles works. **ANGUS DEAYTON**

I wish I had been Bob Geldof. **PRINCE CHARLES**

What do you get the Prince of Wales as a gift? You can't give a silver
ashtray, the man owns Fabergé eggs. The last gift I gave him was
coffee beans made from Cambodian weasel vomit – a real delicacy.
STEPHEN FRY

My parents were Victorians and I have been an Edwardian, a Georgian
twice over and now an Elizabethan. Should Prince Charles accede to the
throne, I shall doubtless be a Right Charlie. **ELSIE POTTER**

The Latin American carnival of grief over Diana, Princess of Wales,
has dwindled and become, as religions tend to become, the preserve of
children, homosexuals and lonely housewives. The majority will allow
her to sink into oblivion. **A.N. WILSON**

Prince Charles is just as entitled to be underwhelmed by the prospect
of ruling over a fourth-class nation as the rest of us are at the prospect
of living in it. **ANTHONY JAY**

Camilla could have done so much better. **INDIA KNIGHT**

Princess Anne's poisonous spittle could stop a camel in its tracks at
20 paces and blind a press photographer for life at twice the distance.
AUBERON WAUGH

Being a member of the Royal Family is just an accident of birth,
a cross we have to bear. **PRINCE ANDREW**

I declare this thing open – whatever it is.
PRINCE PHILIP, OPENING A NEW ANNEX AT VANCOUVER CITY HALL

The trouble with being a princess is that it's so hard to have a pee.
PRINCESS DIANA

The Queen Mother was an upmarket Alf Garnett. **FORMER COURTIER**

Scotland…corgis…broken marriages…so long as the Royal Family don't
look as if they're having fun they will be accepted. **IAN HISLOP**

Prince Harry will call me sir. And I will call him sir. But he will be the
one who means it.
WARRANT OFFICER FIRST CLASS VINCE GAUNT, IN CHARGE OF PRINCE HARRY AT SANDHURST

ARISTOCRACY AND UPPER CLASSES

We had to put a stop to the presentation of debutantes at Court.
Every tart in London was getting in. **PRINCESS MARGARET**

—I am the son of one of Italy's oldest and most aristocratic families.
—My good man, when your race were still living in caves, my
family had been homosexual for a thousand years. **ANON**

There is very little pure blood left in this country, as most of it is tainted
with cocaine. **JENNY ECLAIR**

Those comfortable padded lunatic asylums which are known,
euphemistically, as the stately homes of England. **VIRGINIA WOOLF**

'But I must have ghosts,' said Mrs Spottishworth. 'Don't tell me there
aren't any?' 'There's what we call the haunted lavatory on the ground
floor,' said Rory. 'Every now and then, when there's nobody near it, the
toilet will suddenly flush and when a death is expected in the family it
just keeps going and going. But we don't know if it's a spectre or just a
defect in the plumbing.' **P.G. WODEHOUSE**

The English lord marries for love, and is rather inclined to love where money is. NANCY MITFORD

I used to lead a leisurely life, the life of a duchess, until I married and
became a duchess. It's all work, work, work. **DUCHESS OF BEDFORD**

It is probably much happier to live in a small house, and have Warwick
Castle to be astonished at, than to live in Warwick Castle and have
nothing to be astonished at. **JOHN RUSKIN**

Not many of our old families can boast that a Savile Row tailor calls four
times a year at their country estate to measure the scarecrows in the fields
for new suits. **J.B. MORTON**

Nobody seemed quite clear whether the expression 'drunk as a lord' should be taken as a compliment or an insult.   **LORD STORMONT MANCROFT**

I had a terrible day two years ago when the Duke of Marlborough's grapes beat mine at the fruit show, then I got back to my club to read that the Duke of Beaufort was now the best-dressed duke.

DUKE OF DEVONSHIRE

In England, if you are a duchess, you don't need to be well-dressed – it would be thought quite eccentric.   **NANCY MITFORD**

To think that Grantleigh Manor is in the hands of a man who has no interest in farming, doesn't go to church and now it turns out hasn't heard of Winnie the Pooh. You think A.A. Milne is a motoring organisation I suppose.   **AUDREY FFORBES-HAMILTON**, *TO THE MANOR BORN*

MIDDLE CLASSES

Signs you're middle class: You live in the suburbs; you have a brass door knocker; you have different gardening clothes for your front and back garden.   **PAUL COLE**

Polishing your car is so middle-class. I prefer my cars to look scruffy.

ALAN CLARK

Middle class? I came home last night to find my nine-year-old daughter soaking her conkers in half a litre of *balsamic* vinegar.

JOHN DUCKWORTH

The suburbs which once seemed to me so lovely with their freckled tennis girls and their youths in club blazers have spread so far in the wake of the motor-car that there is little but suburb left.

SIR JOHN BETJEMAN

Suburbs have nothing to do with geography but are states of mind.

PAUL HICKEY

The only place you were really entitled to hang out your washing was in your car.

MALCOLM BRADBURY

We should impose a tax on people who have names as well as numbers on their garden gates.

SIR EDWARD CLARKE

Slums may well be breeding grounds of crime, but middle class suburbs are incubators of apathy and delirium.

CYRIL CONNOLLY

In the middle classes, where the segregation of the artificially limited family in its little brick box is horribly complete, bad manners, ugly dresses, awkwardness, cowardice, peevishness and all the petty vices of unsociability flourish like mushrooms in a cellar.

GEORGE BERNARD SHAW

Ultimately, the lower middle classes are the most deviant. That's why they have net curtains; they have things to hide.

JENNY ECLAIR

There are few who would not rather be taken in adultery than in provincialism.

ALDOUS HUXLEY

LOWER CLASSES

There is no way of life so utterly without redeeming features, so completely lacking in emotional, aesthetic, spiritual or cultural sustenance, so devoid of character as that of people in the lower depths of British society.

THEODORE DALRYMPLE

The age of the Common Man has taken over a nation which owes its existence to uncommon men.

NOËL COWARD

Really, if the lower orders don't set us a good example, what on earth is the use of them? They seem, as a class, to have absolutely no sense of moral responsibility.   **OSCAR WILDE**

There you go again Hilda. Lowering the rateable value wherever you go.
ELSIE TANNER, *CORONATION STREET*

The best way that man could test his readiness to encounter the common variety of mankind would be to climb down a chimney into any house at random, and get on as well as possible with the people inside. And that is essentially what each one of us did on the day that he was born.

G.K. CHESTERTON

God must hate the common people, because he made them so common.

PHILIP WYLIE

You can be in the Horseguards and still be common, dear.

TERRENCE RATTIGAN

Don't knock Bingo. It's the only chance working-class people will ever have of owning a giant ceramic cheetah.   **JOHNNY VEGAS**

We are told that we live in the age of the common man. He is not the common man, but the average man, which is far worse.   **SIR JOHN BETJEMAN**

I have on many occasions been profoundly moved by plays about the Common Man, as in my 50-odd years of restaurant-going I have frequently enjoyed tripe and onions, but I am not prepared to admit that an exclusive diet of either would be completely satisfying.   **NOËL COWARD**

In my day, the working classes didn't try to be beautiful. **LADY DIANA COOPER**

If you bed people of below-stairs class, they will go to the papers.

JANE CLARK, WIFE OF ALAN CLARK

Don't be intimidated by the fancy name 'vol-au-vents'. Eric and
June Selby from Chorley, Lancs avoided vol-au-vents for 20 years,
ignorant of the fact that they are merely pastry with a simple filling.
This is a common mistake amongst working-class folk. Such a shame!

MRS MERTON

SERVANTS

The butler entered the room, a solemn procession of one. **P. G. WODEHOUSE**

He's been trained as a gentleman's gentleman – they're always much more
reliable than gentlemen. **NOËL COWARD**

Parker stood in the doorway, trying to look as like a piece of furniture as
possible – which is the duty of a good butler. **P.G. WODEHOUSE**

How shall we ever know if it's morning if there's no servant to pull up
the blind? **J.M. BARRIE, *THE ADMIRABLE CRICHTON***

Gentlemen are requested, and servants are commanded, to keep off
the grass. **SIGN IN LONDON PARK, 19TH CENTURY**

His Lordship may compel us to be equal upstairs, but there will never be
equality in the servants' hall. **J.M. BARRIE, *THE ADMIRABLE CRICHTON***

Not everyone has the outrageous aplomb of an old friend of mine, born
to servants but through necessity reduced to answering his own front
door. The unwelcome neighbour would receive the politest of smiles and
the simple statement: 'I am not at home.' **JUDY FROSHAUG**

TRADESMEN

The five most terrible words in the English language are: 'We've got the builders in.' **GODFREY SMITH**

I rang up a building firm, and said: 'I want a skip outside my house.' He said, 'I'm not stopping you.' **TOMMY COOPER**

Trades're in. This morning Tate and Lyle delivered sugar by the lorry load. **JACK DEE**

Builder's bum is one of Britain's great institutions. **FRANK DOUGLAS**

Builder's bum: The protrusion of sweaty arse cheeks above the sagging waist of the jeans. Common among builders, council workmen and top fashion designer Alexander McQueen. a.k.a. Bricky's Crack, Dagenham Smile. *VIZ*

—Why have you erected my windbreak in the wrong place?...Did you, or did you not, see a pale blue envelope sellotaped to the handle of your pick-axe?
—Yes I did.
—And what was written on that envelope?
—N.B.
—Well?
—Well, I'm not N.Bailey, I'm Arthur Bailey – A.B.
—You stupid man.
—You can't talk to me like that.
—I can because I pay your wages. And get off the carpet. For your information N.B. means Nota Bene. It's Latin.
—Well, I'm from Balham.

MARGOT LEADBETTER AND ARTHUR BAILEY, *THE GOOD LIFE*

When I asked you to build me a wall, I was hoping rather than just dumping the bricks in a pile, I was wondering if you could find the time to cement them together, you know, in the traditional fashion, one on top of the other?

BASIL FAWLTY, *FAWLTY TOWERS*

SNOBBERY

—Have English class barriers broken down?
—Of course they have, otherwise I wouldn't be sitting here talking to someone like you. **SANDRA HARRIS INTERVIEWING DAME BARBARA CARTLAND**

My auntie was a bit of a social climber – although very much on the lower slopes. I was once on a tram with her going past the gas works in Wellington Road and she said, 'Alan, this is the biggest gas works in England. And *I* know the manager.' **ALAN BENNETT**

I heard a woman bragging: 'Our village was in the paper today. Turns out we're the most in-bred village in England.' **MARK STEELE**

Princess Michael of Kent is far too grand for the likes of us. QUEEN ELIZABETH II

Never keep up with the Joneses. Drag them down to your level. It's cheaper.

QUENTIN CRISP

If there's one thing I can't stand it's snobbism. People who pretend they're superior make it so much harder for those of us who really are.

HYACINTH BUCKET, *KEEPING UP APPEARANCES*

I am not a snob, but I wear a bowler hat in the bath because you never know who might call. **SPIKE MILLIGAN**

Prince Andrew and Sarah met on the polo field – doesn't everybody?

SUSAN BARRANTES, MOTHER OF SARAH FERGUSON

The nice thing about living in Gloucestershire is that none of us have our curtains made by people who haven't got a title. **ANNE ROBINSON**

Yes, but does your swimming pool have an underwater sound system?

ANNE ROBINSON TO JONATHAN ROSS

Don't you sit there and sigh gal like you was Lady Nevershit.

ARNOLD WESKER

The trouble with Michael Heseltine is that he has had to buy all his furniture.

MICHAEL JOPLING

How could you love an Onslow? He sings on coach trips.

HYACINTH BUCKET, *KEEPING UP APPEARANCES*

He's been had up for exposing himself in Sainsbury's doorway. As mother said, Tesco's you could understand it. **ALAN BENNETT**

Our customer at 'Topman' is the everyday 18-year-old lad. Hooligans or whatever. Very few of our customers have to wear suits to work. They will be for his first interview or first court case.

DAVID SHEPHERD, A DIRECTOR OF TOPMAN MENSWEAR

It's my sister, Violet. She's the one with the Mercedes, swimming pool, and room for a pony. **HYACINTH BUCKET, *KEEPING UP APPEARANCES***

I have nothing against undertakers personally. It's just that I wouldn't want one to bury my sister. **JESSICA MITFORD**

He would certainly have despised Christ for being the son of a carpenter, if the New Testament had not proved in time to be such a howling commercial success. **GRAHAM GREENE**

—When I see a spade I call it a spade.
—I am glad to say I have never seen a spade. It is obvious that our social spheres have been widely different. **OSCAR WILDE**

Make sure Onslow's got a shirt on, otherwise it will be like watching some bad Italian film. **HYACINTH BUCKET, *KEEPING UP APPEARANCES***

One could never make love to a woman with a glottal stop. **BRIAN SEWELL**

Anybody seen on a bus after the age of 30 has been a failure in life. **LOELIA, DUCHESS OF WESTMINSTER**

Who would get married in a registry office? It's like a crematorium. **LORD ST JOHN OF FAWSLEY**

It was not Café Society, it was Nescafé Society. **NOËL COWARD**

I could never bear to be buried with people to whom I had not been introduced. **NORMAN PARKINSON**

My uncle had dyslexia before it became all the rage. **KEITH BARRET, *MAKING DIVORCE WORK***

Are we a nation of snobs? The question to ask yourself is this: Would you accept an unsolicited parcel of horse manure from the Queen?

SPIKE MILLIGAN

HONOURS

—Why do you call yourself *Dame*?
—I don't. The Queen does. **AMERICAN INTERVIEWER AND EDITH SITWELL**

—Have you been playing music a long time?
—It must be 45 years now. **THE QUEEN KNIGHTING ERIC CLAPTON**

I've been offered titles but I think they get one into disreputable company.
GEORGE BERNARD SHAW

What has Rex Harrison ever done for England, except live abroad,
refuse to pay taxes, and call everybody a cunt?
HAROLD FRENCH ON THE ANNOUNCEMENT OF REX'S KNIGHTHOOD

Honours range from CMG (known sometimes in Whitehall as
'Call Me God') to KCMG ('Kindly Call Me God') to the GCMG
('God Calls Me God'). **ANTHONY SAMPSON**

The last civil servant to refuse an honour was back in 1496. And the
reason why he refused was because he'd already got one.
BERNARD WOOLLEY, *YES, MINISTER*

Titles distinguish the mediocre, embarrass the superior, and are disgraced
by the inferior. **GEORGE BERNARD SHAW**

What I like about the Order of the Garter is that there's no damn merit
about it. **LORD MELBOURNE**

Lots of people who complained about us receiving the MBE received
theirs for heroism in the war – for killing people. We received ours for
entertaining other people. I'd say we deserved ours more, wouldn't you?
JOHN LENNON

When I received notification of my MBE I thought it was a parking fine because it came in the same sort of envelope. **CHRISTINE TRUMAN**

It is not the title that counts. I will be the same shape in the bath as before. **MR GEORGE THOMAS**

When I want a peerage, I shall buy it like an honest man. **LORD NORTHCLIFFE**

AWARDS

I'd like to thank me mam and dad. If it wasn't for them I wouldn't have low self-esteem and have to follow this empty and shallow profession.

JOHNNY VEGAS

I'm an award-winning comedian. Unfortunately, the award was for swimming. **ARTHUR SMITH**

On the mantelpiece in my parlour I've got a whole row of silver cups. They're for my pussy. Do you know, it wins a prize every time I show it! **MRS SLOCOMBE,** *ARE YOU BEING SERVED?*

The books will finally stop falling on the other side of the shelf. **MICHAEL CAINE ON WINNING HIS SECOND OSCAR**

My father, Kingsley, always had doubts about the Booker Prize although they evaporated on the announcement that he had won it.

MARTIN AMIS

To refuse awards is another way of accepting them – with more noise than usual. **PETER USTINOV**

There is a little touch of vulgarity in the thought of any reward – for anything, ever. **WILLIAM CORY**

PEOPLE AND RELATIONSHIPS

PEOPLE

The world is divided into two sorts of people: those who divide the world into two sorts of people and those who do not. I fall resolutely into the latter category.
STEPHEN FRY

Have you ever thought what a fine world this would be if it weren't for the people in it?
EDEN PHILPOTTS

I sometimes think that God in creating man overestimated his ability.
OSCAR WILDE

I hate mankind for I think myself one of the best of them, and I know how bad I am.
SAMUEL JOHNSON

The closest to perfection a person ever comes is when he fills out a job application.
STANLEY RANDALL

I do not want people to be very agreeable, as it saves me the trouble of liking them a great deal.
JANE AUSTEN

We wouldn't care so much what people thought of us if we knew how seldom they did.
JOHN LANCHESTER

MEN

Men, my dear, are very queer animals – a mixture of horse-nervousness, ass-stubbornness and camel-malice.
THOMAS HENRY HUXLEY

'Ave you ever tried mekin' his belly suffer? It works wonders wi' my Stan – three days o' burnt dinner an' no drippin' in the pantry an' he's like putty in me 'ands.
HILDA OGDEN, *CORONATION STREET*

Talking with a man is like trying to saddle a cow. You work like hell, but what's the point?   **GLADYS UPHAM**

I have always wanted to be a man, if only for the reason that I would like to have gauged the value of my intellect.   **MARGOT ASQUITH**

A man is two people, himself and his cock. A man always takes his friend to the party. Of the two, the friend is the nicer, being more able to show his feelings.   **BERYL BAINBRIDGE**

I love the male body; it's better designed than the male mind.
                                                        ANDREA NEWMAN

I wouldn't kidnap a man for sex, but I'm not saying I couldn't use someone to oil the mower.   **VICTORIA WOOD**

'Tis strange what a man may do, and a woman yet think him an angel.
                                        WILLIAM MAKEPEACE THACKERAY

What every woman knows and no man can ever grasp is that even if he brings home everything on the list, he will still not have got the right things.   **ALLISON PEARSON**

The first time Adam had a chance he laid the blame on woman.
                                                          NANCY ASTOR

WOMEN

—Can you name the woman who would epitomise the English rose?
—Never met any.   **INTERVIEWER AND LORD HEALEY**

English women are elegant until they are ten years old, and perfect on grand occasions.   **NANCY MITFORD**

Honoria Glossop was one of those robust girls with the muscles of a welterweight and a laugh like a squadron of cavalry charging over a tin bridge.

P.G. WODEHOUSE

She smoked 120 gaspers a day, swore like a fisherman, drank like a fish, and was promiscuous with men, women and Etonians.

QUENTIN CRISP

It takes all sorts to make a sex.

SAKI

Aristotle maintained that women have fewer teeth than men; although he was twice married, it never occurred to him to verify this statement by examining his wives' mouths.

BERTRAND RUSSELL

We know of course that women are habitually constipated, but to represent them in fiction as being altogether devoid of a back passage seems to me really an excess of chivalry.

W. SOMERSET MAUGHAM

Of course Celia shits! And how much worse if she didn't.

D.H. LAWRENCE

Sphinxes without secrets.

OSCAR WILDE

Brigands demand your money or your life; women require both.

SAMUEL BUTLER

Women never look so well as when one comes in wet and dirty from hunting.

R.S. SURTEES

Men play the game; women know the score.

ROGER WODDIS

Can the fact that Our Lord chose men as his Twelve Apostles be lightly dismissed?

THE BISHOP OF WINCHESTER

The great and almost only comfort about being a woman is that one can always pretend to be more stupid than one is and no one is surprised.

FREYA STARK

Woman, without her man, is nothing.
Woman: without her, man is nothing.

STATEMENTS SHOWING THE IMPORTANCE OF PUNCTUATION

Why are women so much more interesting to men than men are to women?

VIRGINIA WOOLF

I'm glad I'm a woman because I don't have to worry about getting men pregnant.

NELL DUNN

It goes far towards reconciling me to being a woman when I reflect that I am thus in no danger of marrying one.

LADY MARY WORTLEY MONTAGU

A woman, especially if she have the misfortune of knowing anything, should conceal it as well as she can.

JANE AUSTEN

Women used to have time to make mince pies and had to fake orgasms. Now we can manage the orgasms, but we have to fake the mince pies.

ALLISON PEARSON

It will be a pity if women in the conventional mode are phased out, for there will never be anyone to go home to.

ANITA BROOKNER

A woman who looks like a girl and thinks like a man is the best sort, the most enjoyable to be and the most pleasurable to have and to hold.

JULIE BURCHILL

Certain women should be struck regularly, like gongs.   **NOËL COWARD**

All women become like their mothers. That is their tragedy. No man does. That's his.   **OSCAR WILDE**

I look on the opposite sex with something like the admiration with which I regard the starry sky on a frosty December night. I admire the beauty of the Creator's workmanship, I am charmed with the wild but graceful eccentricity of the motions, and then I wish both of them goodnight.

ROBERT BURNS

MEN AND WOMEN

What's the difference between men and women? Well, I've never seen a man who looked good in a pinafore dress. Unless it's very, very plain with no bust darts.   **VICTORIA WOOD**

The war between the sexes is the only one in which both sides regularly sleep with the enemy.   **QUENTIN CRISP**

In the sex war, thoughtlessness is the weapon of the male, vindictiveness of the female.   **CYRIL CONNOLLY**

I'm a modern man. I've got no problem buying tampons. But apparently women don't consider them a proper present.   **JIMMY CARR**

Cricket week: A five day test, when a gentleman must 'bowl from the pavilion end' while his wife is 'padded up'.   **VIZ**

In her world, men loved women as the fox loves the hare. And women loved men as the tapeworm loves the gut.   **PAT BARKER**

A woman who does a man's work is just a lazy cow.   **JO BRAND**

A man can be happy with any woman as long as he does not love her.

OSCAR WILDE

FEMINISM

A gasket is £100. A gasket, darlin', is £200.   **JO BRAND**

'You worked in an office once didn't you, Jill?' a feminist once asked earnestly. 'Did men ever harass you?' 'Yes,' I replied, 'but not nearly enough.'   **JILLY COOPER**

I could never be a feminist/lesbian as there is nothing more pleasurable to me than the sight of the bottom of the washing basket on a washday.

MRS MERTON

GENDER AND SEXUALITY

Mad About The Boy   **NOËL COWARD, SONG TITLE**

What's the difference between a gay guy and a straight guy? About three double vodkas.   **PAUL DALTON**

Being gay is a lot like being a taxi-driver: you spend a lot of time looking at the back of someone's head.   **COLIN MCALLISTER**

Oh, how can I put this delicately? I'm not really in the vagina business.

PETER MORTON, *PETER'S FRIENDS*

—So, you're a shirt-lifter.
—I prefer sewage-canoeist.   **STAN BOARDMAN AND SCOTT CAPURRO**

I became one of the stately homos of England.   **QUENTIN CRISP**

Bourneville boulevard: 'Cadbury alley', 'fudge tunnel', 'arse'. Used to denote homosexuality. 'I believe he strolls down the Bourneville boulevard.'

VIZ

In Istanbul I was known as 'English Delight'.

NOËL COWARD

We think they're marvellous. And besides, if we didn't have any here, we'd have to go self-service.

THE QUEEN MOTHER ON GAYS

A survey shows that the best time to pull a member of the opposite sex is 10.48pm. And the best to pull a member of the same sex is just before the park closes.

JONATHAN ROSS

When impertinent reporters ask if I'm gay, I say, 'I'm mildly cheerful.'

ARTHUR C. CLARKE

Nick Brown, MP for Newcastle-Upon-Tyne, has been 'outed' as gay. If he'd confessed to being a Sunderland supporter, that would really have been it.

MEMBER OF NEWCASTLE LABOUR CLUB

Most transvestites are just regular guys, who occasionally like to eat, drink and be Mary.

JOE JOSEPH

How many gays does it take to change a lightbulb? Never mind the bulb let's talk about the shade.

GRAHAM NORTON

You can get gay anything now: gay coffee, gay lager – it's like straight lager, it just goes down much easier.

GRAHAM NORTON

I thought men like that shot themselves.

KING GEORGE V

I have heard some say homosexual practices are allowed in France.
We are not French...we are British – thank God!

FIELD MARSHAL VISCOUNT MONTGOMERY

England has always been disinclined to accept human nature.   **E.M. FORSTER**

—I'm a lesbian trapped in a man's body.
—A bit like Martina Navratilova.   **EDDIE IZZARD AND FRANK SKINNER**

My wife's mother tells people I'm effeminate. I don't mind because
compared to her, I am.   **LES DAWSON**

ATTRACTION

Ding dong!   **LESLIE PHILLIPS AS JACK BELL, *CARRY ON NURSE***

When I glimpse the backs of women's knees I seem to hear the first
movement of Beethoven's Pastoral Symphony.   **CHARLES GREVILLE**

Thy breath is like the steame of apple-pyes.   **ROBERT GREENE**

The Owl looked up to the stars above,
And sang to a small guitar,
'O lovely Pussy! O Pussy my love,
What a beautiful Pussy you are,
        You are,
        You are!
What a beautiful Pussy you are!'   **EDWARD LEAR, *THE OWL AND THE PUSSYCAT***

The girl in the omnibus has one of those faces of marvellous beauty which
are seen casually in the streets but never among one's friends. Where do
these women come from? Who marries them? Who knows them?

THOMAS HARDY

I couldn't believe it the other day when I picked up a British newspaper and read that 82 per cent of men would rather sleep with a goat than me.

SARAH FERGUSON, THE DUCHESS OF YORK

Were it not for imagination, Sir, a man would be as happy in the arms of a chambermaid as of a Duchess. SAMUEL JOHNSON

Chaque à son goût – as the farmer said when he kissed the pig.

GEORGE CARMAN QC

I'd say that you were the perfect combination of imperfections. I'd say that your nose was just a little too short, your mouth just a little too wide. But yours was a face that a man could see in his dreams for the whole of his life. I'd say that you were vain, selfish, cruel, deceitful. I'd say that you were…Sibella. **LOUIS MAZZINI,** *KIND HEARTS AND CORONETS*

'Tisn't beauty, so to speak, nor good talk necessarily. It's just IT. Some women will stay in a man's memory if they once walked down a street.

RUDYARD KIPLING

Those hot pants of hers were so damn tight I could hardly breathe.

BENNY HILL

Busts and bosoms have I known
Of various shapes and sizes
From grievous disappointments
To jubilant surprises.

ANON

I like women with gaps in their front teeth. They are so damnably useful when it comes to scraping carrots.

PETER TINNISWOOD

Men have charisma; women have vital statistics. **JULIE BURCHILL**

Let me give you a bit of advice, Daisy. You'll not find this in your romantic novels, but if you're going to wear a see-through nightie, DON'T WEAR A VEST. **ONSLOW,** *KEEPING UP APPEARANCES*

O, she is the antidote to desire. **WILLIAM CONGREVE**

She would serve after a long voyage at sea. **WILLIAM SHAKESPEARE**

I have always found girls fragrant in any phase of the moon. **NOËL COWARD,** *BOOM*

You've got to take that job in the chippie. The thought of you smelling of chip fat morning, noon and night – what a turn-on that would be. **LES BATTERSBY TO CILLA BROWN,** *CORONATION STREET*

Phoebe Lucas plays a glamorous courtesan with about as much sex appeal as a haddock. **NOËL COWARD**

If you really like a girl and she says, 'I love you like a brother,' suggest a weekend in Norfolk – unless you're from Norfolk in which case you probably *are* her brother. **JIMMY CARR**

I am attracted to thin, tall, good-looking men who have one common denominator. They must be lurking bastards. **EDNA O'BRIEN**

So how're you going to impress Deborah now? Or are you going to fall back on your cheese impressions? **GARY,** *MEN BEHAVING BADLY*

What is wrong with a little incest? It is both handy and cheap. **JAMES AGATE**

—Onslow, why don't you grow a moustache?
—You want a moustache – why don't *you* grow one?

DAISY AND ONSLOW, *KEEPING UP APPEARANCES*

Things you'll never hear a woman say: 'My, what an attractive scrotum.'

JEFF GREEN

I know a girl who says the way to drive a man wild is to nibble on his ears for hours and hours. I think it's bollocks. **JIMMY CARR**

Graze on my lips, and if those hills be dry,
stray lower, where the pleasant fountains lie. **WILLIAM SHAKESPEARE**

It is my hideous destiny to be madly loved at first sight by every woman I come across. **W.S. GILBERT,** *THE MIKADO*

Wherever there are rich men trying not to feel old there will be young girls trying not to feel poor. **JULIE BURCHILL**

The best aphrodisiac for women is eating oysters because if you can swallow oysters, you can swallow anything. **HATTIE HAYRIDGE**

What attracts us in a woman rarely binds us to her. **JOHN COLLINS**

SEX

Nothing in our culture, not even home computers, is more overrated than the epidermal felicity of two featherless bipeds in desperate congress.

QUENTIN CRISP

I'd rather have a cup of tea. **BOY GEORGE**

When I hear Charles' steps outside my door I lie down on my bed, close my eyes, open my legs, and think of England. **LADY ALICE HILLINGDON**

Even the men lie back and think of England *THE CONSULTANTS*, **BBC RADIO 4**

No Sex Please, We're British

ANTHONY MARRIOTT AND ALISTAIR FOOT, TITLE OF FARCE

It has to be admitted that we English have sex on the brain, which is a very unsatisfactory place to have it. **MALCOLM MUGGERIDGE**

Did I sleep with her? Not a wink, Reverend Father, not a wink. **BRENDAN BEHAN**

This morning I woke up with Miss Givings. **KEN DODD**

Sex can be a dirty postcard, a cane, a sauna, clothes on a washing line, a locked drawer, an address book, cash on the mantelpiece, a gentleman's lavatory, a frantic exposure, the consummation of love, a peeping Tom.

ROBERT MORLEY

Sexual intercourse is like having someone else blow your nose.

PHILIP LARKIN

I would be greatly in the debt of the man who could tell me what could ever be appealing about those damp, dark, foul-smelling and revoltingly tufted areas of the body that constitute the main dishes in the banquet of love. **STEPHEN FRY**

I would be content that we might procreate like trees. **SIR THOMAS BROWNE**

Who is this Greek chap Clitoris they're talking about? **LORD ALBERMARLE**

Sex is only the liquid centre of the great Newberry Fruit of friendship.

JILLY COOPER

The pleasure is momentary, the position ridiculous, and the expense damnable. **LORD CHESTERFIELD**

Sex is like supermarkets – overrated. Just a lot of pushing and shoving and you still come out with very little at the end. *SHIRLEY VALENTINE*

Sex, on the whole, was meant to be short, nasty and brutish. If what you want is cuddling, you should buy a puppy. **JULIE BURCHILL**

It's an extraordinary way of bringing babies into the the world. I don't know how God thought of it. **WINSTON CHURCHILL**

My wife screams when she is having sex. Especially when I walk in on her. **ROY 'CHUBBY' BROWN**

The only reason my wife has an orgasm is so she'll have something else to moan about. **BOB MONKHOUSE**

Are you going to come quietly or do I have to use earplugs? **SPIKE MILLIGAN**

Why do girls fake orgasms? Because they think we care. **BOB GELDOF**

Prostitutes for pleasure, concubines for service, wives for breeding and a melon for ecstasy. **SIR RICHARD BURTON**

A lady does not move. **LORD CURZON**

The way to tell if a man is sexually excited is if he's breathing. **JO BRAND**

It had an erotic appearance, like the inside of a giraffe's ear or a tropical fruit not much prized by the locals. **KINGSLEY AMIS ON THE VAGINA**

She was looser than an MFI wardrobe. **ROY 'CHUBBY' BROWN**

Nudge-nudge, wink-wink, say no more, know what I mean? **ERIC IDLE,** *MONTY PYTHON'S FLYING CIRCUS*

Chasing the naughty couples down the grassgreen gooseberried double bed of the wood. **DYLAN THOMAS**

He kissed her hand with a sound like a mackerel being replaced clumsily on a fishmonger's slab, and withdrew. **J.B. MORTON**

So I kissed Lucy, and was very surprised to feel her tongue pop out. It was my first real snog and I loved it. You can imagine that I fell in love instantly. Sadly the next year Lucy developed distemper and had to be put down. **HUGH LAURIE**

She had heard that men only wanted one thing, but had forgotten for the moment what it was. **BARBARA PYM**

I'm not against naked girls – not as often as I'd like to be. **BENNY HILL**

—I'd like to make love to you.
—Well, if you do and I ever get to hear about it, I shall be very cross indeed. **GARY MILLS**

Sex at noon taxes. **PALINDROME**

He in a few minutes ravished this fair creature, or at least would have ravished her, if she had not, by a timely compliance, prevented him.

HENRY FIELDING

He was a womaniser – as opposed to a woman who does this, who is not a maniser, but a right old slapper.

JO BRAND

Show me a man who loves football and nine times out of ten you'll be pointing at a really bad shag.

JULIE BURCHILL

I have a really big problem, I cannot have sex with men with little dicks. Oh, I've tried, but I just can't do it. Thus, I have not had sex for two years.

TRACEY EMIN

There was a young lady of Ongar
Who was fucked in the sea by a conga
Her sister in Deal
Said, 'How did it feel?'
'Just like a man, only longer.'

ANON

Bit of rough: sexual partner, usually male, from a lower echelon. One who would wipe his cock on your curtains. e.g. Mellors, Lady Chatterley's Lover.

VIZ

For flavour, instant sex will never supersede the stuff you have to peel and cook.

QUENTIN CRISP

People today say you cannot be happy unless your sex life is happy. That makes about as much sense as saying you cannot be happy unless your golf life is happy.

EVELYN WAUGH

By the time I'd finished with her, she was like a blancmange after a children's party. **SWISS TONI**

As soon as I get home I'm going to rip my wife's bra off. The elastic is killing me. **ROY 'CHUBBY' BROWN**

I thought a *femme fatale* was a dead French woman. **BOB MONKHOUSE**

The best women, like Rolls-Royces, should be delivered to the customer fully run in.
LEO COOPER

The greatest discovery of the age is that women like it too.
HUGH MACDIARMID

Beat me on the bottom with a *Woman's Weekly*.
Let's do it! Let's do it! Let's do it tonight! **VICTORIA WOOD**

You were born with your legs apart. They'll send you to your grave in a Y-shaped coffin. **JOE ORTON**

She's like the old line about justice – not only must be done, but must be seen to be done. **JOHN OSBORNE**

—It doesn't suit women to be promiscuous.
—It doesn't suit men for women to be promiscuous.
NOËL COWARD, RELATIVE VALUES

I hoovered the carpet in the lounge dressed only in bathing trunks.
It was very daring and the atmosphere was charged with sex.
KENNETH WILLIAMS

I don't think one *could* go too far with Priscilla. She has no distance.

NOËL COWARD

I was a convent girl and didn't lose my virginity until I was 21 so I had no knowledge of sex at 20. At 30 it was getting better, 40 a bit better, 50 good and 60 terrific. In fact, I might do a sex video.

ANNE ROBINSON

If I was the Virgin Mary, I would have said no.   **STEVIE SMITH**

I'll wager you that in ten years it will be fashionable again to be a virgin.

DAME BARBARA CARTLAND

He said it was artificial respiration, but now I find I am to have his child.

ANTHONY BURGESS, *INSIDE MR ENDERBY*

Masturbation! The amazing availability of it!   **JAMES JOYCE**

I always thought it was going to be my mum who caught *me* masturbating...   **JIMMY CARR**

Women tend not to dress up in leather aprons and nail each other to coffee tables in their spare time.   **JULIE BURCHILL**

I'm not into all that bondage stuff. Tying people up is such a palaver.

BOY GEORGE

A woman told me she would fulfil my ultimate fantasy for £100. I asked her to paint my house.   **SEAN O'BRYAN**

IKEA bulb: A lady that blows first time one turns her on.   **VIZ**

They're known as the Belgrano Sisters on account of the number of sailors they've been down on. **PETER KAY**

I don't give blowjobs because I find it really off-putting, seeing a grown man look that pathetically grateful. **JENNY ECLAIR**

I never thought of myself as a wicked brothel-keeper. I thought of myself as a welfare worker. **CYNTHIA PAYNE**

It doesn't matter what you do in the bedroom as long as you don't do it in the street and frighten the horses. **MRS PATRICK CAMPBELL**

My own belief is that there is hardly anyone whose sex life, if it were broadcast, would not fill the world at large with surprise and horror. **W. SOMERSET MAUGHAM**

I don't know why I find it intensely erotic to stand naked before an open fridge, but I do. Maybe it's that the spill of light on my body makes me feel like a professional stripper. **STEPHEN FRY**

The trouble with orgies is that you have to spend so much time holding your stomach in. **JOHN MORTIMER**

It's probably easier to come out as a member of a satanic abuse ritual than to come out as a celibate. People seem to think that there's something wrong with you if you don't indulge in these frothy, squelchy activities. **STEPHEN FRY**

What is wrong with pornography is that it is a successful attempt to sell sex for more than it is worth. **QUENTIN CRISP**

There's only one good test of pornography. Get twelve normal men to read the book, and then ask them, 'Did you get an erection?' If the answer is 'Yes' from a majority of the twelve, then the book is pornographic.

W.H. AUDEN

I'm afraid Mr Mouse didn't come out to play.

THE 10TH DUKE OF MARLBOROUGH

Impotence in old age has not been a problem. It's like being unchained from a lunatic.

GEORGE MELLY

Have the British become a nation of porn-watching, vibrator-owning exhibitionists, or is it still the land of stiff upper zips? I would have thought the answer was obvious: we're all sex maniacs now.

COSMO LANDESMAN

COURTSHIP

My great-grandmother was your great-great-grandfather's mistress – so how about it?   **CAMILLA PARKER-BOWLES TO PRINCE CHARLES [ATTRIB]**

I have always felt that English women had to be approached in a sisterly manner, rather than an erotic manner.   **ANTHONY BURGESS**

It is assumed that a woman must wait motionless, until she is wooed. That is how the spider waits for the fly.   **GEORGE BERNARD SHAW**

Without you, life was like *Hamlet* without the balcony scene.

HUMPHREY LYTTELTON

Mrs West is a great prude, having but two loves at one time; I think those are Lord Haddington and Mr Lindsay, the one for use, the one for show.

LADY MARY WORTLEY MONTAGU

I have been in steady relationships with men since I was 18, with not a week off for good behaviour. **JULIE BURCHILL**

Phoning someone up and ringing off isn't a relationship. **DAVID QUANTICK**

My ex-boyfriend came round last night, which was a bit weird because I didn't even know he was in a coma. **JO BRAND**

There is no fury like a woman searching for a new lover. **CYRIL CONNOLLY**

—I'm finished with men! They're nothing but trouble and heartache.
—I know what you mean, dear. I can never get Richard to fold his pyjamas. **ROSE, AND HYACINTH BUCKET,** *KEEPING UP APPEARANCES*

British men take you to McDonald's, make you pay and ask if anyone is dating your sister. **MINNIE DRIVER**

That's it! I've had enough of men. There isn't one worth shaving your legs for. I'm going back to being a virgin. **ROSE,** *KEEPING UP APPEARANCES*

People always talk of a love affair as if lovers spent all their time in bed. **ANTHONY POWELL**

It is explained that all relationships require a little give and take. This is untrue. Any partnership demands that we give and give and give and at the last, as we flop into our graves exhausted, we are told that we didn't give enough. **QUENTIN CRISP**

It's no good pretending that any relationship has a future if your record collections disagree violently or if your favourite films wouldn't even speak to each other if they met at a party. **NICK HORNBY**

While I never admired Edith as much as when I was with Sibella,
I never longed for Sibella as much as when I was with Edith.

LOUIS MAZZINI, *KIND HEARTS AND CORONETS*

We weren't having an affair. He was just lying on top of me to get the
creases out of my negligée.

TRIXIE, *VICTORIA WOOD*

She reflected that all relations with men seemed to lead in the end to
cramp and pins and needles.

A.P. HERBERT

LOVE

Where does one look to find eternal love? The English ladies' tennis team
scoreboard would be an obvious start.

HUMPHREY LYTTELTON

Love: a mutual misunderstanding.

OSCAR WILDE

My girlfriend says, 'You never tell me how much you love me.' I don't
want to upset her.

JIMMY CARR

Love is just a system for getting someone to call you darling after sex.

JULIAN BARNES

One should always be in love. That is the reason one should never marry.

OSCAR WILDE

It is a curious thought, but it is only when you see people looking
ridiculous that you realise just how much you love them.

AGATHA CHRISTIE

Love is someone you can be silly with.

CECIL BEATON

The test for true love is whether you can endure the thought of cutting
your sweetheart's toenails.

W.N.P. BARBELLION

Is not general incivility the very essence of love? **JANE AUSTEN**

Being loved can never be a patch on being murdered. That's when someone gives their all for you. **QUENTIN CRISP**

He loves her as if she were dead. **GERALDINE ENDSOR JEWSBURY**

Sex is a momentary itch; love never lets you go. **KINGSLEY AMIS**

I met my husband when I worked in a delicatessen on the King's Road. He had come in to buy an apple pie. I sold him a meat pie by mistake and we fell in love over a plate of steak and kidney and custard. **ALICE THOMAS ELLIS**

Love gratified is love satisfied, and love satisfied is indifference begun.

SAMUEL RICHARDSON

I have never met anybody who has been made as happy by love as he has been made sad. **ALICE THOMAS ELLIS**

Men have died from time to time and worms have eaten them, but not for love. **WILLIAM SHAKESPEARE**

If you could see my feet when I take my boots off, you'd form some idea of what unrequited affection is. **CHARLES DICKENS**

Women who love the same man do have a kind of bitter freemasonry. **SIR MAX BEERBOHM**

There is nothing in the world like the devotion of a married woman. It's a thing no married man knows anything about. **OSCAR WILDE**

My motto is 'Love and Let Love' – with the one stipulation that people who love in glasshouses should breathe on the windows.

P.G. WODEHOUSE

All my life affection has been showered on me, and every forward step I have made has been taken in spite of it. **GEORGE BERNARD SHAW**

Men love women, women love children, children love hamsters, hamsters don't love anybody. **ALICE THOMAS ELLIS**

HATE

'I hate you, I hate you!' cried Madeline, a thing I didn't know anyone ever said except in the second act of a musical comedy. **P.G. WODEHOUSE**

I hate nobody except Hitler – and that is professional. **WINSTON CHURCHILL**

He hates me or I hate him – the same thing. **ALAN BENNETT**

Oh, you are awful...but I like you. **DICK EMERY**

It does not matter much what a man hates provided he hates something.

SAMUEL BUTLER

He left a bad taste in my mind. **GERALDINE ENDSOR JEWSBURY**

Haven't you noticed how we all specialise in what we hate most?

KINGSLEY AMIS

I have only one regret remaining now in this matter. It is simply that I was unable to look down upon her open coffin and, like the bird in the Book of Tobit, drop a good, large mess in her eye.

JOHN OSBORNE ON THE DEATH OF HIS EX-WIFE, JILL BENNETT

Perhaps hate is recycled love.

JEFFREY BERNARD

My dislike is purely platonic.

HERBERT BEERBOHM TREE

MARRIAGE

It is a truth universally acknowledged, that a single man in possession of a good fortune must be in want of a wife.

JANE AUSTEN

Damnit, it's your duty to get married. You can't be always living for pleasure.

OSCAR WILDE

Marriage is popular because it combines the maximum of temptation with the maximum of opportunity.

GEORGE BERNARD SHAW

It's just handy to fuck your best friend.

JOHN LENNON ON YOKO ONO

Marriage is like the witness protection programme: you get all new clothes, you live in the suburbs and you're not allowed to see your friends anymore.

JEREMY HARDY

A lady's imagination is very rapid; it jumps from admiration to love, from love to matrimony in a moment.

JANE AUSTEN

I don't believe that people would ever fall in love or want to be married if they hadn't been told about it. It's like abroad: no one would want to go there if they hadn't been told it existed.

EVELYN WAUGH

Marriage, well, I think it's a marvellous thing for other people, like going to the stake.

PHILIP LARKIN

If I were married to a hogshead of claret, matrimony would make me hate it.

SIR JOHN VANBRUGH

The surest way to hit a woman's heart is to take aim kneeling.

DOUGLAS JERROLD

I was engaged to a contortionist but she broke it off.   **LES DAWSON**

It is always incomprehensible to a man that a woman should ever refuse an offer of marriage.   **JANE AUSTEN**

No man ever saw a man he would be willing to marry if he were a woman.

GEORGE GIBBS

I was in hopes that Lord Illingworth would have married Lady Kelso. But I believe he said her family was too large. Or was it her feet? I forget which.   **OSCAR WILDE**

Having a wedding without mentioning divorce is like sending someone to war without mentioning that people are going to get killed.

RICHARD CURTIS

Splendid couple – slept with both of them.   **MAURICE BOWRA AT A WEDDING**

Nothing to me is more distasteful than that entire complacency and satisfaction which beam in the countenances of a newly married couple.

CHARLES LAMB

The bride's attitude towards her betrothed can be summed up in three words: Aisle. Altar. Hymn.   **FRANK MUIR**

My wife of eleven years – and that's quite old for a Filippino…   **JIM TAVARE**

She married in haste and repented at Brixton.   **NOËL COWARD**

I left home to marry a man whom no one liked, and after I married him I didn't like him either. **MARGERY ALLINGHAM**

We were happily married for eight months. Unfortunately we were married for four years. **NICK FALDO**

A loving wife is better than making 50 at cricket or even 99; beyond that I will not go. **SIR JAMES BARRIE**

Anniversaries are like toilets – men usually manage to miss them. **JO BRAND**

I have often wanted to drown my troubles, but I can't get my wife to go swimming. **ROY 'CHUBBY' BROWN**

—Was Elaine a trial?
—No, more of a jury. **CYRIL CONNOLLY AND KENNETH TYNAN**

Her essential value to her husband was that she laughed at his jokes. **THE TIMES**

Changeable women are more endurable than monotonous ones; they are sometimes murdered but rarely deserted. **GEORGE BERNARD SHAW**

The penalty for getting the woman is that you must keep her. **LIONEL STRACHEY**

I've been married to Florence for 80 years. The secret of a happy marriage is: 'Yes, dear.' **PERCY ARROWSMITH**

The secret of marital happiness is simple: drink in different pubs to your other half. **JILLY COOPER**

If you cannot have your dear husband for a comfort and a delight, for a breadwinner and a crosspatch, for a sofa, chair, or hot water bottle, one can use him as a Cross to be borne.   **STEVIE SMITH**

The concept of two people living together for 25 years without a serious dispute suggests a lack of spirit only to be admired in sheep.   **A. P. HERBERT**

We've managed 24 years of marriage – with a lot of broken crockery along the way.   **EILEEN ATKINS**

A dentist got married to a manicurist. They fought tooth and nail.   TOMMY COOPER

Marriage is like wine. It is not properly judged until the second glass.   **DOUGLAS JERROLD**

To dare to live alone is the rarest courage; since there are many who had rather meet their bitterest enemy in the field, than their own hearts in their closet.   **CHARLES CALEB COLTON**

The extreme penalty for bigamy? Two mothers-in-law.   **LORD CHIEF JUSTICE RUSSELL**

English law prohibits a man from marrying his mother-in-law. This is a perfect example of totally unnecessary legislation.   **CLEMENT FREUD**

I never married because there was no need. I have three pets at home which answer the same purpose as a husband. I have a dog which growls every morning, a parrot which swears all afternoon, and a cat that comes home late at night.   **MARIE CORELLI**

Bigamists seldom look capable of getting one woman to marry them, let alone two.   **MONICA DICKENS**

ADULTERY

Must we, if we love an apple, nevermore desire a peach?   **JOHN GAY**

My mother said, 'I wouldn't trust my husband with a young woman for five minutes, and he's been dead for 25 years.'   **BRENDAN BEHAN**

A mistress should be like a little country retreat near the town, not to dwell in constantly, but only for a night and away.   **WILLIAM WYCHERLEY**

It is better taste somehow that a man should be unfaithful to his wife away from home.   **BARBARA PYM**

Next to the pleasures of taking a new mistress is that of being rid of an old one.   **WILLIAM WYCHERLEY**

What men call gallantry, and gods adultery,
Is much more common where the climate's sultry.   **LORD BYRON**

You know, of course, that the Tasmanians, who never committed adultery, are now extinct.   **W. SOMERSET MAUGHAM**

DIVORCE

After I won the Million Dollar Challenge in South Africa, I asked my wife if she'd like a Versace dress, diamonds or pearls as a present, but she said, 'No!' When I asked her what she did want, she said, 'A divorce,' but I told her I wasn't intending to spend that much.   **NICK FALDO**

Greater luck hath no man than this, that he lay down his wife at the right moment.
SAMUEL BUTLER

Judges, as a class, display, in the matter of arranging alimony, that reckless generosity which is found only in men who are giving away someone else's cash.
P.G. WODEHOUSE

My acquaintance is divided fairly evenly between those who are desperate to get married and those who are equally desperate to get divorced.
ALICE THOMAS ELLIS

All women are stimulated by the news that any wife has left her husband.
ANTHONY POWELL

After Simon Raven had broken with his wife she telegraphed: 'WIFE AND BABY STARVING.' Simon is supposed to have wired back: 'EAT BABY.'
FRANCES PARTRIDGE

FAMILY

—You will end up childless and alone.
—Well, fingers crossed, yeah.
CHRISTINE AND WILL, *ABOUT A BOY*

—Do you know, a yoghurt pot of my semen could repopulate the whole of Ireland?
—Haven't they had a tragic enough history without you turning up at the border with your yoghurt pot?
GARY AND DOROTHY, *MEN BEHAVING BADLY*

I looked up some of the symptoms of pregnancy: moody, irritable, big bosoms. I've obviously been pregnant for 36 years.
VICTORIA WOOD

Yes, I did father a child with Wendy Craig. It all happened in the 1960s. We were very excitable then.
JOHN MORTIMER

What do I think of impending fatherhood? Well, however happy
I am during the day, at night there is a foetus with an axe.

STEVE TAYLOR, *COUPLING*

He that doth get a wench with child and marries her afterwards it
is as if a man should shit in his hat and then clap it on his head.

SAMUEL PEPYS

My best mate's girlfriend is six months pregnant. She said to me, 'Do you want to feel the baby?' On reflection I think she meant on the *outside*. JIMMY CARR

Parents are the last people on earth who ought to have children.

SAMUEL BUTLER

To lose one parent may be regarded as a misfortune; to lose both looks
like carelessness. OSCAR WILDE

Having children accentuates more marital faults than adultery does.

JULIE BURCHILL

My friend spent 50 quid on a baby alarm and *still* got pregnant.

LINDA SMITH

Let all babies be born. Then let us drown those we do not like.

G.K. CHESTERTON

They say men can never experience the pain of childbirth. They
can if you hit them in the goolies with a cricket bat. For 14 hours.

JO BRAND

He said he had been born in the saddle. It must have been hard on
his mother. TOMMY COOPER

My first words, as I was being born...I looked up at my mother and said,
'That's the last time I'm going up one of those!' STEPHEN FRY

All babies are supposed to look like me – at both ends. WINSTON CHURCHILL

—She's got your eyes.
—Has she? I wondered where they'd gone. SPIKE MILLIGAN

I've got my figure back after giving birth. Sad, I'd hoped to get
somebody else's. CAROLINE QUENTIN

For some months after my birth I led a happy, useful, and productive life,
lying nude on an astrakhan rug, eating coal.
JON PERTWEE, MOON BOOTS

Never hold a naked baby boy up in front of you because he will urinate
in your face. JEREMY HARDY

My father was the only person I ever knew who addressed babies in their
prams as if they were his contemporaries. He spoke as he would to a
bank manager or a bishop; friendly but respectful. JOYCE GRENFELL

I love children – especially when they cry, for then someone takes them away.
NANCY MITFORD

My sister just had a baby. She said, 'Do you want to wind him?'
I said, 'I'll give him a dead leg, shall I?' JIMMY CARR

I was much distressed by next door people who had twin babies and played the violin: but one of the twins died, and the other has eaten the fiddle – so all is peace.

EDWARD LEAR

—Vicky, where's your baby?
—Swapped it for a Westlife CD.
—How could you do such a thing?
—I know, they're rubbish.

SOCIAL WORKER AND VICKY POLLARD, *LITTLE BRITAIN*

If you want to get a pet for your child, I suggest a chicken so that when they get bored of it after a couple of days at least you can have a nice roast dinner.

JO BRAND

Things a mother should know: how to comfort a son without exactly saying Daddy was wrong.

KATHARINE WHITEHORN

Motherhood brought many joys, but catching sight of the underneath of my neck in the mirror of the Tommee Tippee Activity Centre wasn't one of them.

VICTORIA WOOD

Things a mother should know: how to drive a car safely with the children's hands over her eyes.

KATHARINE WHITEHORN

A kid loses his mum in Tesco's. The supervisor says, 'What's she like?' The kid says, 'Big dicks and vodka.' ANON

Make bathtime as much fun for kiddies as a trip to the seaside, by chucking a bucket of sand, a bag of salt, a dog turd and a broken bottle into the bath with them.

A HITCH, *VIZ*, TOP TIP

There was a kid crying in the supermarket so I said to the mother, 'Did you hit this child?' She said, 'No.' I said, 'Why not?'   **DAVE SPIKEY**

It is every mother's duty to embarrass her child. There are several ways you can do this: you can buy the whole family matching anoraks and insist on walking up and down the high street together holding hands. Or you can put on loads and loads of weight then run in the school sports day's mums and daughters race – in your knickers.   **JENNY ECLAIR**

I can only regard children as defective adults.   **EVELYN WAUGH**

Children of Progressive Parents Admitted Only on Leads
   NOTICE IN LONDON RESTAURANT

Both the aunt and the children were conversational in a limited, persistent way. Most of the aunt's remarks seemed to begin with 'Don't', and nearly all of the children's remarks began with 'Why?'   **SAKI**

When I consider how little of a rarity children are, I cannot for my life tell what cause for pride there can possibly be in having them.
   CHARLES LAMB

The trouble with children is that they are not returnable.   **QUENTIN CRISP**

I know a dozen boys at least whom I would willingly exchange for the intimacy of a pair of long-tailed tits.   **E.V. LUCAS**

Their eldest son was such a disappointment to them; they wanted him to be a linguist, and spent no end of money on having him taught to speak – oh, dozens of languages! – and then he became a Trappist monk.
   SAKI

When people have far more children than is either convenient or necessary, the babies always exhibit extraordinary vitality. Nothing seems to kill them.   **SIR JOHN HANKIN**

My father woke me up at three o'clock in the morning and said, 'Son, I've never shot a tiger.' 'Oh, why did you have to tell me?' He said, 'I've got to tell somebody.'   **SPIKE MILLIGAN**

Few misfortunes can befall a boy which bring worse consequences than to have a really affectionate mother.

W. SOMERSET MAUGHAM

My mum says, 'Give me three rings to let me know you're safe and after the second ring she picks up the phone – what's the point of that?
PETER KAY

My mother was a vengeful person. She used to get up in the morning, and say: 'The Lord tells us to turn the other cheek, but there are only so many cheeks in a day.'   **JEANETTE WINTERSON**

I'd be the worst possible godfather. I'd probably drop her on her head at the christening. I'd forget all her birthdays until she was 18. Then I'd take her out, get her drunk and, quite possibly, try to shag her.
WILL, *ABOUT A BOY*

It is almost nicer being a godfather than a father, like having white mice but making your nanny feed them for you.   **THOMAS HANBURY WHITE**

As a rule there is only one person an English girl hates more than she hates her eldest sister, and that's her mother.   **GEORGE BERNARD SHAW**

The kid took to me right away. It could be because on our first meeting I took her to the zoo, and shook her upside down. I wish all relationships with human beings were that easy. **WILL,** *ABOUT A BOY*

My little sister Lily is a whore in Piccadilly
My mother is another in the Strand
My father hawks his arsehole
Round the Elephant and Castle
We're the finest fucking family in the land. **ANON**

Relations are simply a tedious pack of people who haven't got the remotest knowledge of how to live, nor the smallest instinct about when to die. **OSCAR WILDE**

—How do you feel that your mum's so worried about your addiction?
—If I was a teetotal vicar, she'd be equally worried that my bicycle-clips were too tight. **KIRSTY WARK AND PETE DOHERTY**

The sisters entered the drawing-room in the full fervour of sisterly animosity. **R.S. SURTEES**

I hate my brother. The only reason I speak to him is because you never know when you might need a kidney. **LILY SAVAGE**

I knew her mother was coming round. I saw the canary throw itself in the cat's mouth. **ROY 'CHUBBY' BROWN**

It is no use telling me that there are bad aunts and good aunts. At the core they are all alike. Sooner or later, out pops the cloven hoof. **P.G. WODEHOUSE**

Peter remained on friendly terms with Christ notwithstanding Christ's
having healed his mother-in-law.   **SAMUEL BUTLER**

However much you dislike your mother-in-law you must not set fire to her.
                                                    ERNEST WILD

Everyone has an aunt in Tunbridge Wells.   **BRIAN JOHNSON**

When my mother-in-law was born, they fired 21 guns. The only trouble
was, they all missed.   **LES DAWSON**

My grandma was in her seventies when she came to live with us and
had suffered two strokes since her arrival. My brothers used to say,
'At the third stroke, she will be 70-something.'   **JULIE WALTERS**

—I don't think I have told you anything about my grandchildren.
—For which, madam, I am infinitely grateful.
                        ROSE KENNEDY AND WINSTON CHURCHILL

SEX EDUCATION

—If you want, I'll show you my fanny.
—Nah, I'm alright.   **DEBBIE WILKINSON AND BILLY ELLIOT, *BILLY ELLIOT***

My father once attempted to give a very straightforward account of the
whole reproductive process. To his amusement, I rushed out of the room
to be sick before he was half finished.   **JOHN OSBORNE**

She'd been told the facts of life and didn't think much of them.   **DODIE SMITH**

The only talk I've had on sex was from an embarrassed headmaster
about the reproduction of lupins. I'm as ready as can be if ever I fall in
love with a lupin.   **MILES KINGTON**

As I congratulated a friend on his marriage, my young son turned to him and said, 'When are you going to give your pollen to her?'

CHRISTIAN LORIMER

A friend of mine, when leaving Harrow, was assailed at the beginning of a serious talk from his housemaster with the words, 'I don't know if you've ever noticed, but between your legs…'

TIM BROOKE-TAYLOR

I've never even had sex apart from that one time eight months ago but apart from that I'm a complete virgin.

VICKY POLLARD, *LITTLE BRITAIN*

The headmaster summoned all the boys who had reached the age of puberty to his study and, after reassuring himself that the door was firmly secured, made the following brief announcement: 'If you touch it, it will fall off.'

PETER USTINOV

The only sex education I got at school was just as we were about to leave, a master said, 'Don't fornicate in Old Etonian braces.' It was as good advice as any.

ROBERT MASON

The headmaster used to have a private talk with individual leavers which we presumed would be mutually embarrassing, but turned out to be a homily on evacuating the bowels thrice daily.

ARTHUR MARSHALL

Sex education at my school was a muttered warning about the janitor.

FRANKIE BOYLE

Losing your real virginity is when you first come with someone, I believe. A bit like the Queen having two birthdays.

JULIE BURCHILL

Sex was not a subject we discussed in our family. I didn't even realise I had a vagina. The loss of my virginity was a process so lengthy and so painful that I thought, Oh, I see, the man actually has to make the hole by pounding away with his penis.

JULIE WALTERS

There was a young girl from Cape Cod,
Who thought babies all came from God.
But it wasn't the Almighty
Who lifted her nightie
It was Roger, the lodger, the sod.

ANON

I knew nothing at all about sex and simply thought that masturbation was a unique discovery on my part.

JEFFREY BERNARD

I sometimes wonder if there aren't advantages in missing some of the facts of life.

WILLIAM DOUGLAS-HOME

HOME

I'm buying a house at the moment so I've just had a survey done. Eighty per cent of people said I should go ahead.

SEAN HUGHES

Experts have spent years developing weapons which can destroy people's lives but leave buildings intact. They're called mortgages.

JEREMY HARDY

Always live in the ugliest house in the street – then you don't have to look at it.

DAVID HOCKNEY

Samantha lives quietly in a small converted cottage in East Sussex. The cottage is her great passion, and she is lucky to have a professional roofer living next door in case she needs to get felt laid down in the loft.

HUMPHREY LYTTELTON

People's backyards are much more interesting than their front gardens, and houses that back on to railways are public benefactors.

SIR JOHN BETJEMAN

'An Englishman's home is his castle' so the saying goes, which means it should be a ruin with a gift shop.   **JEREMY HARDY**

How very different from the home life of our own dear Queen!

RONALD FIRBANK

All was calm at Wretch Manor. The Colonel was dozing in his study, with a copy of *Horse, Gun, and Rod* in his lap. Mrs Wretch was cutting out of a newspaper a recipe for turnip omelette.   **J.B. MORTON**

—Well, what can I tell you, I moved around a lot, saw a lot of army bases.
—Oh, was your dad in the military?
—No, no, just a coincidence.

MANNY BIANCO AND FRAN KATZENJAMMER, *BLACK BOOKS*

Addresses are given to us to conceal our whereabouts.   **SAKI**

I come from a poor neighbourhood. If anyone ever paid their rent, the police immediately come round to see where they got the money from.

ALEXEI SAYLE

Our neighbourhood was so rough, any cat with a tail was considered posh.

LES DAWSON

I wouldn't say my neighbourhood's rough, but the local paper has a column for forthcoming deaths.   **BOB MONKHOUSE**

INTERIOR DESIGN

Have you seen this décor? It's like being up Zandra Rhodes's bottom.

JUSTIN RYAN

The look I've gone for is classic late Victorian meets My Little Pony.

ALICE TINKER, *THE VICAR OF DIBLEY*

There are some lace curtains popular nowadays that are gathered up for some reason in the middle. They look to me like a woman who's been to the lav and got her underskirt caught up behind her.   **ALAN BENNETT**

I hate minimalism. It's so clinical – like being in an STD clinic. Not that I've ever been in one of them places.   **PAUL O'GRADY**

IKEA's 'Chuck Out Your Chintz' advertising campaign wasn't just against Victoriana. It was against one-nation conservatism. The myth of Little England. John Bull. An obsession with the aristocracy, the monarchy. The chintz aesthetic is determined by upper-middle-class aspirations – people wanting to have a country house, even if they live in a semi.

MITCHELL BATES

Whilst shopping at a DIY store I was interested to note the availability of 'Georgian Style' light switches.   **EMMA COLEMAN**

You think you'll do some little job, perfectly simple… Fate isn't going to have it. I once sat down to put some new cotton wool in a cigarette lighter, and before I'd finished I'd got all the floorboards up in the spare bedroom.   **BASIL BOOTHROYD**

—I hope you'll sleep all right; it's rather a busy wallpaper in the bedroom.
—It'll be fine. I always sleep with my eyes closed.

UNNAMED HOST AND GEORGE BERNARD SHAW

She's an interior designer on that show *Pet Surprise*, you know, the one where they take the dog out for a walk, he thinks it's a normal walk and when he gets back the kennel's got a patio and french doors, and he's, like, 'OH MY GOD!'
BERNARD BLACK, *BLACK BOOKS*

TASTE AND VULGARITY

If you'd spent most of your life on a warship you would not know about taste either.
QUEEN MOTHER ON THE DÉCOR OF THE DUKE OF YORK'S SUNNINGHILL HOME

Taste can be vulgar, but it must never be embarrassing.
NOËL COWARD

Nothing is more debasing for a real man than a plastic apron.
COUNTESS SPENCER

'Whoever has opened the window has opened it too wide,' said Miss Brodie. 'Six inches is perfectly adequate. More is vulgar.'
MURIEL SPARK, *THE PRIME OF MISS JEAN BRODIE*

Bad taste is, specifically, gladioli, cut-glass flower-bowls, two-tone motor cars and dollies to hide telephones. Good taste is, frankly, what I think is good taste.
DAVID HICKS

I don't think I've got bad taste. I've got no taste.
GRAHAM NORTON

I have never believed that jewels, any more than motor cars, can be called vulgar just because they are gigantic.

DENISA, LADY NEWBOROUGH

HOUSEWORK

—Look, I've just cut my finger clipping your blasted hedge.
—Don't swear, Jerry. And don't bleed in the sink, I've just cleaned it.

JERRY AND MARGOT LEADBETTER, *THE GOOD LIFE*

Wagner summoned his charwoman. 'Look here,' he said angrily, 'I can write my name in dust on this piano!' 'It's a grand thing to be so educated,' replied the charwoman. **J.B. MORTON**

Everything must be put back in its proper disorder. **BARBARA PYM**

Have you ever taken anything out of the clothes basket because it has become, relatively, the cleaner thing? **KATHARINE WHITEHORN**

How do you know if it's time to wash the dishes and clean the house? Look inside your pants. If you find a penis in there, it's not time. **JO BRAND**

Handing over the Hoover to my mother was like distributing highly sophisticated weapons to an underdeveloped African nation.

ALAN BENNETT

My mother refused to have a Hoover in the house. She said it sucked all the goodness out of the carpet. **IVY COMPTON-BURNETT**

Ten Things You Wish You'd Never Started: Number 6: Trying out a sample of carpet shampoo. *YOU* **MAGAZINE**

Increase the life of your carpets by rolling them up and keeping them in the garage. **A. ALLIED,** *VIZ,* **TOP TIP**

My mum told me I'd better get a toilet brush, so I did. I've been using it for a week, but I think I'm going back to paper. **DAVE SPIKEY**

Neither of us ever attempted to do much about the house. Once a large and rather expensive pork pie inexplicably went missing here. Though we searched and, over the years, always half expected its re-emergence, it has not yet turned up.   **JOHN BAYLEY**

One of the advantages of being disorderly is that one is constantly making exciting discoveries.   **A.A. MILNE**

Cleanliness is almost as bad as godliness.   **SAMUEL BUTLER**

There is no need to do any housework at all. After the first four years the dirt doesn't get any worse.   **QUENTIN CRISP**

At worst, a house unkept cannot be so distressing as a life unlived.

ROSE MACAULAY

NEIGHBOURS

'In *that* direction,' the Cat said, waving its right paw round, 'lives a Hatter: and in *that* direction,' waving the other paw, 'lives a March Hare. Visit either you like: they're both mad.'

LEWIS CARROLL, *ALICE'S ADVENTURES IN WONDERLAND*

[*on the phone*] Hello, is that Mr Akbar? Mrs Slocombe here, your next door neighbour. I wonder – would you do me a little favour? Would you go to my front door, bend down, look through the letterbox...and if you can see my pussy, would you drop a sardine on the mat?

MRS SLOCOMBE, *ARE YOU BEING SERVED?*

There's a woman who lives opposite me who plays pop music very loudly all weekend with her windows wide open and I can't tell her off because she is black. I resent that. Not being able to tell her off, I mean.

JEFFREY BERNARD

The Bible tells us to love our neighbours, and also to love our enemies; probably because they are generally the same people. **G.K. CHESTERTON**

My dad was raised in a close-knit village community and used to complain, 'Neighbours – they know who you've hit and when you shit.' **CAITLIN MORAN**

FRIENDS AND ENEMIES

I noticed your hostility towards him. I ought to have guessed you were friends. **MALCOLM BRADBURY**

I do not believe that friends are necessarily the people you like best, they are merely the people who got there first. **PETER USTINOV**

Laughter is not a bad beginning for a friendship, and it is by far the best ending for one. **OSCAR WILDE**

We cherish our friends not for their ability to amuse us, but for ours to amuse them. **EVELYN WAUGH**

The feeling of friendship is like that of being comfortably filled with roast beef; love, like being enlivened with champagne. **SAMUEL JOHNSON**

The only people I care to be very intimate with are the ones you feel would make a good third if God asked you out to dinner. **NANCY MITFORD**

D.H. Lawrence has an odd propensity to vomit his friends after a certain period. **LADY OTTOLINE MORRELL**

Mrs Montagu has dropt me. Now, sir, there are people whom one should like very well to drop, but would not wish to be dropt by. **SAMUEL JOHNSON**

So much for James and Maggie Preston. At least we won't have to listen to any more of those interminable stories about her womb.

MARGOT LEADBETTER, *THE GOOD LIFE*

I lost closer friends than 'darling Georgie' the last time I was deloused.

CAPTAIN BLACKADDER, *BLACKADDER GOES FORTH*

A true friend stabs you in the front.

OSCAR WILDE

A hedge between keeps friendship green.

ENGLISH PROVERB

Often we have no time for our friends but all the time in the world for our enemies.

LEON URIS

Lifelong enemies are, I think, as hard to make and as important to one's well-being as friends.

JESSICA MITFORD

The only thing that helps me maintain my slender grip on reality is the friendship I share with my collection of singing potatoes.   **HOLLY,** *RED DWARF II*

WORK

One must have some sort of occupation nowadays. If I hadn't my debts I shouldn't have anything to think about.

OSCAR WILDE

Wanted: Knife-thrower's assistant with more faith than the Pope.

ADVERTISEMENT BY THE COTTLE AND AUSTEN CIRCUS

I ran away to the circus. Circus people loved me: I was the only one who could get the tent back in the bag.

KEN DODD

Some of us will want to follow in father's footsteps…but we can't sign on for ever can we?

PAULINE CAMPBELL-JONES, *THE LEAGUE OF GENTLEMEN*

I though I would enter the priesthood, though not for any better reason than that I looked like a vicar. A few years later, when I had started wearing glasses, I nearly became a don on the same dubious principle.

ALAN BENNETT

It is wonderful when a calculation is made, how little the mind is actually employed in the discharge of any profession. SAMUEL JOHNSON

Fred Elliott at your service, I say, at your service. Weatherfield's butcher, I'm known for my meaty sausage and spicy ring.

FRED ELLIOTT, *CORONATION STREET*

—We're just filling in as book publishers. Normally, if you'll forgive the expression, we're actors by trade.
—But trade's been a bit rough lately, so we've had to take whatever we can get. SANDY AND JULIAN, *ROUND THE HORNE*

If I had been someone not very clever, I would have done an easier job like publishing. That's the easiest job I can think of. A.J. AYER

I was working in Burger King when Andrew Lloyd Webber walked in. He said, 'Give me two whoppers.' I said, 'You're good looking and your musicals are great.' TIM VINE

—What is your profession?
—I'm a gentleman farmer.
—I suppose that means you're neither. INTERVIEWEE AND GILBERT HARDING

I'm a sociable worker. BRENDAN BEHAN

The chief occupation of the job of strawberry picking was the ability to whistle. The young pickers were supposed to whistle all the time to prove they were not eating the strawberries.   **HARRY LAUDER**

The most dangerous job in the world is the man who has to put the first cone out in the fast lane of the A1.   **LEE EVANS**

I once had a job painting the white lines down roadways, but I packed it in before I went round the bend.   **TOMMY COOPER**

There's only one thing worse than an estate agent but at least that can be safely lanced, drained and surgically dressed.   **STEPHEN FRY**

If I were a grave-digger or even a hangman, there are some people I could work for with a great deal of enjoyment.   **DOUGLAS JERROLD**

The dole is a venerable socialist institution, we've all been on it. Money for drugs – don't knock it.   **JOHN PERRY**

One cannot walk through an assembly factory and not feel that one is in Hell.   **W. H. AUDEN**

I am deeply indebted to my lack of shorthand and typing. It probably saved me from a lifetime of hard work.   **PATRICK CAMPBELL**

I like work; it fascinates me. I could sit and look at it for hours.   **JEROME K. JEROME**

In a survey of British schoolchildren under the age of twelve, when asked what they wanted to be when they grew up, 97 per cent said they wanted to be famous and the other three referred the question to their agents.

BEN THOMPSON

Work harder! Millions on welfare depend on you.

R.U. SEERIUS, ELECTION SLOGAN, MONSTER RAVING LOONY PARTY

Anybody who works is a fool. I don't work, I merely inflict myself on the public.

ROBERT MORLEY

Work is like what cats are supposed to be: if you dislike it and fear it and try to keep out of its way, it knows at once and seeks you out.

KINGSLEY AMIS

IDLENESS

I suppose that there is no nation in the world which has so little capacity for doing nothing gracefully, and enjoying it, as the English.

A.C. BENSON

He did nothing in particular, and did it very well.

W.S. GILBERT

Idling has always been my strong point. I take no credit to myself – it is a gift.

JEROME K. JEROME

It was not in his nature to make the mistake of doing something when there was nothing to be done.

ROBERT SPEAIGHT

Idleness is only a coarse name for my infinite capacity for living in the present.

CYRIL CONNOLLY

It is impossible to enjoy idling thoroughly unless one has plenty of work to do.

JEROME K. JEROME

I am constitutionally lazy. Millais used to say of me, when we were young men, that when I began to work, I was too lazy to stop.

WILFRID SCAWEN BLUNT

SPORT AND
LEISURE

SPORT – GENERAL

The only way of preventing civilised men from beating and kicking their wives is to organise games in which they can kick and beat balls.

GEORGE BERNARD SHAW

The ball is man's most disastrous invention, not excluding the wheel.

ROBERT MORLEY

Serious sport has nothing to do with fair play. It is bound up with hatred, jealousy, boastfulness, disregard of all rules and sadistic pleasure in witnessing violence. In other words, it is war minus the shooting.

GEORGE ORWELL

Like most people I lived for a long time with my mother and father. My father liked to watch the wrestling. My mother liked to wrestle.

JEANETTE WINTERSON

I was watching Sumo wrestling on the television for two hours before I realised it was darts.

HATTIE HAYRIDGE

It couldn't be more exciting if Elvis walked in and asked for a bag of chips.

SYD WADDELL COMMENTATING ON A SNOOKER MATCH

This lad can pot them from anywhere, even standing in a hammock.

SYD WADDELL COMMENTATING ON A SNOOKER MATCH

Swimming pools in Britain have very strict rules: no bombing, no petting, no ducking, and no fondue parties.

TOM BAKER, NARRATOR, *LITTLE BRITAIN*

—Ten miles he swam – the last three were agony.
—They were over land.

GREENSLADE AND SEAGOON, *THE GOON SHOW*

The members of Ashton Conker Club, the organising body for the World Conker Championship, are far from despondent about the men's title going to Germany. The day of the Euroconker is here.

J.A. HADMAN

Cads have always a grandmother who is the Duchess of Blank hem hem. They are inclined to cheat at conkers having baked them for 300 years in the ancestral ovens. **GEOFFREY WILLANS AND RONALD SEARLE**

World Dart Players are beer-swilling, gold-chain-wearing, aftershave-reeking, 16-months-pregnant gentlemen (most of whom probably haven't seen their penises since last millennium) supported by the sort of women who only wear knickers to keep their feet warm.

VICTOR LEWIS-SMITH

Squash – that's not exercise, that's flagellation. **NOËL COWARD**

Grand Prix driving is like balancing an egg on a spoon while shooting the rapids. **GRAHAM HILL**

Driving a racing car is like lying in the bath with your feet on the taps but not as comfortable. **DAVID COULTHARD**

Nigel Mansell is the only man who goes to Nick Faldo for charisma lessons. **NICK HANCOCK**

Pooh Sticks is a highly competitive art form, a precision skill that requires not only near-perfect hand-eye co-ordination and a plentiful supply of the proper equipment (sticks) but, crucially, the will and ability to cheat.

STEFANIE MARSH

Skiing is buying two thousand pounds' of silly clothes and equipment and travelling a thousand miles through snow in a coach to stand around in a disco getting drunk.

PHILIP HOWARD

There is no rule to say that dog-racing must be done by greyhounds. In fact, there is no reason why one shouldn't have Pekinese chasing an electric éclair.

ANTHONY ARMSTRONG

Plainly no way has yet been found to stop long-jump commentaries sounding like naughty stories after lights-out in the dorm – 'Ooooh! It's enormous. It was so long!'

RUSSELL DAVIES

Murphy did the 100 meters in record time. He got six months. They were gas meters.

FRANK CARSON

The only athletic sport I have ever mastered is backgammon.

DOUGLAS JERROLD

Nowadays the only serious aquatic sport that I indulge in is the occasional game of Pooh-sticks.

ARTHUR MARSHALL

What we need is a unique sport we can beat the world at. Does any other country play Quidditch?

TONY KILEEN

CRICKET

Neil Harvey's at slip, with his legs wide apart, waiting for a tickle.

BRIAN JOHNSTON

What a magnificent shot! No, he's out.

TONY GREIG

A.R. Gover, the Surrey captain, while pulling his sweater over his head, made a catch between his legs.

J.L. CARR

There is a widely held and quite erroneous belief that cricket is just another game.

PRINCE PHILIP

Cricket is a game which the English, not being a spiritual people, have invented in order to give themselves some conception of Eternity.

LORD STORMONT MANCROFT

I don't play cricket. It requires one to adopt such indecent postures.

OSCAR WILDE

I tend to believe that cricket is the greatest thing that God ever created on Earth…certainly greater than sex although sex isn't too bad either. But everyone knows which comes first when it's a question of cricket or sex.

HAROLD PINTER

J.L. Carr switched allegiance from soccer to cricket because cricket is a game of second chances.

SIMON JENKINS

Here is a game so doggedly peculiar and dangerous that no foreign nations have ever adopted it.

PETER USTINOV

If Stalin had learned to play cricket, the world might now be a better place.

BISHOP RICHARD DOWNEY

To have some idea what it's like facing a fast bowler, stand in the outside lane of a motorway, get your mate to drive his car at you at 95 mph and wait until he's twelve yards away, before you decide which way to jump.

GEOFFREY BOYCOTT

I read a history book once (forget which) which said that cricket is what made the industrial revolution a bloodless one and thus so effective.

SIMON BARD

I discovered to my surprise that the MCC blazer was not red, white and blue.

HERBERT FARJEON

It's a funny kind of month, October. For the really keen cricket fan it's when you discover that your wife left you in May.

DENIS NORDEN

The members seated in the Pavilion at the Test Match refused to join in the Mexican Wave. Well, when you get to a certain age, every time you just get out of your chair, it's a bit of an adventure.

HENRY BLOFELD

Pitches are like wives, you never know how they're going to turn out.

SIR LEN HUTTON

The seats at Lord's are uncommonly hard, and a *Daily Telegraph*, folded twice and placed beneath one, brings something of the solace which good literature will always bring.

A.A. MILNE

He often fielded at deep third man on the slope. He could not see the game, and the other players could not see him. He got his own back for this indignity by rolling the ball in a fresh cowpat.

JAMES PRESTON

They asked me what I wanted to call my autobiography. I suggested: The Definitive Volume on the Finest Bloody Fast Bowler That Ever Drew Breath.

FRED TRUEMAN

Len Hutton's bat was part of his nervous system.

HAROLD PINTER

This bowler's like my dog: three short legs and balls that swing each way.

BRIAN JOHNSTON

Asif Masood approaches the wicket like Groucho Marx chasing after a pretty waitress.

JOHN ARLOTT

And when you rub the ball on rump or belly,
Remember what it looks like on the telly.

A.P. HERBERT

The batsman's technique was like an old lady poking her umbrella at a wasps' nest.

JOHN ARLOTT

The umpire is like the geyser in the bathroom; we cannot do without it, yet we notice it only when it is out of order.

NEVILLE CARDUS

'Dickie' Bird arrived on earth from the Planet Looney to become the best and fairest of all umpires. Great bloke, completely bonkers.

IAN BOTHAM

I cannot for the life of me see why the umpires, the only two people on a cricket field who are not going to get grass stains on their knees, are the only two people allowed to wear dark trousers.

KATHARINE WHITEHORN

Yorkshire 232 all out – Hutton ill, I'm sorry – Hutton 111.

JOHN SNAGGE, SPORTS ANNOUNCER

Personally, I have always looked upon cricket as organised loafing.

WILLIAM TEMPLE

England will win if Camilla Parker bowls.

AUSTRALIAN FANS' BANNER

Cricket is the only game that you can actually put on weight when playing.

TOMMY DOCHERTY

Drink is a serious problem, particularly on cricket tours, for it can be said, without fear of contradiction, that nothing yet devised by man is worse for a sick hangover than a day's cricket in the summer sun.

MICHAEL PARKINSON

I play for an amateur cricket team. At the end of each season we give out prizes for 'Best Catch Taken While Smoking' and 'Baldest Player of the Year.'

ARTHUR SMITH

When 'It isn't cricket' has become an anachronism and a smear, cricket will be close to its deathbed.

J.M. KILBURN

I'll tell you what pressure is. Pressure is a Messerschmitt up your arse. Playing cricket is not.

KEITH MILLER

My wife had an uncle who could never walk down the nave of an abbey without wondering whether it would take spin.

SIR ALEC DOUGLAS-HOME

God wears white flannels.

JAMES CAMERON

Medieval theologians used to dispute how the angels in heaven spent their time, when not balancing on needle points and singing anthems to the Lord. I know. They slump glued to their clouds, glasses at the ready, as the Archangel Michael (that well-known slasher) and stonewalling St Peter open against the Devil's XI. It could not be Heaven, otherwise.

JOHN FOWLES

Oh God, if there be cricket in heaven, let there also be rain.

SIR ALEC DOUGLAS-HOME

HORSE RACING

Owning a racehorse is probably the most expensive way of getting on to a racecourse for nothing.   **CLEMENT FREUD**

One way to stop a runaway horse is to bet on him.   **JEFFREY BERNARD**

John McCririck looks like Worzel Gummidge after an incident with a letter bomb.   **VICTOR LEWIS-SMITH**

There is only one race greater than the Jews – and that is the Derby.
VICTOR SASSOON

I have no intention of watching undersized Englishmen perched on horses with matchstick legs race along courses planned to amuse Nell Gwynn.
GILBERT HARDING

Red Rum is the greatest thing on four legs since Pegasus.   **JEAN ROOK**

A real racehorse should have a head like a lady and a behind like a cook.   **JACK LEACH**

What a pity people don't take as much trouble with their own breeding as intelligent racehorse owners do. But then I suppose it is bordering on fascism to think like that.   **JEFFREY BERNARD**

If you want to understand the effect of weight on a horse, try running for a bus with nothing in your hands. Then try doing it with your hands full of shopping. Then think about doing that for four and a half miles.
JENNY PITMAN

Ten of The Most Pointless Things in the World: No 3: Urging your horse on while watching the Grand National on TV.   *YOU* **MAGAZINE**

—What are your immediate thoughts after winning, Walter?
—I don't have any immediate thoughts at the moment.

BROUGH SCOTT AND WALTER SWINBURN

If Jesus Christ rode his flaming donkey like you just rode that horse, then he deserved to be crucified. **FRED RIMELL TO AMATEUR JOCKEY, JIM OLD**

Having seen the Grand National, it was always my ambition to throw a saddle over the owner of the course and ride them over the appalling Aintree fences. **ARTHUR ASKEY**

With some justification the Jockey Club has been described as 'the purest example of the 18th century to survive in Britain'. **JOHN PURVIS**

Her Majesty is not delighted to have to miss a day's racing at Ascot for the State of Opening of Parliament. It seems that nothing is sacred any more. **ROYAL ADVISER**

BOXING

Boxers don't have sex before a fight. You know the reason why? They don't fancy each other. **JIMMY CARR**

In boxing, the right cross-counter is distinctly one of those things that it is more blessed to give than to receive. **P.G. WODEHOUSE**

Boxing is just show business with blood. **FRANK BRUNO**

In his prime, Joe Bugner had the physique of a Greek statue but he had fewer moves. **HUGH MCILVANNEY**

I'm going down so often these days you'd think I was making a blue movie. **JOHN CONTEH**

—You're aware that the press are saying you weren't trying against Ali.

—Get me Jesus Christ and I'll fight him tomorrow!

—Joe, you're only saying that because you know he's got bad hands.

HUGH MCILVANNEY AND JOE BUGNER

Were you as surprised as we all were when Steven Collins came from behind and licked you in the ring?

MRS MERTON TO CHRIS EUBANK

Mohammed Ali had the incandescent quality of the real star which would have made him famous, even if his gift was knitting not fighting.

MICHAEL PARKINSON

ROWING

The only Oxford and Cambridge Boat Races ever remembered are those in which one side has gratifyingly sunk. **MILES KINGTON**

Either Oxford or Cambridge is leading. **JOHN SNAGGE, COMMENTATOR**

Ah, isn't that nice, the wife of the Cambridge president is kissing the cox of the Oxford crew. **HARRY CARPENTER, COMMENTATOR**

Eight minds with but a single thought – if that!

SIR MAX BEERBOHM ON THE OXFORD ROWING CREW

Rowing seems to me to be a monotonous pursuit, and somehow wasteful to be making all that effort to be going in the wrong direction.

PETER USTINOV

RUGBY

Rugby is a game for the mentally deficient... That is why it was invented by the British. Who else but an Englishman could invent an oval ball?

PETER POOK

Rugby League is war without the frills. **ANON**

Rugby is a good occasion for keeping 30 bullies far from the centre of the city. **OSCAR WILDE**

A bomb under the West car park at Twickenham on an international day would end fascism in England for a generation. **PHILIP TOYNBEE**

England's coach Jack Powell, an immensely successful businessman, has the acerbic wit of Dorothy Parker and, according to most New Zealanders, a similar knowledge of rugby. **MARK REASON**

Look what these bastards have done to Wales. They've taken our coal, our water, our steel. They buy our houses and they only live in them for a fortnight every twelve months. What have they given us? Absolutely nothing. We've been exploited, raped, controlled and punished by the English – and that's who you are playing this afternoon.

PHIL BENNETT, PRE-GAME PEP TALK BEFORE FACING ENGLAND

No leadership, no ideas. Not even enough imagination to thump someone in the line-up when the ref wasn't looking.

J.P.R. WILLIAMS ON WALES LOSING 28–9 AGAINST AUSTRALIA, 1984

That has capped a superb season. It was an emotional high and I have only one complaint: both of the streakers were men. **COLIN TODD**

There's no doubt about it, he's a big bastard. **GAVIN HASTINGS ON JONAH LOMU**

Winger, Simon Geoghegan, resembles Mother Brown, running with a high knee-lift and sometimes not progressing far from the spot where he started. **MARK REASON**

Every time I went to tackle Phil Horrocks-Taylor, Horrocks went one way, Taylor went the other, and all I got was the bloody hyphen. **NICK ENGLAND**

The pub is as much a part of rugby as is the playing field. **JOHN DICKENSON**

Men do not greet one another like this ... except perhaps at rugby club dinners. **ALAN COOPER, DEFENCE COUNSEL, SUMMING UP DURING THE DOLPHIN-HOOKS-PENIS-ROUND-MAN'S-LEG INDECENT SEXUAL ACT COURT CASE, 1991**

FOOTBALL

There's 52,000 people here at Maine Road tonight, but my goodness me, it seems like 50,000. **BYRON BUTLER**

We murdered them nil-nil. **BILL SHANKLY**

The natural state of the football fan is bitter disappointment, no matter what the score. **NICK HORNBY**

A survey shows that English men are more afraid of watching England crash out of Euro 2004 on penalties than of losing their wallet, job or even hair. Only losing a partner would cause greater distress than another penalty shootout disaster. **NEC RESEARCH**

Football and cookery are the two most important subjects in this country. **DELIA SMITH**

Go to see Chelsea play. Makes you proud to be British. **DES O'CONNOR**

Nature hating a vacuum like the average English mind, it has hastened to fill it with football.   **THEODORE DALRYMPLE**

And now the worst news of all. Gay men are getting interested in football. What a catastrophe. One became homosexual to get away from this sort of thing.   **MATTHEW PARRIS**

Let's face it, football is a game for commoners. As soon as you get a mortgage you start liking tennis.

JONATHAN ROSS

I don't know much about football. I know what a goal is, which is surely the main thing about football.   **VICTORIA BECKHAM**

My doctor told me I should have a complete break from football so I became manager of Wolves.   **TOMMY DOCHERTY**

I promised I'd take Rotherham out of the second division. I did. Into the third division.   **TOMMY DOCHERTY**

I wouldn't say I was the best manager in the business, but I was in the Top One.   **BRIAN CLOUGH**

I know Dixie Dean's funeral is a sad occasion but I think that Dixie would be amazed to know that even in death he could draw a bigger crowd than Everton can on a Saturday afternoon.   **BILL SHANKLY**

—What's he going to be telling his team at half time, Denis?
—He'll be telling them that there are 45 minutes left to play.

DICKIE DAVIES AND DENIS LAW

Bobby Robson's natural expression is that of a man who fears he may have left the gas on. **DAVID LACEY**

As a manager, you always have a gun to your head. It's a question of whether there is a bullet in the barrel. **KEVIN KEEGAN**

Like Boudicca rousing the Iceni before they sacked Colchester, Ms Delia Smith strode on to the pitch at half-time to get the crowd back behind the team. 'Where are you?' she yelled. 'Let's be 'aving you!' If this sounded a bit like a pub landlady at chucking-out time, it was purely coincidental. Unhappily, Norwich's defence retains the properties of a kitchen colander and after having a player sent off they lost. Maybe it would have worked had Norwich been playing Colchester. **DAVID LACEY**

I never comment on referees and I'm not going to break the habit of a lifetime for that prat. **RON ATKINSON**

An atheist is a person who watches a Liverpool versus Everton football match and doesn't care who wins. **BILL SHANKLY**

At Glasgow Rangers I was third choice left-back behind an amputee and a Catholic. **CRAIG BROWN**

Glenn Hoddle will probably be doomed to come back as Glenn Hoddle. **TONY BANKS**

Me and about eight mates went up Chelsea last February. Bill Clinton was bloody furious. **FRANK SKINNER**

Being thick isn't an affliction if you're a footballer, because your brains need to be in your feet. **BRIAN CLOUGH**

When Glenn Hoddle was manager of Tottenham he was telephoned by the fire brigade in the middle of the night to tell him there was a fire at the stadium. 'Save the cups, please, save the cups!' pleaded Hoddle. 'Don't worry,' said the policeman, 'the fire hasn't reached the canteen yet.'

ANON

I think Charlie George was one of Arsenal's all time great players. A lot of people might not agree with that, but I personally do.

JIMMY GREAVES

George Best's feet were as sensitive as a pickpocket's hands.

HUGH MCILVANNEY

Watching Wayne Rooney score a debut hat-trick for Manchester United was like seeing your missus with another fella. **ROGER GULLEN, EVERTON FAN**

He's not Thierry Henry...but not many people are. **MARTIN TYLER**

I was watching Germany and I got up to make a cup of tea. I bumped into the telly and Klinsmann fell over. **FRANK SKINNER**

You have to get your priorities right. Women are around all the time but World Cups come only every four years. **PETER OSGOOD**

The English football team – brilliant on paper, shit on grass. ARTHUR SMITH

Argentina are the second-best team in the world, and there's no higher praise than that. **KEVIN KEEGAN**

Don't tell those coming in now the result of that fantastic match. Now let's have another look at Italy's winning goal. **DAVID COLEMAN**

Football hooligans are a compliment to the English martial spirit.

ALAN CLARK

Now that we don't have a war, what's wrong with a good punch-up? We are a nation of yobs. Without that characteristic, how did we colonise the world?...With so many milksops, left-wing liberals and wetties around, I just rejoice that there are people who keep up our historic spirit.

THE DOWAGER MARCHIONESS OF READING

I personally look forward to the day when we have a British football team. We might start winning some games.

JACK STRAW

TENNIS

Oh, I say!

DAN MASKELL

The three most depressing words in the English language: 'Come on, Tim!'

KATE ADIE

Ten of The World's Greatest Rarities: No. 4: A British tennis player with a can of silver polish.

YOU MAGAZINE

Tim Henman is so anonymous. He's like a human form of beige.

LINDA SMITH

Have you ever thought about the person who designed the sports skirt? Somebody sat down, drew a fantasy and made it compulsory uniform. I can never watch Wimbledon without thinking of that man.

INSPECTOR MORSE

In lawn tennis mixed, the basic chivalry move is to pretend to serve less fiercely to the woman than to the man. This is particularly useful if your first service tends to be out in any case.

STEPHEN POTTER

Hardy Amies once told me that the sexiest thing he had seen was nuns playing tennis.   **PRUDENCE GLYNN**

I was asked to be a linesman at the Wimbledon tennis championship. I excused myself by expressing myself flattered by the offer, but begged them to renew it when my eyesight had deteriorated sufficiently to be able to make wrong decisions with absolute conviction.   **PETER USTINOV**

The Gullikson twins are here. An interesting pair, both from Wisconsin.
                                                                DAN MASKELL

Some people are a bit unkind about some of the female tennis players, but I've met Lindsay Davenport and he's a lovely feller.   **JONATHAN ROSS**

We haven't had any more rain since it stopped raining.   **HARRY CARPENTER**

GOLF

Soccer is a simple-minded game for simple people; golf is merely an expensive way of leaving home.   **MICHAEL PARKINSON**

Golf is an ineffectual attempt to direct an uncontrollable sphere into an inaccessible hole with instruments ill-adapted to the purpose.
                                                            WINSTON CHURCHILL

A game in which you can claim the privileges of age, and retain the playthings of childhood.   **SAMUEL JOHNSON**

—I've been waiting for years to get into that golf club.
—I believe they're awfully particular.
                        CAPTAIN MAINWARING AND SERGEANT WILSON, *DAD'S ARMY*

My most common mistake at St Andrews is just turning up.   **MARK JAMES**

Only the other day I actually saw someone *laugh* on a posh golf course in Surrey. **MICHAEL GREEN**

It is almost impossible to remember how tragic a place this world is when one is playing golf. **ROBERT LYND**

My favourite shots are the practice swing and the conceded putt. The rest cannot be mastered. **LORD ROBERTSON**

My backswing off the first tee put him in mind of an elderly lady of dubious morals trying to struggle out of a dress too tight around the shoulders. **PATRICK CAMPBELL**

When male golfers wiggle their feet to get their stance right they look exactly like cats preparing to pee. **JILLY COOPER**

I know it was an easy putt but I had the sun in my eyes – and then I have such light eyelashes. **A.C. BENSON**

The least thing upsets him on the links. He missed short putts because of the uproar of the butterflies in the adjoining meadows. **P.G. WODEHOUSE**

The uglier a man's legs are, the better he plays golf. It's almost a law. **H.G. WELLS**

—How do you think golf could be improved?
—I always feel that the hole is too small. **INTERVIEWER AND MARK JAMES**

What is needed instead of all these instructional books on how to play golf is a walloping good book on how to give it up. **MICHAEL GREEN**

Playing with your spouse on the golf course runs almost as great a marital risk as getting caught playing with someone else's anywhere else.

PETER ANDREWS

The only time Nick Faldo opens his mouth is to change feet.   **DAVID FEHERTY**

Golf balls are attracted to water as unerringly as the eye of a middle-aged man to a female bosom.   **MICHAEL GREEN**

The secret of missing a tree is to aim straight at it.   **MICHAEL GREEN**

No new golf joke has been invented for 40 years.   **MICHAEL GREEN**

GAMES

What is the fastest game in the world? It's played in Belfast pubs, and it's called Pass the Parcel.   **DAVE ALLEN**

Games are the last resort of those who do not know how to idle.

ROBERT LYND

If PacMan had affected us as kids, we'd be running around in dark rooms, munching pills and listening to repetitive music.   **MARCUS BRIGSTOCKE**

This week's prize is just the thing for the small rodent enthusiast who likes to keep his pets minty-fresh – it's a bottle of Listerine Mousewash.

HUMPHREY LYTTELTON

—Hey, wouldn't it be amazing if all this money was real?
—That is the single most predictable and boring thing that anyone could ever say whilst playing Monopoly.   **RICK AND VYVYAN, *THE YOUNG ONES***

What do you call a female cow?   **LARRY GOGAN, QUIZ QUESTION**

It is impossible to win gracefully at chess. No man has yet said 'Mate!' in a voice which failed to sound to his opponent bitter, boastful and malicious.

A.A. MILNE

Battenburg cake, cut into 16 slices then arranged into a square, makes an ideal emergency chessboard.

GRAHAM CARTER, *VIZ,* **TOP TIP**

True or false: Niagara Falls is turned off at night.

BOB MORTIMER, *SHOOTING STARS*

—Who was finally found on the banks of Lake Tanganyika in 1871?
—Homo sapiens.

JOHN HUMPHRYS AND EDWINA CURRIE, *CELEBRITY MASTERMIND*

—Name the BBC's Grand Prix commentator? I'll give you a hint. It's something you suck.
—Dickie Davies.

LARRY GOGAN AND CONTESTANT [CORRECT ANSWER: MURRAY WALKER]

The answers to the pub quiz are as follows: John Leslie; John Leslie; Stan Collymore; Ulrika Jonsson; Cruising; Kevin Spacey; Catherine Zeta Jones; Rent Boys; Fred Elliot; Ann Widdecombe (half a point if you put Les Dawson).

EDDIE, *EARLY DOORS*

The crossword puzzle threatens western civilisation. If it became widespread, it would make devastating inroads on the working hours of every rank of society.

THE TIMES, **1925**

It's all fun and games until somebody loses an eye. Then it's just a game: Find The Eye.

FRANK KNOX

If you've understood Mornington Crescent, nothing else in your life makes sense.

JEREMY HARDY

HOBBIES – GENERAL

There is nothing – absolutely nothing – half so much worth doing as
simply messing about in boats.   **KENNETH GRAHAME**

Sir Matthew spent the morning designing mausoleums for his enemies.
                                                  ERIC LINKLATER

Recreations: smoking, drinking, swearing, pressing wild flowers.
                                          STEPHEN FRY, *WHO'S WHO*

Lord Queensberry's hobbies were: finding homosexuals, boxing,
and heckling sermons.   **LEO MCKINSTRY**

Recreations: making love, ends meet, and people laugh.
                                    NICHOLAS FAIRBAIRN, *WHO'S WHO*

'I suppose the best thing about model aeroplanes is watching your little
brother's reaction when you smash them,' – as my big brother used to
say. Before he drowned.   **ARDAL O'HANLON**

Recreations: picking up litter.   **MARY ARCHER,** *WHO'S WHO OF WOMEN*

Old contact lenses make ideal 'portholes' for small model boats.
                                          F. JOHNSON, *VIZ,* **TOP TIP**

Recreations: cinema, science fiction, thinking while gardening,
natural history.   **KEN LIVINGSTONE,** *WHO'S WHO*

Recreations: rocking horses, buying vintage underwear, watching people
at the Jesus Green Lido.
                ROWAN PELLING, FOUNDING EDITOR OF *THE EROTIC REVIEW, WHO'S WHO*

His Grace the Duke of Dunstable's hobbies are pokerwork, omelette making, and training racing pigs.

P.G. WODEHOUSE

Recreations: torpedoing pretension, hounding hypocrisy.

MARTIN BELL

I have a Scottish correspondent who spends his leisure hours collecting the registration numbers of bassoons.

PATRICK MOORE

Recreations: researching athletics, history, visiting teashops.

PETER LOVESEY

Interests include collection of thistledown for pillows; the science and art of scything.

SIR STEPHEN TALLENTS

Recreations: merry-making, wild flowers, music, mongrels.

JILLY COOPER, *WHO'S WHO*

I hate people who play bridge as if they were at a funeral and knew their feet were getting wet.

W. SOMERSET MAUGHAM

Lord Shortcake collected stamps as well as goldfish – but only English twopenny stamps. He had no interest in foreign stamps, which, he said, should be left to foreigners.

J.B. MORTON

Recreations: hunting, fishing, shooting, food, rugby, men.

CLARISSA DICKSON WRIGHT

Before he was a playwright, Tom Stoppard was a journalist, and he was once interviewed by the editor for a job on the *Evening Standard*. On his C.V. he had listed 'politics' as one of his interests. 'Who is the Home Secretary?' asked the editor. 'I said I was *interested*,' replied Stoppard, 'I didn't say I was obsessed.'

MARK STEVENS

Recreations: tidying.

VICTORIA WOOD, *WHO'S WHO*

Plainspotters Do It Looking Up.

CAR BUMPER STICKER

Recreations: few.

A.L. KENNEDY

My interests are DIY, watching telly and keeping regular bowel movements.

JASPER CARROTT

FISHING

A fishing-rod is a stick with a hook at one end and a fool at the other.

SAMUEL JOHNSON

Fishing is a way of life. It's like Transcendental Meditation.

ALAN AYCKBOURN

Dr Strabismus (Whom God Preserve) of Utrecht is carrying out research work with a view to crossing salmon with mosquitoes. He says it will mean a bite every time for fishermen.

J.B. MORTON

Maybe the fish goes home and brags about the size of the bait he stole.

GARY SWAN

HUNTING

The English country gentleman galloping after a fox – the unspeakable in full pursuit of the uneatable.

OSCAR WILDE

If foxes, like women, had a vote, I think they would vote unanimously for the keeping up of fox-hunting.

COLONEL SIR LANCELOT ROLLESTON

Hunting is all that's worth living for. It's the sport of kings, the image of war without its guilt and only 25 per cent of its danger.

R.S. SURTEES

No sportsman wants to kill the fox or the pheasant as I want to kill him when I see him doing it. GEORGE BERNARD SHAW

One of the main arguments in favour of fox hunting is that foxes kill chickens. But so does Bernard Matthews and nobody advocates chasing him across the country with a pack of dogs and tearing him to pieces.

ALEXEI SAYLE

If we pro-hunting protestors were a tribe in the South American rainforest or some village in Africa, we'd have Sting and Bob Geldof putting on concerts to save us, but because we're from the home counties no one gives a stuff. **PRO-HUNTING DEMONSTRATOR, BBC NEWS REPORT**

Anti-hunt campaigners would be a lot more honest if they simply poured pots of paint over Volvos and BMWs. That's closer to what they are all about: a them-and-us situation. **ANNE ROBINSON**

Saying foxhunting is egalitarian because of stable lads and kennel maids is like saying The Ritz hotel is egalitarian because it employs toilet cleaners.

MARK THOMAS

I am weary of the endless kerfuffle over fox hunting. I am told there is a technical term for my condition: tallyhosis. **P.D. CLARKE**

When a man wants to murder a tiger, it's called sport; when the tiger wants to murder him, it's called ferocity. **GEORGE BERNARD SHAW**

The fascination of shooting as a sport depends almost wholly on whether you are at the right or wrong end of the gun.   **P. G. WODEHOUSE**

Deer hunting would be a fine sport, if only the deer had guns.   **W.S. GILBERT**

The depressing thing about an Englishman's traditional love of animals is the dishonesty thereof – get a barbed hook into the upper lip of a salmon, drag him endlessly around the water until he loses his strength, pull him to the bank, hit him on the head with a stone, and you may well become fisherman of the year. Shoot the salmon and you'll never be asked again.
CLEMENT FREUD

The fine art of wasp-shooting is alive and well in Britain, but there is division over whether shooting a trapped wasp is sporting. While some recommend a target laced with jam, Alan Witherby argued that conserve is against the rules of natural justice. 'Surely every self-respecting sportsman knows one does not shoot a sitting wasp. In Hampshire we shoot the driven wasp, high and fast flying. In a good summer I have been known to bag as many as one.'   **DAVID DERBYSHIRE**

Drag-hunting is like kissing your sister.   **MICHAEL COLVIN**

Uncle Matthew had four magnificent bloodhounds, with which he used to hunt the children. Two of us would go off with a good start to lay the trail, and Uncle Matthew and the rest would follow the hounds on horseback.   **NANCY MITFORD**

GARDENING

Why is the sky blue? Because if it was green, an Englishman wouldn't know where to stop mowing.   **JACK HARPER**

'I want to be a lawn.' Greta Garbo.   **W.C. SELLAR AND R.J. YEATMAN**

Only the other day I was inquiring of an entire bed of old-fashioned roses, forced to listen to my ramblings, on the meaning of the universe as I sat cross-legged in the lotus position in front of them.   **PRINCE CHARLES**

A humane way to repel moles is to detach the battery-operated cell from a musical greeting card and drop it into the excavation.

DENISE DEW-HUGHES

Britain is the last outpost of the genuine lawnmower; a weighty beast with a sturdy roller and a meticulous cylinder action, snipping the grass with the delicacy of a hairdresser, and styling it into verdant stripes.

JASON HAZELEY

As an advocate of the consumption of grass-mowings, I have eaten them regularly for over three years, and off many lawns. The sample I am eating at present comes off a golf green on Mitcham common. I mix them with lettuce leaves, sultanas, currants, rolled oats, sugar, and chopped rose-petals, with uncut rose-petals sprinkled over the whole.

J.B. BRANSON

One of the most pleasing sounds of Springtime, to be heard all over the country, is the contented cooing of osteopaths as Man picks up his garden spade.   **OLIVER PRITCHETT**

I am not a dirt gardener. I sit with my walking stick and point things out that need to be done. After many years, the gardener is now totally obedient.   **HARDY AMIES**

Nothing grows in our garden, only washing.   **DYLAN THOMAS**

There is already enough potential trouble in a garden without having one of those smug, self-satisfied, rosy-cheeked little bastards squatting year after year at the edge of the goldfish pond pretending he's fishing.

ALAN MELVILLE ON GARDEN GNOMES

The idea of Prince Charles conversing with vegetables is not quite so amusing when you remember that he's had plenty of practice chatting to members of his own family.

JACI STEPHENS

Have you noticed that when the garden looks good it is due to the season, and when it doesn't it is due to the gardener.

H. NEEL

How do you stop a neighbour's cat scratching up your garden? Concrete one or the other over.

RIMMER, *RED DWARF*

My rose tree is dead, as is my fern, and perhaps the liveliest thing in this flat is my plaster bust of Nelson.

JEFFREY BERNARD

For sale: Bonsai tree. Large. £80.

JIMMY CARR

Perennials are the ones that grow like weeds, biennials are the ones that die this year instead of next, and hardy annuals are the ones that never come up at all.

KATHARINE WHITEHORN

Flowers are simply tarts; prostitutes for the bees. **UNCLE MONTY,** *WITHNAIL AND I*

Whoever heard of a serious crime being committed by a gardener?

HARRY GRAHAM

The best time to take cuttings is when no one is looking. **BOB FLOWERDEW**

Gardeners' Film Club: *Back to the Fuchsia* starring Michael J. Foxglove; *The Plums of Navarone*; *Sleeping With the Anemone*; *Rebel Without a Cos*; *Clay Jones and the Temple of Doom*.

I'M SORRY I HAVEN'T A CLUE

Lord Illingworth told me this morning that there was an orchid in the conservatory as beautiful as the seven deadly sins.

OSCAR WILDE

No man should plant more garden than his wife can hoe. **ENGLISH SAYING**

To a gardener there is nothing more exasperating than a hose that just isn't long enough.

CECIL ROBERTS

[*to a salesperson at a garden centre*] Do you have anything that will kill Alan Titchmarsh?

CARTOON, *THE SPECTATOR*

The best place to seek God is in the garden. You can dig for him there.

GEORGE BERNARD SHAW

Rummaging in an overgrown garden will always turn up a bouncy ball.

PETER KAY

I was sat at the bottom of the garden a week ago, smoking a reflective cheroot, thinking about this and that – mostly that, and I just happened to glance at the night sky and I marvelled at the millions of stars glistening like pieces of quicksilver thrown carelessly onto black velvet. In awe I watched the waxen moon ride across the zenith of the heavens like an amber chariot towards the void of infinite space wherein the tethered bolts of Jupiter and Mars hang forever in their orbital majesty, and as I looked at all this, I thought, 'I must put a roof on this lavatory.'

LES DAWSON

I have a children's playhouse in the garden which I intend in due course to make into an Old Buffer's Shed. I will relocate there when my daughters become teenagers and re-emerge when they become socially acceptable again, around the age of 30.

ANDREW STILTON

PLEASURE

The British are not good at having fun. I get overexcited if there's a pattern on my kitchen roll.

VICTORIA WOOD

Deprivation is to me what daffodils were to Wordsworth.

PHILIP LARKIN

Americans have fun. The English merely stare about them, and wonder
if they should have brought a mac.   MICHAEL BYWATER

The old English belief that if a thing is unpleasant it is automatically
good for you.   OSBERT LANCASTER

People must not do things for fun. We are not here for fun. There is no
reference to fun in any Act of Parliament.   A.P. HERBERT

The hurroosh that follows the intermittent revelation of the sexual goings-
on of an unlucky MP has convinced me that the only safe pleasure for a
parliamentarian is a bag of boiled sweets.   JULIAN CRITCHLEY MP

—Do you know what good clean fun is?
—I give up. What good is it?   TOMMY COOPER

If there is one thing an intellectual can't stand, it is the sight of a common
man enjoying himself.   ANTHONY DANIELS

The only pleasure an Englishman has is passing on his cold germs.
                                                     GERALD DURRELL

You can't get a cup of tea big enough or a book long enough to suit me.
                                                     C.S. LEWIS

There is nothing I like better than looking up a word in the dictionary.
                                                     MARTIN AMIS

If I were to begin life again, I would devote it to music. It is the only
cheap and unpunished rapture on earth.   REVD SYDNEY SMITH

This afternoon I painted streaks in my hair with process white; later blew
up a paper bag and popped it. It made a splendid noise.

                              BARBARA PYM, DIARY ENTRY, 5 OCTOBER 1954

If I had no duties, and no reference to futurity, I would spend my life in driving briskly in a post-chaise with a pretty woman. **SAMUEL JOHNSON**

One of the minor pleasures in life is to be slightly ill. **HAROLD NICOLSON**

At the age of 80, there are very few pleasures left to me, but one of them is passive smoking. **BARONESS TRUMPINGTON**

But for pure joy, you can't beat a catch I held running in 20 yards from deep mid-off to extra cover. That was 15 years ago. **JEFFREY BERNARD**

One half of the world cannot understand the pleasures of the other.

JANE AUSTEN

She was so glad to see me go that I have almost a mind to come again, that she may again have the same pleasure. **SAMUEL JOHNSON**

No man is a hypocrite in his pleasures. **SAMUEL JOHNSON**

If you eliminate smoking and gambling, you will be amazed to find that almost all an Englishman's pleasures can be, and mostly are, shared by his dog. **GEORGE BERNARD SHAW**

To relax, I put Smarties tubes on cats' legs to make them walk like a robot. If I'm really in the mood for fun, I make them walk down stairs. **JIMMY CARR**

If you find life a bit dull at home and want to amuse yourself, put a stick of dynamite in the kitchen fire. **JOYCE CARY**

Nothing is more hopeless than a scheme of merriment. **SAMUEL JOHNSON**

I can sympathise with people's pains, but not with their pleasure.
There is something curiously boring about somebody else's happiness.

ALDOUS HUXLEY

It is always wiser to consider not so much why a thing is not enjoyable, as
why we ourselves do not enjoy it.

G.K. CHESTERTON

The most intolerable pain is produced by prolonging the keenest pleasure.

GEORGE BERNARD SHAW

One of my pleasures is to read in bed every night a few pages of
P.G. Wodehouse, so that if I die in my sleep it will be with a smile on
my face.

ARTHUR MARSHALL

Drinking the best tea in the world in an empty cricket ground – that,
I think, is the final pleasure left to man.

C.P. SNOW

SHOPPING

The best shopping is done when it is unpremeditated. Virginia and Tony
went out one Saturday morning to buy a reel of cotton and came back
with a Bentley car.

JOYCE GRENFELL

We live in an age when unnecessary things are our only necessities.

OSCAR WILDE

Confectioners caught on that customers would happily buy a hole if it
had a bit of mint round it.

FRANK MUIR

I went window shopping today.
I bought four windows.

TOMMY COOPER

CHRISTMAS

A Happy Christmas to one and all. Why not invite an old person into your home this Christmas time? Spoil them with turkey and all the trimmings, and I think £14.50 is about right to charge them.   **MRS MERTON**

Christmas is a three-day festival dedicated to the birth of Bing Crosby.
WILLIS HALL

Baldrick, I want you to go out and buy a turkey so large you'd think its mother had been rogered by an omnibus.
EDMUND BLACKADDER, *BLACKADDER'S CHRISTMAS CAROL*

I won't be having turkey for Christmas. I'll be having Rohypnol. Two. Bit of stuffing. Unconscious till New Year's Day.   **LILY SAVAGE**

I got her implants for Christmas. She didn't want 'em. She wanted a Dyson.   **ROGER KAVANAGH, *THE ROYLE FAMILY***

I said to my four-year-old daughter, 'Let's write a letter to Santa Claus and put it up the chimney.' She said, 'Can't we just text him?'
ULRIKA JONSSON

A dog is for life, not just for Christmas. So do be careful at the office party.
JIMMY CARR

My granddaughter proudly announced that she is an icicle in her school's Christmas play. 'What do you have to say?' I enquired. 'Nothing, I just drip.'   **CAROLYN ANDERSON**

I can only properly enjoy carol services if I am having an illicit affair with someone in the congregation. Why is this? Because they are essentially pagan, not Christian, celebrations.   **ALAN CLARK**

The crackers contained, as usual, paper hats, none of which ever suited my grandmother and made her look either like Napoleon on a bad day or a member of the French Revolution en route for Versailles with a grievance.   **ARTHUR MARSHALL**

Claustrophobia: fear of Father Christmas.   **ANDY HAMILTON**

This year an old friend came around for lunch, and I'm afraid I snapped at him after he said, for the hundredth time, 'Is there anything I can do?' There was. Stay out of the kitchen and drink your bloody whisky.

JEFFREY BERNARD

If I sent a Christmas card to Gilbert Harding he would add to the words 'from Hubert Gregg' the words 'and Gilbert Harding', and send it to someone else.   **HUBERT GREGG**

My only objection to the custom of giving books as Christmas presents is perhaps the selfish one that it encourages and keeps in the game a number of writers who would be far better employed if they abandoned the pen and took to work.   **P.G. WODEHOUSE**

Christmas beat all records this year: I managed to have a family argument even though I haven't spent the day with any of them.

MARK LAMARR

'I spent Christmas Day cleaning out the kennels,' said the General. 'Went to Early Service. Then I got into my oldest clothes and had a thorough go at them. Had luncheon late and a good sleep after. Read a book all the evening. One of the best Christmas Days I've ever had.'

ANTHONY POWELL, *AT LADY MOLLY'S*

The only way to spend New Year's Eve is either quietly with friends or in a brothel. Otherwise when the evening ends and people pair off, someone is bound to be left in tears.   **W.H. AUDEN**

HOLIDAY

There's sand in the porridge and sand in the bed,
And if this is pleasure we'd sooner be dead.   **NOËL COWARD**

Please, no more bank holidays. We have enough cold, damp, miserable
days as it is.   **PETER TITHER**

No holiday is ever anything but a disappointment...There is nothing
like an unsatisfactory holiday for reconciling us to a life of toil.

ARNOLD BENNETT

The best part of a holiday is perhaps not so much to be resting yourself,
as to see all the other fellows busy working.   **KENNETH GRAHAME**

There's never been a holiday like this. For £30 you can join the ranks
of 40 paying prisoners of war at a chillingly realistic Colditz style
concentration camp.   **GREAT BRITISH ALTERNATIVE HOLIDAY CATALOGUE**

A good holiday is one spent among people whose notions of time are
vaguer than yours.   **J.B. PRIESTLEY**

PARTIES

Of course I don't want to go to a cocktail party. If I wanted to stand
around with a load of people I don't like eating bits of cold toast I can
get caught shoplifting and go to Holloway.   **VICTORIA WOOD**

I delight in the idea of a party but find no pleasure in the reality.
The result is that I can neither keep away from parties nor enjoy them.

J. B. PRIESTLEY

I once heard a lady discussing who should be invited to a party, say, 'Oh, don't let's have him. He's always the Life and Soul.' **PAUL JENNINGS**

I no longer dine in private houses, I can't stand the repressed sex and overt violence. **SUE TOWNSEND**

—You can have your standing-up-running or your sitting-down-with-knife-and-fork...
—I think a cold buffet is best.
—Would you like us to lay on a turkey?
—Well I hadn't planned on a cabaret. **JULIAN AND KENNETH, ROUND THE HORNE**

Dinner parties are given mostly in the middle classes by way of revenge. **WILLIAM THACKERAY**

If the soup had been as warm as the claret, if the claret had been as old as the chicken, if the chicken had been as fat as the host, it would have been a splendid meal. **DONALD MCCULLOUGH**

For dessert we had ice-cream: it was the only dish that was served hot. **LADY BEACONSFIELD**

The greatest mistake made about parties is to think guests are going to be grateful to their hosts. **MICHAEL GREEN**

The Life and Soul, the man who will never go home while there is one man, woman or glass of anything not yet drunk. **KATHARINE WHITEHORN**

That's just typical. Five minutes before the most important party of my life and the house is destroyed by a giant sandwich. **RICK, THE YOUNG ONES**

EDUCATION
AND
INTELLIGENCE

PUBLIC SCHOOL

You can't expect a boy to be depraved until he has been to a good school.

SAKI

Public school boys wore their hair in lank 'bangs', brushed down to one eye; they left their mouths gaping open when not talking, as if they had just run a race; they tended to barge their way to the front of the dinner queue, bellowing 'Sorry'; and when they couldn't hear you they shouted 'What?' (pronounced 'Wart?')...As for accent, they pronounced toast 'taste'.

BEVIS HILLIER

The ape-like virtues without which no one can enjoy a public school.

CYRIL CONNOLLY

At Harrow, John Mortimer wore a monocle, carried a cane and, to amuse the other boys, grew mustard and cress in his top hat.

NIGEL FARNDALE

George Melly sings like an old negress, which comes so naturally to those educated at Stowe.

JOHN MORTIMER

I was interviewing candidates for a vacant post. One was a Wykehamist, who seemed obtuse and conceited. He did not get the job. A few days later I received a letter from the frustrated applicant, abusing me roundly for turning him down, pointing out that it was bad manners to reject Wykehamists and that I must mend my ways.

JAMES PALMES

Ken Russell was also at Pangbourne, and I am glad to say that it threw me into the arms of Soho, Sandown Park and Smirnoff and not into making bizarre films about the likes of Wagner.

JEFFREY BERNARD

Tony Blair was my fag at Fettes school. He made particularly good toast.

MICHAEL GASCOIGNE

Let me protest against recent attacks on the fagging system at public schools. In all my four years I can recall only eleven deaths by fagging.

J.B. MORTON

The purpose of a Downside education is to prepare one for death.

AUBERON WAUGH

He has glaring faults and they have certainly glared at us this term.

STEPHEN FRY'S SCHOOL REPORT

Writing – The dawn of legibility in your son's handwriting reveals his total inability to spell.
Geography – He does well to find his way home.
Swimming – Tends to sink.
ARTHUR MARSHALL, SCHOOL REPORT

Intelligence was a deformity which must be concealed; a public school taught one to conceal it as a good tailor hides a paunch or a hump.

CYRIL CONNOLLY

When I was at school, education could go hang. As long as a boy could hit a six, sing the school song very loud and take hot crumpet from behind without blubbing.
LIEUTENANT GEORGE, *BLACKADDER GOES FORTH*

Nine o'clock was the customary time for morning prayers, one of which, I remember, began, 'Dear Lord, doubtless Thou knowest that in the *Daily Telegraph* this morning...'
JOHN MONTGOMERY

He shows great originality, which must be curbed at all cost.
PETER USTINOV'S SCHOOL REPORT

At school I never minded the lessons. I just resented having to work terribly hard at playing.
JOHN MORTIMER

A mother telephoned the school to ask if her son was homesick. 'I very much hope that he is,' replied the Headmaster, 'I shouldn't think much of his home if he wasn't.'

JOHN PRITCHARD

No matter what the weather or time of year, so many schools always smelt of wet linoleum and mackintoshes and, even when it had not been served for weeks, cabbage.

ARTHUR MARSHALL

Stewed prunes and custard were a too-regular feature of the school lunch. On Fridays there was a sort of bread-and-butter pudding, known as Resurrection Pudding, as it was felt that everything left over during the week was put into it.

JOHN MONTGOMERY

Assistant masters came and went. Some liked little boys too little and some too much.

EVELYN WAUGH

O vain futile frivolous boy. Smirking. I won't have it. I won't have it. Go find the headmaster and ask him to beat you within an inch of your life. And say please.

ALAN BENNETT

The only real drawback of the school was the fact that the headmaster happened to be a sadist. LORD BERNERS

My office. 9:20. Executions.

JOHN CLEESE AS BRIAN STIMPSON, *CLOCKWISE*

To the public school people, the grammar school boys were oiks with uncouth accents, blazers sewn with college badges and a battery of Parker pens in the front top pocket to assert status. Worse, they wore the collars of open-necked shirts outside their jacket collars and rode bicycles with low handlebars.

BEVIS HILLIER

There is now less flogging in our great schools than formerly, but then less is learned there; so that what the boys get at one end they lose at the other.

SAMUEL JOHNSON

One master had his classroom on the second floor and he dangled a boy outside the window by his hair. Another master got drunk one evening and tried to remove the appendix of a boy with a penknife.

ARTHUR MARSHALL

J.L. Carr was against beating – except for parents, for which purpose he kept a cricket bat in his study.

SIMON JENKINS

A minor infringement of a trivial school rule inspired the Head Mistress to call the girls 'second-class whores'. One girl wrote to her mother in high dudgeon and she replied equally indignantly: 'With all the money we're paying you should be first-class by now.'

SUSAN TAYLOR

A public schoolboy must be acceptable at a dance and invaluable in a shipwreck.

ALAN BENNETT

When Lord Berners returned, many years later, to visit his old school, he was astonished to observe nothing but smiling faces, only to learn that it was a school no more and that the building was a lunatic asylum.

ARTHUR MARSHALL

EDUCATION – GENERAL

The main aim of education should be to send children out into the world with a reasonably sized anthology in their heads so that, while seated on the lavatory, waiting in doctors' surgeries, on stationary trains or watching interviews with politicians, they may have something interesting to think about.

JOHN MORTIMER

You should be able to detect when a man is talking rot, that is the main, if not the sole, purpose of education.   **HAROLD MACMILLAN**

The Department of Education officials favour comprehensive education because it ensures that when their own children leave their public schools they have minimal competition for places at Oxford and Cambridge.

SIR HUMPHREY APPLEBY, *YES, MINISTER*

Education has always been a minority interest in England. The English have generally preferred to keep the bloom of their ignorance intact and on the whole have succeeded remarkably well, despite a century and a quarter of compulsory schooling of their offspring.   **THEODORE DALRYMPLE**

The only time my education was interrupted was when I was at school.

GEORGE BERNARD SHAW

My education was the liberty I had to read indiscriminately and all the time, with my eyes hanging out.   **DYLAN THOMAS**

Education isn't everything. For a start, it isn't an elephant.   **SPIKE MILLIGAN**

I've over-educated myself in all the things I shouldn't have known at all.

NOËL COWARD

Lack of education is an extraordinary handicap when one is being offensive.

JOSEPHINE TAY

Nothing that is worth knowing can be taught.   **OSCAR WILDE**

The first time you leave your child at school you're faced with a tough decision – down the pub or back to bed?   **JO BRAND**

I wish I'd been a mixed infant. **BRENDAN BEHAN**

He pursued his studies but never overtook them. **H.G. WELLS**

Grammar schools are public schools without the sodomy. **TONY PARSONS**

My son, Sam, is being educated not so as to enjoy himself, but so other people will enjoy him. **ROGER SCRUTON**

Spoon-feeding in the long run teaches us nothing but the shape of the spoon. **E.M. FORSTER**

I was teacher's pet. She kept me in a cage at the back of the class. **KEN DODD**

My school report said that I was every inch a fool. Fortunately I was not very tall. **SIR NORMAN WISDOM**

An inflatable boy goes to an inflatable school with an inflatable teacher and an inflatable headmaster. One day the inflatable boy runs amok with a drawing pin going pop, pop, pop! The inflatable headmaster summons him to his study and says, 'I'm so disappointed in you. You've let me down, you've let yourself down, and you've let the school down.'
REVD GERALDINE GRANGER, *THE VICAR OF DIBLEY*

Examiners are dispassionate, but if you succeed in infiltrating one semi-colon into an essay, they will be so filled with nostalgic delight that a pass grade is assured. **ERIC DEHN**

Examinations are pure humbug from beginning to end. If a man is a gentleman, he knows quite enough, and if he is not a gentleman whatever he knows is bad for him. **OSCAR WILDE**

In examinations those who do not wish to know ask questions of those who cannot tell.   **WALTER RALEIGH**

If we have to have an exam at eleven, let us make it one for humour, sincerity, imagination, character – and where is the examiner who could test such qualities?   **A.S. NEILL**

It will be a great day when our schools have all the resources they need and the air force has to hold a cake-sale to buy a bomber.   **LOTHIAN PARENTS ACTION GROUP**

UNIVERSITY

The exquisite art of idleness, one of the most important things that any university can teach.   **OSCAR WILDE**

I chose a single-sex Oxford college because I thought I'd rather not face the trauma of men at breakfast.   **THERESA MAY**

At Oxford we drank to ludicrous excess and threw up over some of the most beautiful buildings in Britain.   **STEVEN NORRIS**

The birds are not worthy of the cage. **JOHN STRACHEY ON OXFORD ARCHITECTURE**

The real Oxford is a close corporation of jolly, untidy, lazy, good-for-nothing humorous old men, who have been electing their own successors ever since the world began and who intend to go on with it. They'll squeeze under the Revolution or leap over it when the time comes, don't you worry.   **C.S. LEWIS**

Oh my head...feels like the time I was initiated into the Silly Buggers Society at Cambridge. I misheard the rules and tried to push a whole aubergine up my earhole.   **LIEUTENANT GEORGE,** *BLACKADDER GOES FORTH*

I find Cambridge an asylum, in every sense of the word. **A.E. HOUSMAN**

If a man is a fool, you don't train him out of being a fool by sending him to university. You merely turn him into a trained fool, ten times more dangerous. **DESMOND BAGLEY**

UMIST DEGREES. PLEASE TAKE ONE.
WRITTEN ON THE TOILET ROLL DISPENSER IN THE UNIVERSITY OF MANCHESTER INSTITUTE OF SCIENCE AND TECHNOLOGY UNIVERSITY STUDENTS' UNION TOILETS

A Master of Art
Is not worth a fart. **ANDREW BOORDE, 1690**

TEACHER

I dreamed last night I was teaching again – that's the only bad dream that ever afflicts my sturdy conscience. **D.H. LAWRENCE**

Everybody who is incapable of learning has taken to teaching. **OSCAR WILDE**

For every person wishing to teach there are 30 not wishing to be taught.
W.C. SELLAR AND R.J. YEATMAN

Headmasters have powers at their disposal with which Prime Ministers have never yet been invested. **WINSTON CHURCHILL**

A really successful headmaster could have run a departmental store, a battleship, or a brigade with success. And vice versa. **COMMANDER C.B. FRY**

INTELLIGENCE

How many never think, who think they do. **JANE TAYLOR**

There are only two kinds of people who are really fascinating: people who know absolutely everything and people who know absolutely nothing.

OSCAR WILDE

—Someone said I had the wit and intellect of a donkey.
—Oh, an absurd suggestion, sir, unless it was a particularly stupid donkey.

PRINCE GEORGE AND BLACKADDER, *BLACKADDER III*

You must have taken great pains, sir; you could not have naturally been so stupid.

DR SAMUEL JOHNSON

There is, and there always has been, an unusually high and consistent correlation between the stupidity of a given person and that person's propensity to be impressed by the measurement of IQ.

CHRISTOPHER HITCHENS

It was revealed to me many years ago with conclusive certainty that I was a fool and that I had always been a fool. Since then I have been as happy as any man has a right to be.

ALISTAIR SIM

The greatest lesson in life is to know that even fools are sometimes right.

WINSTON CHURCHILL

Thinking is the most unhealthy thing in the world, and people die of it just as they die of any other disease. Fortunately, in England at any rate, thought is not catching. Our splendid physique as a people is entirely due to our national stupidity.

OSCAR WILDE

A great many people think they are thinking when they are merely rearranging their prejudices.

WILLIAM JAMES

It's quite a three-pipe problem, and I beg that you won't speak to me for 50 minutes.

SHERLOCK HOLMES, *THE ADVENTURES OF SHERLOCK HOLMES,* **ARTHUR CONAN DOYLE**

I don't suppose she would recognise a deep, beautiful thought if you handed it to her on a skewer with tartar sauce. **P.G. WODEHOUSE**

Three minutes' thought would suffice to find this out, but thought is irksome and three minutes is a long time. **A.E. HOUSMAN**

Merely having an open mind is nothing; the object of opening the mind, as of opening the mouth, is to shut it again on something solid.

G.K. CHESTERTON

Never seem more learned than the people you are with. Wear your learning like a pocket watch and keep it hidden. Do not pull it out to count the hours, but give the time when you are asked. **LORD CHESTERFIELD**

Only in Britain could it be thought a defect to be 'too clever by half'. The probability is that too many people are too stupid by three-quarters.

JOHN MAJOR

Lord Birkenhead is very clever, but sometimes his brains go to his head.

MARGOT ASQUITH

He's an intellectual without the intellect. **JOHN MCKENNA**

It has yet to be proven that intelligence has any survival value.

ARTHUR C. CLARKE

To know all is not to forgive all. It is to despise everybody. **QUENTIN CRISP**

LOGIC

First things first, but not necessarily in that order. **DR WHO**

You can't be a rationalist in an irrational world. It isn't rational. **JOE ORTON**

In dealing with Englishmen you can be sure of one thing only, that the logical solution will not be adopted. **DEAN INGE**

'I see nobody on the road,' said Alice. 'I only wish I had such eyes,' the King remarked in a fretful tone. 'To be able to see Nobody! And at that distance too!' **LEWIS CARROLL,** *THROUGH THE LOOKING GLASS*

It is necessary for technical reasons that these warheads should be stored with the top at the bottom, and the bottom at the top. In order that there may be no doubt as to which is the top and which is the bottom, for storage purposes, it will be seen that the bottom of each head has been labelled with the word, 'TOP'. **BRITISH ADMIRALTY INSTRUCTIONS**

'Contrariwise,' continued Tweedledee, 'if it was so, it might be; and if it were so, it would be: but as it isn't, it ain't. That's logic.' **LEWIS CARROLL,** *THROUGH THE LOOKING GLASS*

The insurance man told me that the accident policy covered falling off the roof but not hitting the ground. **TOMMY COOPER**

It is a dreadful pity when a beautifully spacious generalisation is upset by one or two simple facts. **NEVILLE CARDUS**

If you don't know where you are going, any road will get you there.

LEWIS CARROLL

A little nonsense now and then is cherished by the wisest men. **ROALD DAHL**

Poor Enoch Powell, driven mad by the remorselessness of his own logic.

IAN MCLEOD

THE NATURAL WORLD

WEATHER

It is commonly observed, that when two Englishmen meet, their first talk is of the weather; they are in haste to tell each other, what each must already know, that it is hot or cold, bright or cloudy, windy or calm.

SAMUEL JOHNSON

Whenever people talk to me about the weather, I always feel certain that they mean something else.   **OSCAR WILDE**

What about this fog! My pussy's been gasping all night.

MRS SLOCOMBE, *ARE YOU BEING SERVED?*

The English climate: on a fine day, like looking up a chimney; on a rainy day, like looking down it.   **THOMAS MOORE**

If God had intended man to live in England, he'd have given him gills.

DAVID RENWICK

The climate of England has been the world's most powerful colonising influence.   **RUSSELL GREEN**

The rain was gusting against the window as if propelled by a trainee special effects man.   **KINGSLEY AMIS**

In April, in the springtime his lordship would, when it rayned, take his open coach to receive the benefit of the irrigation, which he was wont to say was very wholesome because of the nitre in the aire and the universall spirit of the world.   **JOHN AUBREY ON FRANCIS BACON**

When I mowed my front lawn on 22 April in bright sunshine, it was necessary to break the continuity of the stripes to go around the snowman built the day before by my grandchildren.   **DAVID PUGH**

A dim Scottish sun is out, less day realised than day potential, as if God has left on the pilot light. **WILLIAM MCILVANNEY**

Thunder is the sound of God moving his beer barrels across the floor of the sky. **CYRIL FLETCHER**

Lightning must, I think, be the wit of heaven. **REVD SYDNEY SMITH**

It's spring in England. I missed it last year. I was in the bathroom. **MICHAEL FLANDERS**

Summer has set in with its usual severity. **SAMUEL TAYLOR COLERIDGE**

That divine harbinger of summer – warm rain. **KEVIN MYERS**

It was such a lovely day I though it a pity to get up. **W. SOMERSET MAUGHAM**

Mad Dogs and Englishmen Go Out In The Midday Sun **NOËL COWARD, SONG TITLE**

Heat, ma'am! It was so dreadful here that I found there was nothing left for it but to take off my flesh and sit in my bones. **REVD SYDNEY SMITH**

If it gets much hotter in this country they'll be doing benefits for us in Africa. **JONATHAN ROSS**

Very high and very low temperatures extinguish all human sympathy and relations. It is impossible to feel any affection beyond 78 and below 20 Fahrenheit; human nature is too solid or too liquid beyond these limits. Man only lives to shiver or perspire. **REVD SYDNEY SMITH**

A few summers like this and we'll all be behaving like Italians.

JOHN MORTIMER

It's November 28 and my husband is still not wearing his vest. Is this clear evidence of global warming?   EILEEN M. CLARKE

Listening to Francis Wilson give the weather forecast is like sitting on wet seaweed at Land's End at the end of February.   JEAN ROOK

Cheeky BBC weathergirl Kaddy Lee-Preston turned up the heat when she put 'rude' village names on her TV map on BBC 'South East Today'. Towns like Dover, Margate and Maidstone were replaced with real-life places such as Upper Dicker, Thong, Pratt's Bottom and Clap Hill. But she earned a ticking off from bosses, unamused at her joke. The BBC has yet to receive any complaints about the broadcast. Forecasters around the country could have fun with Slackbottom in Yorkshire, Twatt on the Orkney Islands and Great Cockup in Cumbria. *SUNDAY MIRROR*

The British, he thought, must be gluttons for satire: even the weather forecast seemed to be some kind of spoof, predicting every possible combination of weather for the next 24 hours without actually committing itself to anything specific.   DAVID LODGE

English winters are like the First World War. You start thinking, 'Am I going to die before I get to the end of this?'

JOHN CLEESE

You want to be foretold the weather? It is bad enough when it comes, without our having the misery of knowing about it beforehand.

JEROME K. JEROME

Anthony Eden's father once hurled a barometer out of the window into the pouring rain, yelling, 'See for yourself, you bloody thing.' JILLY COOPER

As soon as they start talking about hearing the cuckoo, it snows.

A.P. HERBERT

I have to go out. It's so cold in my flat that I think it may snow in the kitchen this afternoon. JEFFREY BERNARD

—Prime Minister, I have to report that a minister was found half-naked with a guardsman in Hyde Park last night.
—Last night? The coldest night of the year? Makes you proud to be British. CIVIL SERVANT AND WINSTON CHURCHILL

The snow sounded as if someone was kissing the window all over outside.

LEWIS CARROLL

Everybody talks about the weather, but nobody does anything about it.

CHARLES D. WARNER

We shall never be content until each man makes his own weather and keeps it to himself. JEROME K. JEROME

UMBRELLA

It is the umbrella that has made Englishmen what they are.

SIR MAX BEERBOHM

It is the habitual carriage of the umbrella that is the stamp of Respectability. Robinson Crusoe was rather a moralist than a pietist, and his leaf-umbrella is as fine an example of the civilised mind striving to express itself under adverse circumstances as we have ever met with.

ROBERT LOUIS STEVENSON

Like a true gentleman, I carry an umbrella at all times but I never unfurl it. The only time I opened it was to insert the following note: 'This umbrella was stolen from Lt. Col. A.D. Wintle.'

LT. COL. ALFRED DANIEL WINTLE

A capital method of reviving a shabby silk umbrella: if a black umbrella goes green take a sponge to it loaded with a cupful of cold strong tea to which about ten drops of ammonia have been added.

HOUSEHOLD HINTS, 1897

Don't put up your umbrella until it begins to rain. **LORD SAMUEL**

Umbrellas, like faces, acquire a certain sympathy with the individual who carries them. **ROBERT LOUIS STEVENSON**

Never judge a man by his umbrella. It may not be his.

NOTICE IN ETON MASTER'S SCHOOLROOM

NATURE AND THE COUNTRYSIDE

There's ever such a dainty hellebore by your left plimsoll, Cynthia.

ARTHUR MARSHALL

Can anything more sharply evoke the memory of imperial greatness than the rolling English road, eight feet wide at its blind corners, a cow standing in the middle of it. **ALAN COREN**

The countryside is not a nice frozen picture of a Constable painting.

BEN GILL

Grass is hard and lumpy and damp, and full of dreadful black insects.

OSCAR WILDE

Every time I come up here and see that view, the spirit soars! You can't help thinking what a wonderful place it would be to set up a machine gun! Give me a small squad of hand-picked men and I could defend this place indefinitely!
WALTER 'FOGGY' DEWHURST, *LAST OF THE SUMMER WINE*

Five minutes on even the nicest mountain is awfully long.
W. H. AUDEN

No, I can't do with mountains at close quarters – they are always in the way, and they are so stupid, never moving and never doing anything but obtrude themselves.
D.H. LAWRENCE

Except during the nine months before he draws his first breath, no man manages his affairs as well as a tree does.
GEORGE BERNARD SHAW

I have no relish for the country; it is a kind of healthy grave.
REVD SYDNEY SMITH

My living in Yorkshire was so far out of the way that is was actually twelve miles from a lemon.
REVD SYDNEY SMITH

I'll never understand why anybody agreed to go on being rustic after about 1400.
KINGSLEY AMIS

Anybody can be good in the country.
OSCAR WILDE

Young farmer with 100 acres would be pleased to hear from young lady with tractor. Please send photograph of tractor.
ADVERTISEMENT, *EVESHAM ADVERTISER*

A joke goes a long way in the country. I have known one last pretty well for seven years.
REVD SYDNEY SMITH

It is my belief, Watson, founded upon my experience, that the lowest and vilest alleys of London do not present a more dreadful record of sin than does the smiling and beautiful countryside.

SHERLOCK HOLMES, *THE COPPER BEECHES,* **SIR ARTHUR CONAN DOYLE**

In English villages, you turn over a stone, you never know what will crawl out.

MISS MARPLE, AGATHA CHRISTIE

In this corner of the shires, elderly ladies in bulletproof tweed still wobble down the lanes on dreadnought bicycles.

DAILY TELEGRAPH

It's only the urban middle class who worry about the preservation of the countryside because they don't have to live in it.

SIR HUMPHREY APPLEBY, *YES, MINISTER*

The finest landscape in the world is improved by a good inn in the foreground.

SAMUEL JOHNSON

SEA

To me the sea is never sane. It has too much to do with the moon to be quite compos mentis.

G.A. SALA

I knew an old lady who had never seen the sea, so I took her there. She stared at it a while, then said, 'Is that all it does?'

MICHAEL HOWARD

They had brought a large map representing the sea
without the least vestige of land:
And the crew was much pleased when they found it to be
A map they could all understand.

EDWARD LEAR, *THE HUNTING OF THE SNARK*

My boat, Nitchevo, can sleep six people who know each other very well. Or one prude.

PETER USTINOV

Mrs Thompson told me that she crossed the Channel with Ruskin on a rough day: he recommended jumping as a cure for sea-sickness.

GEOFFREY MADAN

Being on a lighthouse resembled nothing more than being on a spaceship. Perhaps a spaceship co-designed by NASA and the Goons.

PETER HILL, *STARGAZING*

The ships hung in the sky in much the same way that bricks don't.

DOUGLAS ADAMS

The ship is sinking. We must try and save it. Help me get it into the lifeboat.

SPIKE MILLIGAN

What I have never been able to discover is whether the fellows who swim the Channel are obliged to keep their feet off the ground all the way.

E.V. KNOX

The hardest part of sailing round the world? Stepping on dry land.

ELLEN MACARTHUR

Ah, salt water! It's ours.   **LORD HERVEY DIPPING HIS FINGER IN A LAGOON IN ITALY**

ANIMALS – GENERAL

I find penguins at present the only comfort in life. One feels everything in the world so sympathetically ridiculous; one can't be angry when one looks at a penguin.

JOHN RUSKIN

The cow stared at me and called a committee.

G.K. CHESTERTON

All the really good ideas I ever had came to me while I was milking a cow.

GRANT WOOD

The friendly cow, all red and white,
I love with all my heart:
She gives me cream with all her might,
To eat with apple-tart. **ROBERT LOUIS STEVENSON**

—I've never ridden in cars pulled by cows before.
—Bullocks, Mr Belcher.
—No, I haven't, honestly.
JOAN SIMS AND PETER BUTTERWORTH, *CARRY ON UP THE KHYBER*

You can lead a cow upstairs but not down. It's the way their joints don't oppose. But I feel sorry for the poor person who found that out the hard way. 'Come on, Daisy, down you go.' 'I can't go downstairs, it's the way my joints are.' 'I don't care about your joints. My wife's coming home in five minutes. Get down the stairs.' **RICKY GERVAIS**

All the ingenious men, and all the scientific men, and all the fanciful men in the world could never invent, if all their wits were boiled into one, anything so curious, and so ridiculous, as a lobster. **CHARLES KINGSLEY**

A Portsmouth man believes he had found the way to talk to hedgehogs, although he does not know the meaning of what he says to them.
HAMPSHIRE EVENING NEWS

Why do squirrels bury their acorns? It's just what the oak trees want! HARRY HILL

How would Mrs Mockpudding cure an elephant's hiccoughs? My uncle, when up country, used to make the beast drink backwards from a tilted bucket with a rusty axe in it. But this never had any effect. When down country, he tried the same cure, with the same negative result.
J.B. MORTON

The only mention in the Bible of a pet animal is in Tobit 5:16:
'So they went forth both, and the young man's dog with them.'

GEOFFREY MADAN

I dislike monkeys: they always remind me of my poor relations.

HENRY LUTRELL

It does not do to leave a live dragon out of your calculations if you live near him.

J.R.R. TOLKIEN

There was a young lady of Riga
Who rode with a smile on a tiger
They returned from the ride
With the lady inside
And the smile on the face of the tiger.

EDWARD LEAR

The point of installing Lewis the goat in the flat was so we could use the gag: 'A goat in the flat? What about the smell?' 'Oh, he'll get used to that.'

ARTHUR ASKEY

Goldfish immersed in 3.1% alcohol will overturn (lose the righting reflex) within six to eight minutes.

WILLIAM HARTSTON

Thank the Lord you are not a Centipede! Every Sunday morning happens the weekly cutting of toenails and general arrangement of toes. And if that is a bore with ten toes what would it have been if the will of Heaven had made us with a hundred feet!

EDWARD LEAR

And what's a butterfly? At best
He's just a caterpillar dressed.

JOHN GAY

Butterflies only live for three days. Imagine if it was born in B & Q. After three days it dies and goes to heaven and everyone there says, 'What's life on earth like?' And the butterfly goes, 'Well, it's just a do-it-yourself store.'

JOE PASQUALE

What do slugs call snails? Gypsies.

TIM VINE

Leave only three wasps alive in the whole of Europe and the air of Europe will still be more crowded with wasps than space is with stars.

SIR JAMES JEANS

There was a young man of Tralee
Who was stung on the neck by a wasp
When asked if it hurt
He replied, 'Not a bit.
It can do it again if it likes.'

ANON

During 2001, Morton Council Pest Control Officers assisted with the destruction of 5 squirrels, 173 wasps, 1 beetle, 1 wood louse, 1 strawberry weevil, 17 ants, 10 bees, 8 fleas, 5 bedbugs, 1 red spider mite and an unspecified insect believed to be a gnat.

BUCKINGHAMSHIRE ADVERTISER

I have long held the notion that if a vet can't catch his patient there's nothing much to worry about. JAMES HERRIOT

The British, for all their loss of prestige, are not yet afraid of small turtles.

H.F. ELLIS

Exit, pursued by a bear. **WILLIAM SHAKESPEARE, STAGE DIRECTION,** *A WINTER'S TALE*

—Dear Dr Rhubarb, for two days now my rabbit Barlow has lain quite still and motionless. What can be wrong?
—Dead, my dear.

J.B. MORTON

God didn't drive Adam and Eve out of the Garden of Eden, the midges did.

MIKE HARDING

DOG

Percy was the dog's name. His guiding rule in life was 'If it moves, bite it.'

P.G. WODEHOUSE

Do you recollect the Alington poodle? Exactly like a typhoid germ magnified.

GEORGE LYTTELTON

I can't understand why people throw sticks to dogs. Dogs aren't particularly interested in sticks. What they are interested in is crotches.

JENNY ECLAIR

The English Dog Cult now vies with Christianity in the top ten religions.

SPIKE MILLIGAN

The great pleasure of a dog is that you may make a fool of yourself with him and not only will he not scold you, but he will make a fool of himself too.

SAMUEL BUTLER

The nose of the bulldog has been slanted backwards so that he can breathe without letting go.

WINSTON CHURCHILL

You think dogs will not be in heaven? I tell you, they will be there long before any of us.

ROBERT LOUIS STEVENSON

If you've got an Islamic dog muzzle him.

TIM VINE

I once tried to smuggle my Peke, Pinkie Panky Poo, past customs by wrapping him in my cloak. Everything was going splendidly until my bosom barked.   **MRS PATRICK CAMPBELL**

A man loses his dog so he puts an ad in the paper. And the ad says, 'Here boy!'   **SPIKE MILLIGAN**

I wouldn't really call it a cushion, Pekingese is a more common name for them. No, well never mind, he was very old.   **STEPHEN FRY**

The man recovered from the bite – the dog it was that died.
                                                                    OLIVER GOLDSMITH

BIRD

'Listen,' he would say as some feeble quack would be heard from the willow beyond the pond. 'That's an easy one to tell. The frog-pippit.' Then he would add, as a safety measure, 'as I believe they call it in these parts.'   **STEPHEN POTTER**

All I know of birds to this date is that sparrows are the ones that are not pigeons.   **ALAN COREN**

'Fancy that,' said the man who handed a rhinoceros to the pigeon-fancier.
                                                                    J.B. MORTON

Yesterday morning I noticed that a blue-tit had pecked the cap off my milk-bottle. The milk inside was frozen, and the little bird had tiny skates on its feet and was skating round and round on the milk.
                                                                    J.B. MORTON

Did St Francis preach to the birds? Whatever for? If he really liked birds he would have done better to preach to the cats.   **REBECCA WEST**

CAT

The cats clung to him as though he owed them money. **ANTHONY ARMSTRONG**

A cat's got her own opinion of human beings. She don't say much, but you can tell enough to make you anxious not to hear the whole of it.

JEROME K. JEROME

If cats were in the police they'd never come below the ranks of detective.

PAUL JENNINGS

My cat can recognise a cheap label with his eyes closed. **ANN M. FOGGATT**

Drat the cat. And while I'm at it, drat a few other people's cats as well.

ALICE THOMAS ELLIS

It is the neighbour's cat that makes one believe there is a hell. **ROBERT LYND**

Home Wanted: for little fiend in feline form. Willing to do light mousework. **NEREA DE CLIFFORD**

—How do you humanely catch mice?
—It depends on who's throwing them. **HUMPHREY LYTTELTON AND BARRY CRYER**

The cat in gloves catches no mice.

ENGLISH PROVERB

I inadvertently dropped some perfume on my pussy and I had tomcats banging against my catflap all night. **MRS SLOCOMBE, *ARE YOU BEING SERVED?***

Dogs look up to you, cats look down on you. Give me a pig. He just looks you in the eye and treats you as an equal. **WINSTON CHURCHILL**

HORSE

'It's all right, it's just a horse in the bathroom,' he said quietly.

DOUGLAS ADAMS

I know two things about the horse,
and one of them is rather coarse.

NAOMI ROYDE-SMITH

A horse is as it were an extension of a man, ergo part of him. We are
all centaurs.

ANTHONY BURGESS

I live by the maxim, 'Time spent dismounted can never be regained.'

LT.COL. ALFRED DANIEL WINTLE

There is something about the outside of a horse that is good for the inside
of a man.

WINSTON CHURCHILL

A prince can learn no art fully, save the art of horsemanship. The brave
beast knows no flattery, and will throw a prince as soon as its groom.

BEN JONSON

I often used to think I was rather a disappointment to my dear late
father-in-law, because I was not a filly, which would have been much
more interesting for him.

MINETTE MARIN

A correspondent of the *Manchester Sporting Chronicle*, thinking that his
horse was shortsighted, had his eyes examined by an oculist, who certified
that the horse had a No.7 eye, and required concave glasses. They were
obtained and fitted on the horse's head. At first the horse was a little
surprised, but rapidly showed signs of the keenest pleasure, and he now
stands all the morning, looking over the half-door of his stable with his
spectacles on, gazing around him with an air of sedate enjoyment.

THE BANNER, 1888

ARTS AND ENTERTAINMENT

CULTURE

The reaction of the inhabitants to having Glasgow made the Cultural Capital of Europe is a very healthy one: they are quite simply terrified that it will put 20p on the price of a pint of bitter.   **JEFFREY BERNARD**

One of the freedoms of the English is the freedom from culture.

LORD GOODMAN

The arts are like the Church. People don't actually go to Church but they feel better because it's there.   **SIR HUMPHREY APPLEBY,** *YES, MINISTER*

Melvyn Bragg is to the arts what those parasitic birds are to the rhino. Irritating, but ultimately not significant.   **SIR JOHN DRUMMOND**

People flock to Stonehenge on fine weekends, pay their money, take a good, long, meaningless look, and drive off leaving a lot of orange peel and Coke cans, after the manner of culture seekers the world over.

BASIL BOOTHROYD

Had Jerusalem been built in England and the site of the Crucifixion discovered, it would promptly be built over and called the Golgotha Centre.   **ALAN BENNETT**

ART

—Is that picture yours? It's rubbish.
—It's a mirror.   **RIMMER AND LISTER,** *RED DWARF*

When Constable had an exhibition of his work, Henry Fuseli called to his maid, 'Bring me my umbrella – I am going to see Mr Constable's paintings.'   **C.R. LESLIE**

I've come into this 'ouse, more times than I care to remember, cold, wet, tired out, not a penny in me purse, and the sight o' them ducks and that murial, well, they've kept me away from the gas tap an' that's a fact.

HILDA OGDEN, *CORONATION STREET*

All this modern art looks like bollocks so it must be worth something.

EDINA MONSOON, *ABSOLUTELY FABULOUS*

Nothing unites the English like war. Nothing divides them like Picasso.

HUGH MILLS

The English public take no interest in a work of art until it is told that the work in question is immoral. **OSCAR WILDE**

It's amazing in life what we are given. I was given giant tits and a good visual sense. **TRACEY EMIN**

Tracey Emin is a contemporary artist who once exhibited a small tent covered in the names of everyone she had ever slept with, and is now working on a marquee for Peter Stringfellow. **ANGUS DEAYTON**

A critic told us that Damien Hirst's 'A Thousand Years' – an exhibit involving maggots, a cow's head and innumerable flies being zapped on an insectocutor – was a metaphor for the human life cycle, although it seemed to me more like a metaphor for an Italian restaurant I once ate in.

VICTOR LEWIS-SMITH

Modern artists always sign their names at the bottom of their paintings so that people will know which way up to hang them. **FRANK MUIR**

One should either be a work of art, or wear a work of art. **OSCAR WILDE**

I don't think anyone knows about painting any more. Art, like human nature, has got out of hand.   **NOËL COWARD**

There is nothing so terrible as the pursuit of art by those who have no talent.   **W. SOMERSET MAUGHAM**

Tracey Emin should have a health-warning tattooed on her forehead.   **SIR ROY STRONG**

In every community of a thousand souls there will be nine hundred doing the work, ninety doing well, nine doing good, and one lucky dog painting or writing about the other nine hundred and ninety-nine.   **TOM STOPPARD**

I was named as the world's most famous artist only because Rembrandt didn't have his own TV show.   **ROLF HARRIS**

Rolf Harris is a difficult to man to hate but that shouldn't stop us from trying.   **A.A. GILL**

It does not matter how badly you paint so long as you don't paint badly like other people.   **GEORGE MOORE**

—It's a self-portrait.
—Who of?   **TONY HANCOCK AND LANDLADY, *THE REBEL***

—Mr Churchill, I want you to know I got up at dawn and drove a hundred miles for the unveiling of your bust.
—Madam, I want you to know that I would happily reciprocate the honour.   **UNIDENTIFIED WOMAN AND WINSTON CHURCHILL**

I would rather see the portrait of a dog that I know than all the allegorical paintings they can shew me in the world.   **SAMUEL JOHNSON**

Edith Sitwell's interest in art was largely confined to portraits of herself.

JOHN FOWLES

To sit for one's portrait is like being present at one's own creation.

ALEXANDER SMITH

I commissioned my portrait bust from Paravinci. I doubt he will ever get the stone or finish it; if he does it will be the next best thing to having myself stuffed.   **EVELYN WAUGH**

I prefer painting landscapes. A tree doesn't complain that I haven't done it justice.   **WINSTON CHURCHILL**

Graham Sutherland's portrait of me makes me look as if I were straining a stool.   **WINSTON CHURCHILL**

I cannot see the man for the likeness.   **ROGER FRY**

Every portrait that is painted with feeling is a portrait of the artist, not of the sitter.   OSCAR WILDE

People who had never visited the Louvre to see the Mona Lisa came to see the space on the wall from which it had been stolen.   **ROBERT LYND**

When Augustus John invited fellow artist, Adrian Daintrey, to visit his studio he welcomed him inside and said, 'I have to go now, but stay as long as you like.'   *THE DAILY TELEGRAPH*

Buy old masters. They fetch a better price than old mistresses.

LORD BEAVERBROOK

If Botticelli were alive today, he'd be working for *Vogue*.　PETER USTINOV

I'm very deeply depressed to hear that art students are interested in
being successful.　PATRICK HERON

Sculpture: mudpies which endure.　CYRIL CONNOLLY

The Venus de Milo is only what's to be expected if you will go on biting
your nails.　NOËL COWARD

I took my children to see some of Henry Moore's chunky abstract
sculptures in Hyde Park. My daughter, Laura, seven, said, 'Look,
something's fallen off a jumbo jet.'　SPIKE MILLIGAN

I always get it wrong in drawing the hind legs of quadrupeds, so I drew
the soul of the cow.　G.K. CHESTERTON

Art has to move you and design does not, unless it's a good design for a bus.

DAVID HOCKNEY

We plundered and we pillaged the world over. One man took a Doric
column home and used it as a garden roller.　CLARE MASON

To say the Elgin Marbles should be returned to Athens is the equivalent
of saying that if Napoleon had conquered Britain and then sold bits of
Stonehenge to an Italian friend, then the French would have a claim
to Stonehenge.　RICHARD ALLAN

Art? Art? All the art in the world isn't worth a good meat and potato pie.

L.S. LOWRY

He didn't like heads, did he? **JOHN PRESCOTT ON HENRY MOORE SCULPTURES**

ARCHITECTURE

Can anyone draw up a list of five buildings in London worth a detour to see, which have been put up since the war? **JO GRIMOND**

I never weary of great churches. It is my favourite mountain scenery.

ROBERT LOUIS STEVENSON

We shape our buildings; thereafter they shape us. **WINSTON CHURCHILL**

The great point of the tower is that it will be entirely useless.

BARON BERNERS ON BUILDING FARINGDON FOLLY

Members Of The Public Committing Suicide From This Tower Do So At Their Own Risk. **SIGN HUNG BY LORD BERNERS ON FARINGDON FOLLY**

The higher the building, the lower the morals. **NOËL COWARD**

The British love permanence more than they love beauty. **SIR HUGH CASSON**

Brighton Pavilion looks as if St Paul's had gone down to the sea and pupped. **REVD SYDNEY SMITH**

Cinemas and theatres are always bigger inside than they are outside.

MILES KINGTON

There are no rules of architecture for a castle in the clouds. **G.K. CHESTERTON**

Think how uncomfortable Hansel and Gretel must have been in the
Witch's candy house in damp weather!   C.S. LEWIS

MUSIC

The English may not like music, but they absolutely love the noise
it makes.   SIR THOMAS BEECHAM

Music can be made anywhere, is invisible and does not smell.   W.H. AUDEN

Music is like a dog; the nicest thing that can be said about it is that you
wouldn't know it was there.   QUENTIN CRISP

Extraordinary how potent cheap music is.   NOËL COWARD

In the rich cornucopia of their art, it was always Mr Rogers who supplied
the copia and Mr Hammerstein the corn.   BERNARD LEVIN

—Andrew Lloyd Webber wanted you to provide the lyrics for his musical
Cats. Why did you turn down his offer?
—I can't stand his music.   INTERVIEWER AND IAN DURY

If you hear bad music, it is one's duty to drown it by one's conversation.
                                            OSCAR WILDE

Almost the only thing music can represent unambiguously is the cuckoo –
and that it can't differentiate from the cuckoo-clock.   BRIGID BROPHY

Not many sounds in life, and I include all urban and rural sounds,
exceed in interest a knock at the door.   CHARLES LAMB

Too much counterpoint, and what is worse – Protestant counterpoint.
                              SIR THOMAS BEECHAM ON BACH

Composing is like driving down a foggy road toward a house. Slowly you see more details of the house – the colour of the slates and bricks, the shape of the windows. The notes are the bricks and mortar of the house.

SIR BENJAMIN BRITTEN

After playing Chopin, I feel as if I had been weeping over sins that I had never committed, and mourning over tragedies that were not my own.

OSCAR WILDE

Bach almost persuades me to be a Christian. **VIRGINIA WOOLF**

Beethoven always sounds to me like the upsetting of bags of nails, with here and there an also dropped hammer. **JOHN RUSKIN**

Beethoven's Fifth Symphony may be Fate – or Kate – knocking at the door. That is up to you. **C.B. REES**

Beethoven's last quartets were written by a deaf man and should be listened to only by a deaf man. **SIR THOMAS BEECHAM**

I love Beethoven – especially the poems. **RINGO STARR**

If anyone has conducted a Beethoven performance, and then doesn't have to go to an osteopath, then there's something wrong. **SIMON RATTLE**

Benjamin Britten – the most English of composers. Sea songs and boy sopranos. **WILLIAM DONALDSON**

Edward Elgar's Symphony in A Flat is the musical equivalent of St Pancras Station. **SIR THOMAS BEECHAM**

From Mozart I learnt to say important things in a conversational way.

GEORGE BERNARD SHAW

I like listening to Tchaikovsky's Fifth just as I like looking at a fuchsia drenched with rain.

JAMES AGATE

I love Wagner's music better than anybody's. It is so loud that one can talk the whole time without other people hearing what one says. That is a great advantage.

OSCAR WILDE

Stockhausen? I nearly trod in some once.

SIR THOMAS BEECHAM

I learnt from my insurance company that my car had been deemed a write-off after being kept on hold on the telephone with a performance of an extended excerpt from 'In Paradisum' of Fauré's 'Requiem.'

JOHN FENDLEY

The Young Brass Soloist of the Year is on BBC2 tonight. The musicians will be accompanied by the Black Dyke Band – good to see the BBC supporting minorities.

JONATHAN ROSS

Let a short Act of Parliament be passed, placing all street musicians outside the protection of the law, so that any citizen may assail them with stones, sticks, knives, pistols, or bombs without incurring any penalties.

GEORGE BERNARD SHAW

This is a special meeting of the Ladies' Choral to talk about the forthcoming Festival and County Choral Competition. We know the date and we know the set song. It's in two parts for ladies' voices in E flat, 'My Bosom is a Nest'.

JOYCE GRENFELL

Some of Schoenberg's pages resemble a kitchen flypaper during the rush-hour on a hot August afternoon.   **C.W. ORR**

Choristers you must be braver
With your demi-semi-quaver.   **CARYL BRAHMS**

A song now and then is very desirable as it is a relief to conversation; but half a dozen consecutively, even from St Cecilia in person, would become a bore.   **'A LADY OF RANK', *ETIQUETTE GUIDE***

My uncle Toby would never offer to answer this by any other kind of argument than that of whistling half a dozen bars of Lillabullero.   **LAURENCE STERNE**

Voltaire said that what was too silly to be said could be sung. Now you seem to think that what is too delicate to be said can be whistled.   **GEORGE BERNARD SHAW**

I can recognise but one tune, 'God Save the Queen', and then only because people stand up for it.   **W.B. YEATS**

Canon Wetherby can't tell 'Pop Goes the Queen' from 'God Save the Weasel'.   **MARY CHOLMONDELEY**

There was a recital of Baroque music in Ramsden church. A very dry and rarefied programme – it makes one feel like eating sloes, I decided, that astringent feeling in the mouth.   **BARBARA PYM**

The acoustics in Kings' College Chapel would make a fart sound like a sevenfold Amen.   **DAVID WILLCOCKS**

Eighteenth century music sounds like a Pekinese peeing on a mink rug.

NOËL COWARD

Bells are music's laughter.

THOMAS HOOD

My favourite musical instrument is the telephone.

QUENTIN CRISP

I can't type; but if I could type, I'd rather play the harpsichord.

PETER USTINOV

Colin's piano playing is believed by faith-healers to possess miraculous powers. It once made a blind man deaf.

HUMPHREY LYTTELTON

Oh, Julian's a miracle of dexterity on the cottage upright.

SANDY, *ROUND THE HORNE*

My daughter, aged nine, said, 'I always know a Miles Davis record when I hear it because it sounds like a little boy who's been locked out and wants to get in.'

KENNETH TYNAN

The Blues, the most convenient and harmonic progression ever discovered…the most hackneyed, overplayed, obvious musical effect in the world, and yet in some curious way at times the most compelling.

BENNY GREEN

Contemporary music is three farts and a raspberry, orchestrated.

JOHN BARBIROLLI

It was Mr Western's custom every afternoon, as soon as he was drunk, to hear his daughter play on the harpsichord.

HENRY FIELDING

OPERA

I liked everything about the opera but the music.

BENJAMIN BRITTEN ON STRAVINSKY'S *THE RAKE'S PROGRESS*

I do not mind what language an opera is sung in so long as it is a language I don't understand. **SIR EDWARD APPLETON**

The singing man keeps his shop in his throat. **GEORGE HERBERT**

Pavarotti is like someone who has swallowed a Stradivarius. **PETER USTINOV**

That soprano's singing reminds me of a cart coming downhill with the brake on. **SIR THOMAS BEECHAM**

It is said that Emilia Rustiguzzi once blew the slates off a potting-shed while singing one of Grieg's lullabies in a garden in Pisa. **J.B. MORTON**

POP MUSIC

There are two different kinds of people. There are people who like pop music and people who think that Peter Gabriel is a character in *The Archers*. **MILES KINGTON**

—How do you rate your music?
—We're not good musicians. Just adequate.
—Then why are you so popular?
—Maybe people like adequate music. **INTERVIEWER AND THE BEATLES**

Seventeen years and 15 albums later, Spinal Tap is still going strong, and they've earned a distinguished place in rock history as one of England's loudest bands. **MARTI DIBERGI,** *THIS IS SPINAL TAP*

Vince Hill appeared and told us how he nearly didn't record 'Edelweiss'. Ah well, they nearly didn't build Auschwitz; it's just a horror we have to live with.
VICTOR LEWIS-SMITH

All rock 'n' roll singers sound like a nudist backing into a cold-nosed dog – set to music.
ROBERT ORBEN

Most people get into bands for three simple reasons: to get laid, to get fame, and to get rich.
BOB GELDOF

The greatest achievement of Punk rock was the way it made flared trousers unfashionable.
TONY PARSONS

The good thing about the iPod is that you can store 10,000 songs on there – or two Pink Floyd tracks.
STUART MACONIE

Daughters, lock up your mothers, Daniel O'Donnell is in town.
PATRICK MURRAY

Not content to have the audience in the palm of his hand, Frankie Laine goes one further and clenches his fist.
KENNETH TYNAN

Sometimes an orgasm is better than being on stage. Sometimes being on stage is better than an orgasm.
MICK JAGGER

I think Mick Jagger would be astounded and amazed if he realised to how many people he is *not* a sex symbol.
ANGIE BOWIE

—Olivia Newton John is terrific. She's got lovely legs.
—Yes, but legs apart, what do you think of her?
GUEST AND TERRY WOGAN

Enrique Iglesias is greasier than a disorientated gannet swimming away from the Exxon Valdez oil spill straight into Peter Stringfellow's discarded thong.
MARK LAMARR

Dannii Minogue – it's a sad story: when she was a child, a dingo ran off with her talent.

MARK LAMARR

Does Paul McCartney make records just to annoy me personally?

ALEX HARVEY

I am the only man who can say he's been in Take That and at least two members of the Spice Girls.

ROBBIE WILLIAMS

Peter Andre: the most unwelcome comeback since Jimi Hendrix's vomit.

MARK LAMARR

It's a funny old world: someone goes out and shoots John Lennon and lets Des O'Connor live.

ROY 'CHUBBY' BROWN

DANCE

I have always been a magnificent dancer with one foot; the other one, I think, is better on the violin.

SEYMOUR HICKS

Mind you, Hugh Gaitskell was a very good dancer. And to me, that is more important than politics in a man.

BARBARA CASTLE

I'm a great dancer and I love to dance. When I had my fiftieth birthday party the last tune they played was Boney M's 'Ra Ra Rasputin'. I thought right, let's really go for it, so there I was, swinging and moving until I got this terrible pain in my chest and I thought, dear God, I'm going to die on the dance floor, but what a great way to go, it's been a fantastic party. And when I came off the dance floor, I discovered I'd broken my underwired bra.

CLARISSA DICKSON-WRIGHT

She clapped me to her bosom and pushed me on to the dance floor. It was like being lashed to an upholstered pneumatic drill. **RICHARD GORDON**

I'm a dancer trapped in the body of a tree.   **ARDAL O'HANLON**

In a poll to find 'The Best TV Moment Ever', British viewers voted
Ricky Gervais' dance in the sitcom, *The Office*, the overall winner.
The dance beat the Fall of the Berlin Wall and the Apollo Moon Landing.
'Well, that was just one small step compared to what I did,' said Ricky.
                                               BBC NEWS WEBSITE

Have you seen the price of ballet tickets? That's a lot to see buggers jump.
                                               NIGEL BRUCE

I can think of nothing more kinky than a prince chasing a swan around all night.
                                               ROBERT HELPMAN

Do, Do, Do, The Funky Gibbon   **THE GOODIES, SONG TITLE**

That hybrid known as ballroom dancing, an art which is compounded
equally of the lithe, sensuous panther, the lissom, supple gigolo, and the
light-shod, look-slippy waiter who can steer a tray and 24 glasses through
a crowd without slipping.   **JAMES AGATE**

...the zest goes out of a beautiful waltz
When you dance it bust to bust.   **JOYCE GRENFELL,** *STATELY AS A GALLEON*

And hand in hand, on the edge of the sand,
They danced by the light of the moon,
    The moon,
    The moon,
They danced by the light of the moon.   **EDWARD LEAR,** *THE OWL AND THE PUSSYCAT*

The regular and insatiable supporters of ballet are people too sluggish of intellect to listen to a play on the one hand, and too devoid of imagination to listen to fine music without accompanying action, on the other.   **ALAN DENT**

FAME AND CELEBRITY

You know you've made it in showbiz when you're known by one name. Ladies and gentleman, please welcome Kenny Lynch.   **MARK LAMARR**

My rise to fame was like climbing the north face of the Eiger in stiletto heels.   **RUSSELL HARTY**

I do not allow the word 'famous' on the BBC. If a man really is famous, the word is redundant. If he is not, it is a lie.   **LORD REITH**

Twinkle, twinkle, little star,
Who the hell do you think you are?   **FRANK TAYLOR**

There may be wonder in money, but, dear God, there is money in wonder.
                                                              ENID BAGNOLD

Fame, like a wayward girl, will still be coy to those who woo her with too slavish knees.   **JOHN KEATS**

I'm very big in Botswana.   **PATRICIA ROUTLEDGE**

We're more popular than Jesus Christ now. I don't know which will go first. Rock and roll or Christianity.   **JOHN LENNON**

I am a professional object of curiosity.   **NEIL HAMILTON**

Being a personality is not the same as having a personality.   **ALAN COREN**

Kim and Aggie are cleaners who became celebrities – like the Cheekie Girls in reverse.   JONATHAN ROSS

Like all great men when one comes closely in touch with them, the conjurer was quite human, quite like ourselves; so much so that in addition to his fee he wanted his taxi fare both ways.   E.V. LUCAS

There's something so incredibly downmarket about being famous.

LAURENCE LLEWELYN-BOWEN

The trouble with fulfilling your ambitions is you think you will be transformed into some sort of archangel and you're not. You still have to wash your socks.   LOUIS DE BERNIÈRES

The real drawback with television celebrity as far as my own humble share of it is concerned is that it prevents me from ever showing annoyance at terrible service in a restaurant or from tutting with impatience in a supermarket queue. One has to face life's irritations with a benign and foolish grin all over one's face.   STEPHEN FRY

David Dickinson of *Bargain Hunt* looks like the love child of Peter Stringfellow crossed with a mahogany hat stand.   TERRY WOGAN

If Quentin Crisp had not existed it is unlikely that anyone would have had the nerve to invent him.   ANON

Literary fame is very limited; it's like being a famous taxidermist.

IAN MCEWAN

I'm afraid of losing my obscurity. Genuineness only thrives in the dark. Like celery.   ALDOUS HUXLEY

If a terrorist group wanted to hit Britain, all they'd have to do is kill a hundred random celebrities. The country would have a nervous breakdown.

CHRIS MORRIS

These days, celebrities are endorsing all sorts of products. On my packet of sausages I noticed a photo of Anthony Worral Thompson. Underneath it said, 'Prick with a fork'.

HUMPHREY LYTTELTON

One can survive everything, nowadays, except death, and live down everything except a good reputation.

OSCAR WILDE

I always like to compare models to supermodels in the way I compare Tampax to Super Tampax: supermodels cost a bit more and they are a lot thicker.

JO BRAND

D.B. Wyndham-Lewis or 'the wrong Wyndham-Lewis' as the Sitwells called him, to distinguish him from his namesake the American born painter and writer.

RICHARD INGRAMS

FILM

I've got the new *Star Wars* CD, with a bonus 40 minutes taken out.

MARCUS GIBB

The length of a film should be directly related to the endurance of the human bladder.

ALFRED HITCHCOCK

Steven Spielberg returns to the caverns of his nightmare as obsessively as the tongue will return to the tiny cavern vacated by a loose filling.

GILBERT ADAIR

The British film industry is like Anne Robinson – always on the lookout for a new face.

JACK DEE

Beverly Hills is just Golders Green with sunshine. **VIVIAN ELLIS**

A British actor so good looking that his face has been declared a place of natural beauty, which makes it an ideal place to sit – and enjoy a picnic.
STEPHEN FRY ON DANIEL CRAIG

If Peter O'Toole was any prettier, you'd have to call the film *Florence of Arabia*. **NOËL COWARD**

Sometimes people confuse me with Anthony Hopkins. Here's how you tell the difference: I'm the one nailing Mrs Hopkins. **MICHAEL CAINE**

Michael Winner puts the dire into director. **CURT HULSE**

Is it at all widely known that the shooting of the Korda film about Nelson was held up because nobody could remember which arm it was he lost?
ARTHUR MARSHALL

In Hollywood, it's just as important to see which party you don't get invited to. It's like a court, but not King Arthur's – more like Richard III's. **MICHAEL CAINE**

The best research for playing a drunk is being a British actor for twenty years. **MICHAEL CAINE**

What, when drunk, one sees in other women, one sees in Garbo sober.
KENNETH TYNAN

I recommend *Last Orders*, a small, quiet gem of a film, made by an Australian, but as British as the idea of throwing a pal's ashes off Margate pier. Into a stiff wind. **DAVID THOMSON**

Orlando Bloom sounds like the love-child of Virginia Woolf and James Joyce. **QUENTIN COOPER**

We all watched *The Elephant Man* and we were moved to tears, thinking it was a wonderful example of man's humanity to man, and my dad just said, 'Wouldn't he make an amazing novelty rucksack?' **RICKY GERVAIS**

THEATRE AND ACTORS

Why does the cinema feel like a treat and the theatre, so often, like a penance? **MAUREEN LIPMAN**

People go to the theatre because this is the night someone might fall off the wire. **CAROL ANN DUFFY**

Long experience has taught me that in England nobody goes to the theatre unless he or she has bronchitis. **JAMES AGATE**

A WARM HAND ON YOUR OPENING

NOËL COWARD, TELEGRAM TO GERTRUDE LAWRENCE

I'm sustained through a performance by the image of a glass of red wine floating in the middle distance. **SIMON CALLOW**

It is recorded of Charles Lamb, whose stage farce *Mr H* ran for one night, that he joined in the hissing of it. **CRISPIN LACEY**

Two things in that play should be cut. The second act and that child's throat. **NOËL COWARD**

I want you to stand perfectly still and without saying a word, try to convey the idea that you have a brother who drank port in Shropshire.

SEYMOUR HICKS

Ladies, just a little more virginity, if you don't mind. **HERBERT BEERBOHM TREE**

Speak clearly, don't bump into people, and if you must have motivation, think of your pay packet on Friday. **NOËL COWARD**

Dear boy, why not try acting?

LAURENCE OLIVIER TO 'METHOD' ACTOR, DUSTIN HOFFMAN

You mean actors actually rehearse? I thought they just got drunk, stuck on silly hats and trusted to luck. **EDMUND BLACKADDER, BLACKADDER III**

The First Law of Acting: Any line that is cut out of any actor's part is the only good line he has. **P.G. WODEHOUSE**

Show me a congenital eavesdropper with the instincts of a Peeping Tom and I will show you the makings of a dramatist. **KENNETH TYNAN**

I was asked for a play which would make people laugh when their seaside holidays were spoilt by the rain and they came into the theatre to get dry. This seemed to me as worthwhile a reason as any for writing a play.

ALAN AYCKBOURN

When I was once threatened with litigation by a Hollywood film producer, and in no position to bargain from any foreseeable strength, my agent, Robin Fox, advised me: 'Tell him to go fuck himself, dear boy.'

JOHN OSBORNE

O God, send me some good actors – cheap. **LILIAN BAYLIS, THEATRICAL MANAGER**

If I wasn't an actor I'd probably be a psychopath. **TERENCE STAMP**

I come from a long line of performers and actors. It's called the dole queue.

JACK DEE

To be dependent on an agent is like entrusting your most precious future to your mother-in-law or your bookmaker.

JOHN OSBORNE

Don't Put Your Daughter On The Stage, Mrs Worthington

NOËL COWARD, SONG TITLE

I always knew that if all else failed I could become an actor – and all else failed.

DAVID NIVEN

I learned two things at drama school: first, that I couldn't act; second, that it didn't matter.

WILFRED HYDE-WHITE

I love acting. It is so much more real than life.

OSCAR WILDE

If I have occasionally given brilliant performances on the screen, this was entirely due to circumstances beyond my control.

GEORGE SANDERS

Kenneth Tynan said I had only two gestures: left hand up, and right hand down. What did he want me to do, bring out my prick?

JOHN GIELGUD

They say an actor is only as good as his parts. Well, my parts have done me pretty well, darling.

BARBARA WINDSOR

Sid James looked as bad as his acting.

KENNETH WILLIAMS

Possibly because of my shape, the role of Portia always eluded me.

ROBERT MORLEY

When I played drunks I had to remain sober because I didn't know how to play them when I was drunk.   **RICHARD BURTON**

Many of my roles were what I call 'Up periscope' parts. I played opposite more submarines than leading ladies.   **SIR JOHN MILLS**

My roles play into a certain fantasy of what people want English people to be, whereas half the time we're vomiting beer and beating people up.

HUGH GRANT

—Do you think this tribute lunch marks the end of your career?
—What career?   **JOURNALIST AND ROGER MOORE**

The unique thing about Margaret Rutherford is that she can act with her chin alone. Among its many moods I especially cherish the chin commanding, the chin in doubt, and the chin at bay.   **KENNETH TYNAN**

I have no intention of uttering my last words on the stage, darling. Room service and a couple of depraved young women will do me quite nicely for an exit.   **PETER O'TOOLE**

RADIO

The Archers must be the authentic voice of the English shire. We aim, in our grander moments, to write in the tradition of Jane Austen, Laurie Lee and H.E. Bates.   **WILLIAM SMETHURST**

The Archers should be retitled, 'The Grundys and Their Oppressors'.

NEIL KINNOCK

The plot of *The* Archers is squelchy and the dialogue compost...but Shula Archer is trimly stacked, with eyelashes like long grass, and any man would climb a loft ladder for her.   **JEAN ROOK**

Miss Harthill's voice is quintessentially Radio 4, like someone talking down a would-be suicide from a high window-ledge.   *THE LISTENER* **MAGAZINE**

I have always characterised the relationship between my producer and I as that of a man and his dog, each believing the other to be the dog.

JOHN PEEL ON JOHN WALTERS

I am amazed at radio DJs today. I am firmly convinced that AM on my radio stands for Absolute Moron. I will not begin to tell you what FM stands for.   **JASPER CARROTT**

TELEVISION

There was life before *Coronation Street* but it didn't add up to much.

RUSSELL HARTY

Television is the first truly democratic culture – the first culture available to everybody and entirely governed by what the people want. The most terrifying thing is what people do want.   **CLIVE BARNES**

I'll die if I miss Scooby-doo.   **NEIL**, *THE YOUNG ONES*

All the gadgets in my house are controlled from a master switch.
I set the video last night and when I came home it had recorded all the programmes from the washing machine. It was the best night's viewing I ever had.   **BOB MONKHOUSE**

I watched *Countdown* once and I got aroused. It's only seven letters.

BARRY CRYER

Coming up...John Leslie speaks about Ulrika's rape claims, and we taste the food loved by Marie-Antoinette – cockerels' testicles and marzipan vagina cakes.   **RICHARD MADELEY**, *RICHARD AND JUDY*

No! No! No! We're not watching *The bloody Good Life*! Bloody bloody bloody! I hate it! It's so bloody nice! Felicity 'Treacle' Kendal and Richard 'Sugar-Flavoured-Snot' Briers! They're just a couple of reactionary stereotypes, confirming the myth that everyone in Britain is a lovable, middle-class eccentric – and I hate them.

VYVYAN, *THE YOUNG ONES*

I object to all this sex on the television – I mean, I keep falling off. GRAHAM CHAPMAN

The new series of *Kavanagh QC* is so true to life that I fell asleep during the last ten minutes of counsel's speech to the jury.

JUDGE BARRINGTON BLACK

Television influences us? Not true. If it did, we'd all be gourmet chefs by now.

ALLY ROSS

I do not watch drama because it depicts cohabitation, promiscuity, infidelity, adultery and under-age sexual activity as not just normal but as mature and desirable. You may wonder how I know it does that without watching it: the Bishop of Winchester says so.

EDWARD ENFIELD

Seeing a murder on television can help work off one's antagonisms. And if you haven't any antagonisms, the commercials will give you some.

ALFRED HITCHCOCK

I hated the lingering nude scenes in the television adaptation of my book, *The Camomile Lawn*. They simply wouldn't have happened. Nobody had central heating in those days.

MARY WESLEY

The remarkable thing about television is that it permits several million people to laugh at the same joke and still feel lonely.

T. S. ELIOT

Television is as injurious to the soul as fast food is to the body.

QUENTIN CRISP

I don't watch television – I always seem to have something better to do, such as nothing.

HUNTER DAVIES

Television is for appearing on, not looking at.

NOËL COWARD

Wasn't Germaine Greer on one of those programmes that people go on that shouldn't?

STEPHEN FRY

I was too scared to tell my parents I was going on *Big Brother* so I told them I was going on *Countdown*.

KEMAL SHAHIN

I used to love Reality TV but lately I've gone right off it. There's something wrong about being a celebrity and sitting at home watching members of the public on the telly.

FRANK SKINNER

When they ring you up at the BBC and ask you out to lunch then you know you've been fired.

JACK DE MANIO

And a message to all our viewers: Matron will be bringing round your medication shortly.

ANGUS DEAYTON

COMEDY

—What did you think of the comedian?
—He's all right – if you like laughing.

DAVE SPIKEY

The sound of laughter is the most civilised music in the world.

PETER USTINOV

You make the jokes: I see them.

G.K. CHESTERTON

Oh, shut up, Baldrick. You'd laugh at a Shakespearean comedy.

EDMUND BLACKADDER, *BLACKADDER II*

Comedy is the one job you can do badly and no one will laugh at you.

MAX MILLER

Never say a humorous thing to a man who does not possess humour.
He will always use it in evidence against you. **HERBERT BEERBOHM TREE**

There's terrific merit in having no sense of humour, no sense of irony,
practically no sense of anything at all. If you're born with these so-called
defects you have a very good chance of getting to the top. **PETER COOK**

From the silence that prevails I conclude that Lauderdale has been telling
a joke. **RICHARD BRINSLEY-SHERIDAN**

When I make a joke I always laugh quickly, so that there's no doubt
about it. **W. SOMERSET MAUGHAM**

His impressions were perfectly splendid. And I do think it so kind of
him to tell us who he is imitating. It avoids discussion, doesn't it?

OSCAR WILDE

Many a true word is spoken in jest.

ENGLISH PROVERB

Comedy script-writing is one of the few trades that doesn't have to fear
competition from the Japanese. **DENIS NORDEN**

The essence of any blue material is timing. If you sit on it, it becomes
vulgar. **DANNY LA RUE**

It is only the dull who like practical jokes. **OSCAR WILDE**

Oh, I do hope you're not going to spoil everything with lower middle class humour. **HYACINTH BUCKET,** *KEEPING UP APPEARANCES*

When a society has to resort to the lavatory for its humour, the writing is on the wall. **ALAN BENNETT**

I can't stand innuendo. If I see one in the script I whip it out immediately.

KENNETH WILLIAMS

For many years I thought an innuendo was an Italian suppository. **SPIKE MILLIGAN**

Good taste and humour are a contradiction in terms, like a chaste whore. **MALCOLM MUGGERIDGE**

How low and unbecoming a thing laughing is: not to mention the disagreeable noise that it makes, and the shocking distortion of the face. **LORD CHESTERFIELD**

I try to offset any tendency towards the macabre with humour. As I see it, this is a typically English form of humour. It's a piece with such jokes as the one about the man who was being led to the gallows to be hanged. He looked at the trap door in the gallows, which was flimsily constructed, and he asked in some alarm, 'I say, is that thing safe?' **ALFRED HITCHCOCK**

He ought to run a hospital for sick jokes. **ANTHONY POWELL**

Angels can fly because they can take things lightly. **G.K. CHESTERTON**

Comedians often play the person they fear becoming. **JOHN CLEESE**

My New Year's resolution is to refrain from saying witty, unkind things, unless they are really witty and irreparably damaging. **JAMES AGATE**

One should not exaggerate the importance of trifles. Life is much too short to be taken seriously. NICHOLAS BENTLEY

—What would you and Ernie have been if you weren't comedians?
—Mike and Bernie Winters. **MICHAEL PARKINSON AND ERIC MORECAMBE**

Spike Milligan was the great grand-daddy of post-war British comedy. He allowed the British to be silly. **STEPHEN FRY**

The first time I saw The Goons, it suddenly struck me that comedy needn't be funny. **ALEXEI SAYLE**

Anyone who thinks women aren't funny is an idiot: two of my favourite comedians in the last 25 years are Lily Savage and Dame Edna Everage. **RICKY GERVAIS**

We had a topless lady ventriloquist in Liverpool once. Nobody ever saw her lips move. **KEN DODD**

I've worked places you wouldn't throw a petrol bomb in. And if you did, they'd have drunk it. **PAUL O'GRADY**

'How d'you want the lights?' the club-manager said. 'What're my options?' 'On or off.' **PETER KAY**

Advice to stand up comedian? Wear a pair of brown trousers.

BOB MONKHOUSE

Jim Tavare once walked on stage and said, 'Hello, I'm a schizophrenic,' and was greeted by the heckle, 'Well you can both fuck off then!'

MALCOLM HARDEE

My favourite riposte to a heckle is to say, 'Excuse me, I'm trying to work here. How would you like it if I stood yelling down the alley while you're giving blow jobs to transsexuals?'

PAUL MERTON

Bob Monkhouse did for comedy what Gannex raincoats did for flashing.

DENIS NORDEN

Ronnie Corbett is Cary Grant on his knees.

DANNY LA RUE

Descriptions of my face have included comparisons with most root vegetables – usually in an advanced state of decomposition.

FRANKIE HOWERD

Some accountants are comedians, but comedians are never accountants.

GEORGE CARMAN QC, DEFENDING KEN DODD

The trouble with political jokes is they get elected.

TIM BROOKE-TAYLOR

CRITICS

I can take any amount of criticism, so long as it is unqualified praise.

NOËL COWARD

Why is it that a single slam from even the most patent imbecile can undo all the praise of a hundred critics?

P.G. WODEHOUSE

When the critic caused me a somewhat uneasy breakfast, I contented myself with the knowledge that I had given him a perfectly ghastly evening.

JEREMY SINDEN

Don't read your reviews, dear boy. Measure them!   **W. SOMERSET MAUGHAM**

A critic is a man who knows the way but can't drive the car.   **KENNETH TYNAN**

I remember reviewing the singer Frank Ifield under the insane misapprehension he was blind. I often wonder what he thought when he read the review in which I congratulated him on the gallantry with which he had overcome the handicap.   **KENNETH TYNAN**

Milton Shulman would hang-glide to the Orkneys to give a writer a bad review.   **MIKE LEIGH**

A bad review is even less important than whether it is raining in Patagonia.   **IRIS MURDOCH**

After I'd given a less than complimentary review to Noël Coward's *Look After Lulu* I walked alone into a restaurant only to see the playwright himself seated at another table, also alone. He rose at once and came padding across the room to the table behind which I was cringing…'Mr T,' he said crisply, 'you are a cunt. Come and have dinner with me.'   **KENNETH TYNAN**

COMMUNICATION AND LITERATURE

TALK

Talk to a woman as if you loved her, and a man as if he bored you.

OSCAR WILDE

Typical Brit – the only thing that works is the mouth.

JUMBO, *ONLY FOOLS AND HORSES*

I haven't spoken to my wife for over a month. We haven't had a row – it's just that I'm afraid to interrupt her.   **LES DAWSON**

The English really aren't interested in talking to you unless you've been to school or to bed with them.   **LADY NANCY KEITH**

I won't say anything because no one ever listens to me anyway. I might as well be a Leonard Cohen record.   **NEIL,** *THE YOUNG ONES*

No one listened to one unless one said the wrong thing.

SYLVIA TOWNSEND WARNER

Her communication became very subtle, very difficult to follow, like Henry James read aloud on the Underground.   **A.P. HERBERT**

She sat listening to the speech with the stoical indifference with which an Eskimo might accept the occurrence of one snowstorm the more, in the course of an Arctic Winter.   **SAKI**

I tried to be pleasant and chatty. It was like engaging the pyramids in small talk.   **W. SOMERSET MAUGHAM**

I have a notion that it is pleasanter to read Boswell's record of the conversations than it ever was to listen to Doctor Johnson.

W. SOMERSET MAUGHAM

Talk to a man about himself and he will listen for hours.   **BENJAMIN DISRAELI**

Gilbert Gottfried met Jackie Onassis at a party but found that they had little in common. Trying to make small talk, Gottfried unthinkingly asked: 'So, where were you when Kennedy was shot?'   **SIMON FANSHAWE**

My idea of a good conversation is when neither party remembers a word of what was said afterwards.   **E.F. BENSON**

SPEECHES

The most difficult things for a man to do are to climb a wall leaning towards you, to kiss a girl leaning away from you, and to make an after-dinner speech.   **WINSTON CHURCHILL**

A speech is like a love affair: any fool can start one but to end it requires considerable skill.   **LORD STORMONT MANCROFT**

I stand up when he nudges me. I sit down when they pull my coat.   **ERNEST BEVIN**

A good way to start a speech is to say: 'As Henry VIII said to his wives: "I won't keep you long."'   **SIR CLAUS MOSER**

I am the most spontaneous speaker in the world because every word, every gesture, and every retort has been carefully rehearsed.   **GEORGE BERNARD SHAW**

LETTERS

Why waste money on first class stamps? Simply write your letters a few days earlier, and send them second class.   **P. HONK, *VIZ*, TOP TIP**

The perfect way to ensure that any letters I post arrive promptly is simply to disguise them as bills. **B. PREGER**

The post is hopeless and I have given up sending things by post. I have things delivered in my Rolls. **BARBARA CARTLAND**

Correspondences are like smallclothes before the invention of suspenders; it is impossible to keep them up. **REVD SYDNEY SMITH**

I have always thought Evelyn Waugh's immortal phrase 'with love or what you will' as the ultimate end to my correspondence. It has disarmed my sternest critic and redeemed my dullest prose. **PHILIP A. DAVIES**

A Royal Engineer serving overseas, wrote 200 love-letters a week to his girlfriend back home. This Saturday, at All Saints Church, she marries the postman. *THE WEEKLY GAZETTE*

TELEPHONE

My phone was ringing, so I picked it up and said, 'Who's speaking please?' And a voice said, 'You are.' **TIM VINE**

Someone calls Admiral Insurance every six seconds for a quote. What a nutter. **JIMMY CARR**

I have noticed that when someone asks for you on the telephone and, finding you out, leaves a message begging you to call him up the moment you come in, as it's important, the matter is more often important to him than to you. **W. SOMERSET MAUGHAM**

The itemised telephone bill ranks up there with suspender belts, Sky Sports channels and *Loaded* magazine as inventions women could do without. **MAEVE HARAN**

I've often wondered how businessmen used to cope before mobile phones were invented. How did they tell their wives they were on the train?

PETE MCCARTHY

David Beckham loves texting. He was going to text in his vote in the General Election but he couldn't spell X. **LENNY HENRY**

Old telephone directories make ideal personal address books. Simply cross out the names and addresses of people you don't know.

K. SMITH, *VIZ*, TOP TIP

NAMES

—Hello, I'm John Ffolkes – one large one, one small one.
—Hello, I'm George Roper – perfectly normal in every way.

JOHN FFOLKES AND GEORGE ROPER, *GEORGE AND MILDRED*

Well glaze my nipples and call me Rita. **MELCHETT, *BLACKADDER BACK AND FORTH***

I say, it is Wendy Plackett, isn't it? I don't suppose you'll remember me. Yes, that's right, 'Lumpy' Latimer…Isn't that Freesia McSomething?… Oh, there's Fizzy Wiggins! **JOYCE GRENFELL**

—Mr Coward, may I come in?
—Who is it?
—It's me, Yehudi.
—Yehudi who? **YEHUDI MENUHIN AND NOËL COWARD**

—Your name vill also go on zee list. Vot is it?
—Don't tell him, Pike.

GERMAN U-BOAT CAPTAIN AND CAPTAIN MAINWARING, *DAD'S ARMY*

Colin is the sort of name you give your goldfish for a joke. **COLIN FIRTH**

In pidgin-English I am known as 'Fella belong Mrs Queen.'

PRINCE PHILIP

I was born on a council estate but my parents named me 'Jeremy' so we had to move.

JEREMY HARDY

I became a great runner because if you're a kid in Leeds and your name is Sebastian you've got to become a great runner.

SEBASTIAN COE

I was once paged at JFK airport as 'Mr No One.'

PETER NOONE

When I worked as a telephone operator, I was once asked for the number of a 'Mr Go-to-Bed' in Little Snoring.

PHYL AMISON

Seems ages since I had a natter with old Yoko Suji in Tokyo. I wonder how his wife is, what was her name? 'Radiant Flower of the Divine Heavens.' I wonder if her feet are still playing her up.

TONY HANCOCK

When I got married my feminist friends went mad. One sniffed, 'Are you going to take your husband's name?' I said, 'No, because I don't think "Dave" suits me very much.'

JO BRAND

—You have a daughter, I believe?
—Yeah, yeah, Henrietta.
—Did he, did he? I'm sorry to hear that.

STEPHEN FRY AND HUGH LAURIE

I said everyone calls me Ann. Even God calls me Ann. To which he replied, 'God calls me Lord Henley.'

ANN WIDDECOMBE

His name's Angus – the 'g' is silent.

PAUL MERTON

—We're talking this evening to Sir Arthur Greeb-Streebling.
—Streeb-Greebling. The 'T' is silent, as in 'fox'.

DUDLEY MOORE AND PETER COOK

Rupert: An officer whose father bought him a commission
(usually Household Cavalry).
Rodney: An officer who earned his commission.   **BRITISH ARMY SLANG**

The only thing about him that's a mouthful is his name.   **ANGUS DEAYTON**

When I was in the Foreign Office, I would say, 'I'm going to call you
Andrew. You call me Peter.' To which they would then say, 'Yes, Minister.'

PETER HAIN

When you meet a public man who ostentatiously shortens his forename,
make the sign of the Evil Eye and count your spoons.   **BERNARD LEVIN**

Names adopted during the Puritan revolution and listed in the Sussex
register: Performe-thy-Vowes Seers; Stand-fast-on-high Stringer; Weep-not
Billing; Fight-the-good-fight-of-faith White; Kill-sin Pemple; Fly-
fornication Richardson.   **AYTOUN ELLIS**

Proper names are poetry in the raw.
Like all poetry they are untranslatable.

W. H. AUDEN

His intimate friends called him 'Candle-ends',
And his enemies, 'Toasted-cheese'.   **LEWIS CARROLL, *THE HUNTING OF THE SNARK***

Dirk Bogarde called her Snowdrop because, he said, anything less like a
snowdrop you could never wish to meet. Asked what flower he most
resembled he didn't hesitate: 'Holly.'   **JOHN COLDSTREAM**

Nobody ever makes up nicknames, a nickname is your real identity, jumping out from behind you like an afreet. **ROBERT ROBINSON**

There is a rose named after me. The catalogue describes it as 'superb for bedding, best up against a wall'. **JUNE WHITFIELD**

LANGUAGE AND WORDS

Like Henry V and Elizabeth I, Winston Churchill, at a time of great peril to England, addressed the moment in the country's ancestral tongue. In 1940 he told apprehensive Britons, 'We shall fight them on the beaches, we shall fight them on the landing grounds, we shall fight them in the fields and in the streets, shall fight in the hills: we shall never surrender'. Every word is Old English save one: 'surrender' is French. **MELVYN BRAGG**

Personally I like short words and vulgar fractions. **WINSTON CHURCHILL**

How amazing that the language of a few thousand savages living on a fog-encrusted island in the North Sea should become the language of the world. **NORMAN ST. JOHN-STEVAS**

English is the perfect language to sell pigs in. **MICHAEL HARTNETT**

English is the only language you can imagine where 'pathetic' is a term of abuse – imagine 'The Pathetic Symphony'. Tells us a lot about English attitude to emotion. **A.N. WILSON**

If there was graffiti in a lavatory cubicle I had to read every word, and sometimes even corrected the spelling and punctuation. **SUE TOWNSEND**

I spend all my time arguing with spell-check on my computer. **ANN WIDDECOMBE**

American is the language in which people say what they mean, as Italian is the language in which they say what they feel. English is the language in which what a character means or feels has to be deduced from what he or she says, which may be quite the opposite. **JOHN MORTIMER**

In a British hotel, the words, 'Can I help you sir?' mean roughly, 'What the hell do you want?' **KINGSLEY AMIS**

Far from it, as the private said when he aimed at the bulls-eye and hit the gunnery instructor. **DOROTHY L. SAYERS**

Check carefully the correct meaning of words in the dictionary before use: In his poem, 'Pippa Passes', Robert Browning uses the word 'twat' under the misapprehension that it is a nun's hat. **RAYMOND GILL**

A haitch and a hay, two hars and a hi and a hess and a ho and a hen spell 'Arrison. **ANON**

Eskimos have dozens of words for 'snow' but only one for 'patio'. **ROSS NOBLE**

English spelling would seem to have been designed chiefly as a disguise for pronunciation. It is a clever idea, calculated to check presumption on the part of the foreigner. **JEROME K. JEROME**

I will not instruct my daughters in foreign languages. One tongue is sufficient for a woman. **JOHN MILTON**

Everybody has the right to pronounce foreign names as he chooses. **WINSTON CHURCHILL**

Is there anything worse than speaking a foreign language to someone who turns out to be English? **MICHAEL FRAYN**

—Was death instant?
—Instantaneous, Lewis. Coffee may be instant, death may not.

SGT LEWIS AND INSPECTOR MORSE, *INSPECTOR MORSE*

Not 'what', 'who'. Didn't they learn you no grammar at school?

HILDA OGDEN, *CORONATION STREET*

This is the sort of English up with which I will not put. **WINSTON CHURCHILL**

Splitting infinitives is akin to burping; a habit disdained in some company, tolerated in others, and highly esteemed in a few. It's all a matter of upbringing. **FRANCIS GARDOM**

The phrase 'with great respect' invariably implies that the addressee has the IQ of a garden gnome. **NEIL KENNEDY**

There are certain phrases that, when you hear them, strike dread in your heart. One of these is: 'Do you mind if I say something?' **JOYCE GRENFELL**

The worst words in the English language are, '...and while you're up there...' **MARK REAGAN**

The word 'meaningful' when used today is nearly always meaningless.

PAUL JOHNSON

'When I use a word,' Humpty-Dumpty said in rather a scornful tone, 'it means just what I choose it to mean – neither more nor less.'

LEWIS CARROLL, *THROUGH THE LOOKING GLASS*

There are many ways of saying 'Well!' The speaker who had the floor at the moment said it rather in the manner of the prudish queen of a monarch of Babylon who has happened to wander into the banqueting hall just as the Babylonian orgy is beginning to go nicely.   P.G. WODEHOUSE

The trouble with words is that you never know whose mouth they've been in.   DENNIS POTTER

The word 'bush', so lifeless in a gardening programme becomes plump when used in its proper sense of pubic hair.   SIMON NYE

Inventors of words:
Byron:	bored, blasé
G.K. Chesterton:	etiquette, picnic
Coleridge:	pessimism, phenomenal, Elizabethan
Dr Johnson:	comic, literature
Tennyson:	fairy tale

GEOFFREY MADAN

Inspector Morse does crossword puzzles. Knows all sorts of words that nobody ever uses.   SGT LEWIS, GHOST IN THE MACHINE

I have been wondering why Anthony Burgess will insist on using the word 'micturate'. I conclude that he is an English language swank. Whether it is correct or not is neither here nor there. What's wrong with piss?

JEFFREY BERNARD

A simile committing suicide is always a depressing spectacle.   OSCAR WILDE

Euphemisms are unpleasant truths wearing diplomatic cologne.

QUENTIN CRISP

She plunged into a sea of platitudes, and with the powerful breast stroke of a channel swimmer made her confident way towards the white cliffs of the obvious.   W. SOMERSET MAUGHAM

BURMA	Be Upstairs Ready My Angel
NORWICH	Knickers Off Ready When I Come Home
POLO	Pants Off, Legs Open
LOMBARD	Loads of Money But a Right Dickhead
NQOTD	Not Quite Our Type Dear

ACRONYMS

My wife loves the c-word. Sometimes, when the children are listening, she combines it with 'bastard' to create the word 'custard'.

JEREMY CLARKSON

Hobson's choice: the choice of a thing offered or nothing, from 'Tobias Hobson', a Cambridge horsekeeper, who lent out the horse nearest the stable door, or none at all.

CHAMBERS DICTIONARY

I was criticised for swearing on television. The word I used was 'bloody', which, where I come from in Yorkshire, is practically the only surviving adjective.

MAUREEN LIPMAN

—I will not fuck it up again, Mum.
—Bridget! Language!
—Sorry. I will not fuck it up again, *Mother*.

BRIDGET JONES AND MUM, *BRIDGET JONES, THE EDGE OF REASON*

Fuck it the fucking fucker's fucking fucked.

ANTHONY BURGESS QUOTING WHAT A MECHANIC SAID ABOUT THE ENGINE OF HIS CAR

When they told me they wanted to call the show *Two Fat Ladies* I objected strongly: 'ladies', I argued, sounds like a public convenience.

CLARISSA DICKSON-WRIGHT

Eh, toilet mouth, there's a kiddie's bike outside.   **PETER KAY,** *PHOENIX NIGHTS*

The first person to use the colloquial coupling word on television was
Kenneth Tynan. He said it in an arts discussion, to point out how silly it
was he couldn't say it. He was smoking at the time. You can't smoke on
television now, but you can say fuck as often as you like.   **A.A. GILL**

If ever I utter an oath again may my soul be blasted to eternal damnation.
GEORGE BERNARD SHAW

In these politically correct times, it looks as if my theatre company may
have to perform the pantomime, 'Snow White and the Seven Persons of
Restricted Growth' and 'Beauty and the Bodily Challenged'. And I
suppose a Slave of the Ring in 'Aladdin' is out of the question?   **IAN LISTON**

Any stupid remark, quoted often enough, becomes gospel.   **LESLIE CHARTERIS**

If the remarks with which I am credited – and never made – are really
good, I acknowledge them. I generally work myself into the belief that
I originally said them.   **NOËL COWARD**

The quotation of two or three lines from Spenser's *Faerie Queene* is
probably as good a silencer as any.   **STEPHEN POTTER**

DESCRIPTION

Did you ever in your puff see such a perfect perisher?   **P.G. WODEHOUSE**

His smile bathed us like warm custard.   **BASIL BOOTHROYD**

If those are Mr Heckmondwick's own personal pipes they've been lagged
once already.   **N.F. SIMPSON**

She was looking about as pale as a beetroot that has suddenly heard bad news. **SAKI**

Now, where will you perch, Miss Pool? Will you be quite comfy on the leather pouffe? **JOYCE GRENFELL**

'I say, someone's on my cock.' 'It's only my cousin Hilary,' said Delia. 'He won't mind changing, will you, Hilary...' Mr Grant, really quite glad of an excuse to dismount, offered his cock to Lydia, who immediately flung a leg over it, explaining that she had put on a frock with pleats on purpose... 'I know that once Lydia is on her cock nothing will get her off.'
ANGELA THIRKELL, *THE BRANDONS*, DESCRIBING A FAIRGROUND RIDE

Memories are like mulligatawny soup in a cheap restaurant. It is best not to stir them. **P.G. WODEHOUSE**

Louise says, once you get used to it, it's utter utter utter blissikins.
NANCY MITFORD

George Bernard Shaw's exquisite handwriting – like a fly which has been trained at the Russian ballet. **JAMES AGATE**

I am as appreciatively indifferent to Edith Sitwell as I am to the quaint patterns of old chintzes, or the designs on dinner plates. **H.G. WELLS**

He shook Uriah Heep's hand. It felt like a fish in the dark.
CHARLES DICKENS, *DAVID COPPERFIELD*

If he happened to be selling an archangel a pair of wings it would turn out afterwards that the feathers were dropping off. **GEORGE A. BIRMINGHAM**

Veronica would find something to tumble over in the Sahara desert.
JEROME K. JEROME

Debating with Nancy Astor is like playing squash with a dish of scrambled egg.
HAROLD NICHOLSON

WRITER

'I suppose you know a lot of writers,' she said. 'I know some,' he said, 'but I prefer people.'
MALCOLM BRADBURY, *THE HISTORY MAN*

Writers are selfish people, with a love of their own company so passionate that it seems entirely likely that one day one of us just might get ourselves pregnant.
JULIE BURCHILL

A great many people now reading and writing would be better employed in keeping rabbits.
EDITH SITWELL

Writing is hard work. It's mental in every sense of the word.
JULIA DAVIS

An author's first duty is to let down his country.
BRENDAN BEHAN

The true function of a writer is to produce a masterpiece and no other task is of any consequence.
CYRIL CONNOLLY

The only rule I have found to have any validity in writing is not to bore oneself.
JOHN MORTIMER

To write simply is as difficult as to be good.
W. SOMERSET MAUGHAM

The truth is that writing is the profound pleasure and being read the superficial.
VIRGINIA WOOLF

You do your best to delay the moment of creation – Laurie Lee used to copy out all the shipping news from *The Times* before he started a poem.
JOHN MORTIMER

I have yet to meet a writer who wouldn't rather peel a banana than apply himself to a pen. **ALICE THOMAS ELLIS**

The hard part is getting to the top of page 1. **TOM STOPPARD**

Jack Frost dancing bespangled in the sunshine. **WINSTON CHURCHILL ON GEORGE BERNARD SHAW**

Half an hour at his desk, and he'd be on the phone saying, 'Is the patch of wall you're staring at any more interesting than the one I'm staring at?' **ALAN BENNETT ABOUT RUSSELL HARTY**

Gazing at the typewriter in moments of desperation I console myself with three thoughts: Alcohol at six, dinner at eight, and to be immortal you've got to be dead. **GYLES BRANDRETH**

I love deadlines. I like the whooshing sound they make as they fly by. **DOUGLAS ADAMS**

I get all my ideas from a mail order company in Indianapolis. Although I'm not prepared to give you their name. **DOUGLAS ADAMS**

I get my ideas from a warehouse called Ideas R Us. **TERRY PRATCHETT**

As long as the plots keep arriving from outer space, I'll go on with my virgins. **DAME BARBARA CARTLAND**

Whom the gods wish to destroy they first call promising. **CYRIL CONNOLLY**

Ambrose isn't a frightfully hot writer. I don't suppose he makes enough out of a novel to keep a midget in doughnuts for a week. Not a really healthy midget. **P.G. WODEHOUSE**

Thank you for the manuscript; I shall lose no time in reading it.

BENJAMIN DISRAELI

No passion in the world is equal to the passion to alter someone else's draft.

H.G. WELLS

Your manuscript is both good and original; but the part that is good is not original, and the part that is original is not good. **SAMUEL JOHNSON**

BOOKS

Keeping a bar is much better than writing a book. Many an English writer has wished he kept a pub instead of a publisher. **G.K. CHESTERTON**

I feel his books are all written in hotels with the bed unmade. **RONALD FIRBANK**

Naomi Campbell has ghost-written a book. Now if only I could get someone to ghost-read it for me. **MARK LAMARR**

Please buy my book. Forty per cent of profits go to the taxman which goes to fund hospitals for little sick kiddies. **RICKY GERVAIS**

There are two basic reactions. There are those who hate you because they think you put them in your book, and there are those who hate you because they think you didn't put them in your book. **HANIF KUREISHI**

There is a great deal of difference between an eager man who wants to read a book and a tired man who wants a book to read. **G.K. CHESTERTON**

The paperback is very interesting, but I find it will never replace a hardcover book – it makes a very poor doorstop. **ALFRED HITCHCOCK**

It was a book to kill time for those who liked it better dead. **ROSE MACAULAY**

The first book I can remember reading was one of those Rupert annuals I was always given every Christmas. I think I would shoot the creature now. **SIR ROY STRONG**

I was in a bookshop and overheard a father say to his young son: 'I don't know what you want a book for. You don't even feed your rabbit.' **ADRIAN HOLDEN**

They told me how Mr Gladstone read Homer for fun, which I thought served him right. **WINSTON CHURCHILL**

The more I read Socrates, the less I wonder that they poisoned him. **THOMAS BABINGTON MACAULAY**

I am going to read a few chapters of Mrs Gaskell to take the taste of *Howard's End* out of my mouth. **EDMUND GOSSE**

A book for all ages – especially the Stone, Iron and Bronze. **SPIKE MILLIGAN**

A real book is not one that we read, but one that reads us. **W.H. AUDEN**

I've taken up speed-reading. I can read *War and Peace* in two seconds. It's only three words but it's a start. **TIM VINE**

I never read a book before reviewing it. It prejudices one so. **REVD SYDNEY SMITH**

Translations (like wives) are seldom faithful if they are in the least attractive. **ROY CAMPBELL**

One always tends to overpraise a long book because one has got through. **E.M. FORSTER**

To J. Alastair Frisby Who Told Me I Would Never Have A Book
Published And Advised Me To Get A Job Selling Jellied Eels

P.G. WODEHOUSE, BOOK DEDICATION

'You told them you were expecting to sell a hundred thousand copies?'
'We always tell them we're expecting to sell a hundred thousand copies,'
said Richard Clutterbuck, letting him in on one of the secrets of the
publishing trade.

P.G. WODEHOUSE

On another small table stood Zuleika's library. Both books were in covers
of dull gold.

SIR MAX BEERBOHM

I have only read one book in my life, and that is *White Fang*. It's so
frightfully good that I've never bothered to read another.

NANCY MITFORD

I cannot choose one hundred best books because I have written only five.

OSCAR WILDE

If you try to laugh and say 'No' at the same time it sounds like neighing –
yet people are perpetually doing it in novels.

HILAIRE BELLOC

I never read any novels except my own. When I feel worried, agitated or
upset, I read one and find the last pages soothe me and leave me happy.
I quite understand why I am popular in hospitals.

DAME BARBARA CARTLAND

At what point was it decided that Humpty Dumpty was a giant egg man?
It's not in the actual rhyme. It's not, 'Humpty Dumpty the egg man sat
on the wall.'

RICKY GERVAIS

Riddle: If the clocks were to feel that they had no one to talk to or keep
them going, what publisher would they refer to? Answer: We have no one
to Chatto and Windus.

LORD BERNERS

Except for a sense of humour, Hemingway had everything.

QUENTIN CRISP

When somebody in a novel says something like 'I've never been in an air crash', you know this means that five minutes later they will be.

ALAN BENNETT

Jane Austen was in fact a man. A huge Yorkshireman with a beard like a rhododendron bush. **EDMUND BLACKADDER,** *BLACKADDER III*

Pride and Prejudice was the most erotic novel I'd ever read until the wet-shirt version on television reduced it to an ad for Quality Street sweets.

BARBARA TRAPIDO

I loved Mr Darcy far more than any of my own husbands. **RUMER GODDEN**

Frankenstein is a book about what happens when a man tries to have a baby without a woman. **ANNE K. MELLOR**

I was reading a book, *The History of Glue*. Couldn't put it down. **TIM VINE**

—What was Charles Dickens' first novel?
—'White Christmas'? **MELANIE SYKES AND CONTESTANT,** *THE VAULT*

We were put to Dickens as children but it never quite took.
That unremitting humanity soon had me cheesed off. **ALAN BENNETT**

—Which character in literature do you hate most?
—Steerforth in *David Copperfield*. A plausible rat with a yellow streak.
—Which character would you most like to have an affair with?
—Steerforth. **INTERVIEWER AND MATTHEW PARRIS**

Pale Fire was alleged by Nabokov himself to be the hardest of his books to write, but that can't have compared with the pain of having to read it.

JOHN OSBORNE

Since reading *Vanity Fair* at Eton I've always wanted to roger Becky Sharp.

ALAN CLARK

Lady Chatterley's Lover: in this reviewer's opinion this book cannot take the place of J.R. Miller's 'Practical Gamekeeping'.

FIELD AND STREAM MAGAZINE, 1928

Whenever I want a good read I get one of Jeffrey Archer's novels and stand on it, so I can reach the good books. **STEVEN NORRIS**

Books that have become classics – books that have had their day and now get more praise than perusal – always remind me of retired colonels and majors and captains who, having reached the age limit, find themselves retired on half-pay. **THOMAS BAILEY ALDRICH**

Foolish writers and readers were created for each other; and Fortune provides readers as she does mates for ugly women. **HORACE WALPOLE**

If somebody could write a book for the people who never read they would make a fortune. **NANCY MITFORD**

The *Lord of the Rings* is a book for engineering students called Dave. LINDA SMITH

Science fiction is no more written for scientists than ghost stories are written for ghosts. **BRIAN ALDISS**

I'm sure we would not have had men on the Moon if it had not been for H.G. Wells and Jules Verne and the people who write about this and made people think about it. I'm rather proud of the fact that I know several astronauts who became astronauts through reading my books.

ARTHUR C. CLARKE

The oldest books are still only just out to those who have not read them.

SAMUEL BUTLER

The reason why so few good books are written is that so few people who can write know anything.

WALTER BAGEHOT

You cannot tell a man by the lobster he eats, but you can tell something about him by the literature he reads.

A.A. MILNE

Dictionaries are like watches: the worst is better than none, and the best cannot be expected to go quite right.

DR SAMUEL JOHNSON

There is no tribe of human beings more pestiferous than the people who insist on lending you books whether you wish to borrow them or not.

ROBERT LYND

Borrowers of books – those mutilators of collections, spoilers of the symmetry of shelves, and creators of odd volumes.

CHARLES LAMB

A book reads the better which is your own, and has been so long known to us, that we know the topography of its blots, and dog's ears, and can trace the dirt in it to having read it at tea with buttered muffins.

CHARLES LAMB

What readers ask nowadays in a book is that it should improve, instruct, and elevate. My book wouldn't elevate a cow.

JEROME K. JEROME

The good ended happily, and the bad unhappily. That is what Fiction means.

OSCAR WILDE

SHAKESPEARE

He had read Shakespeare and found him weak in chemistry.

H.G. WELLS

William Shakespeare went into a pub. The landlord said, 'Get out, you're barred.' **PETER KAY**

Shakespeare's stuff is different from mine, but that is not to say that it is inferior. **P.G. WODEHOUSE**

The most important thing to remember about Shakespeare is that he was a writer, working on commission. I like to think that if the Bard were alive today he'd be out on the beach in Beverly Hills tapping out high concept movies of the week on his word processor up to his ruff on cocaine. **MAUREEN LIPMAN**

Shakespeare had a sad life; after all, he didn't live long enough to collaborate with Andrew Lloyd Webber. **VICTORIA WOOD**

If Shakespeare were put in the dock and tried by the grammarians, he would be condemned as a rogue and a vagabond. **A.G. GARDINER**

Shakespeare never had six lines together without a fault. Perhaps you may find seven, but this does not refute my general assertion. **SAMUEL JOHNSON**

After dinner to the Duke's house, and there saw *Twelfth Night* acted well, though it be but a silly play, and not related at all to the name or day. **SAMUEL PEPYS**

But Shakespeare one gets acquainted with without knowing him. It is a part of an Englishman's constitution. His thoughts and beauties are so spread abroad that one touches them everywhere, one is intimate with him by instinct. – No man of any brain can open at a good part of one of his plays, without falling into the flow of his meaning immediately. **JANE AUSTEN**

Playing Shakespeare is very tiring. You never get to sit down, unless you're a King. **JOSEPHINE HULL**

—I believe that I could write like Shakespeare, if I had a mind to try it.

—Yes, nothing wanting but the mind.

WILLIAM WORDSWORTH AND CHARLES LAMB

I want my Hamlet to be so male that when I come out on the stage they hear my balls clank. **JOHN BARRYMORE**

A college professor, having seen a touring production of *Hamlet*, asked the director of the piece whether he believed that the Prince of Denmark had ever actually consummated his relationship with Ophelia. 'Yes,' replied the director, 'I think it was during the second week at the Grand Theatre, Wolverhampton.' **MICHAEL SIMKINS**

I would rather have written *Oklahoma!* than *Hamlet*. (Actually, as the records show, I wrote neither, but you get the idea.) **P.G. WODEHOUSE**

The only possible message to be extracted from *Hamlet* is that it doesn't pay to take an after-lunch nap in an orchard. **ARTHUR MARSHALL**

A bad experience of Shakespeare is like a bad oyster – it puts you off for life.

JUDI DENCH

The remarkable thing about Shakespeare is that he really is very good, in spite of all the people who say he is very good. **ROBERT GRAVES**

Do you know how they are going to decide the Shakespeare-Bacon dispute? They are going to dig up Shakespeare and dig up Bacon; they are going to set their coffins side by side, and they are going to get Herbert Beerbohm Tree to recite *Hamlet* to them. And the one who turns in his coffin will be the author of the play. **W.S. GILBERT**

I do not know whether Bacon wrote the works of Shakespeare, but if he did not it seems to me that he missed the opportunity of his life. **J.M. BARRIE**

[*punches Shakespeare*] That is for every schoolboy and schoolgirl for the next 400 years. Have you any idea how much suffering you're going to cause? Hours spent at school desks trying to find one joke in *A Midsummer Night's Dream*. Wearing stupid tights in school plays saying things like, 'What ho, my Lord,' and, 'Oh, look, here comes Othello talking total crap as usual.' Oh and this kick is for Ken Branagh's endless uncut four-hour version of *Hamlet*.

EDMUND BLACKADDER, *BLACKADDER BACK AND FORTH*

POETRY

'As to poetry, you know,' said Humpty-Dumpty…'I can repeat poetry as well as other folk, if it comes to that – ' 'Oh, it needn't come to that,' Alice hastily said. **LEWIS CARROLL, *THROUGH THE LOOKING GLASS***

I do not find, my son, that God has made you a poet; and I am very glad that he has not. **LORD CHESTERFIELD**

Poetry is sissy stuff that rhymes. Weedy people say la and fie and swoon when they see a bunch of daffodils. **GEOFFREY WILLANS**

Je ramblais lonely comme un cloud,
Qui flotte en haut sur dale et hill,
Quand tout à coup je vis un crowd
De touristes dans le Lakeland Grill. **MILES KINGTON**

There are two ways of disliking poetry, one way is to dislike it, the other is to read Alexander Pope. **OSCAR WILDE**

Anyone for Tennyson? **MATTHEW STURGIS**

If you call Le Gallienne a minor poet you might just as well call a street lamp a minor planet.   **EDWARD MARSH**

I would venture to guess that Anon, who wrote so many poems without signing them, was often a woman.   **VIRGINIA WOOLF**

Indifference to poetry is one of the most conspicuous characteristics of the human race.   **ROBERT LYND**

Poems are like people. There are not many authentic ones around.

ROBERT GRAVES

Poets have been mysteriously silent on the subject of cheese.   **G.K. CHESTERTON**

James Elroy Flecker wrote one memorable line: 'Their bosoms shame the roses; their behinds impel the astonished nightingales to sing,' but then struck it out.   **J.L. CARR**

Is Derrick or Smart the better poet? Sir, there is no settling the precedence between a flea and a louse.   **SAMUEL JOHNSON**

George Herbert's 'King of Glory, King of Peace' is very English, like a damp, overgrown churchyard.   **BARBARA PYM**

Lord Byron writes like a housewife on the verge of the vapours.

ROBERT BOLT

W.B. Yeats looked like an umbrella left behind at a picnic.   **GEORGE MOORE**

Why do we need a Poet Laureate at all? We might as well still retain a Court Jester or a Royal Food Taster.   **KEITH WATERHOUSE**

My problem is that I am not allowed to be funny.

ANDREW MOTION, THE POET LAUREATE

You probably won't think it's any good…It's the sort of poetry you can understand. **RITA,** *EDUCATING RITA*

Poetry is talking on tiptoe. **GEORGE MEREDITH**

Ian Dury was the people's poet laureate. **SUGGS, SINGER FROM MADNESS**

There is no money in poetry, but then there is no poetry in money, either. **ROBERT GRAVES**

Poets, like whores, are only hated by each other. **WILLIAM WYCHERLEY**

Your poetry is bad enough, so pray be sparing of your prose. **LADY HOLLAND**

Explaining how you write poetry…it's like going round explaining how you sleep with your wife. **PHILIP LARKIN**

A poet can survive anything but a misprint. **OSCAR WILDE**

Making Cocoa For Kingsley Amis **WENDY COPE, TITLE OF POEM**

Perhaps no person can be a poet, or even can enjoy poetry, without a certain unsoundness of mind. **THOMAS BABINGTON MACAULAY**

Poetry is not the most important thing in life…I'd much rather lie in a hot bath reading Agatha Christie and sucking sweets. **DYLAN THOMAS**

JOURNALISM AND NEWS

—Anything interesting in *The Times*?
—Don't be silly, Charles. **NOËL COWARD,** *BLITHE SPIRIT*

B-52 Bomber Found On The Moon **HEADLINE,** *SUNDAY SPORT*

Freddie Starr Ate My Hamster   HEADLINE, *THE SUN*

You should always believe what you read in newspapers, for that makes
them more interesting.   ROSE MACAULAY

A newspaper consists of the same number of words whether there be any
news in it or not.   HENRY FIELDING

In America, journalism is apt to be regarded as an extension of history;
in Britain, as an extension of conversation.   ANTHONY SAMPSON

This is a very horrible country, England. We invented the Macintosh,
you know. We invented the flasher, the voyeur. That's what the British
press is about.   MALCOLM MCLAREN

The life of a journalist is poor, nasty, brutish and short. So is his style.

STELLA GIBBONS

I would never advise anybody to come to Fleet Street. Learning this trade
is like learning high diving – minus the water. But I wouldn't have missed
it for all the treasures in Araby.   WILLIAM CONNOR

Working at *The Sun* under Kelvin MacKenzie was like stumbling into a
scene from *Mad Max*, with a liberal daily dash of Monty Python, Benny
Hill and *Apocalypse Now*.   PIERS MORGAN

My uncle was a political writer for one of those London tabloids. I can
still remember his biggest scoop. The headline read, 'High Ranking
Politician Caught Wearing Women's Clothing'. Of course you turned to
page two and you found out it was Margaret Thatcher, but by then you'd
already bought the paper.   DAPHNE MOON, *FRASIER*

In old days men had the rack. Now they have the Press. **OSCAR WILDE**

The best leaks always take place in the urinal. **JOHN COLE**

Lord Beaverbrook is a dear old bugger. The accent is on the word bugger.
ANONYMOUS EDITOR

No news is good news; no journalists is even better news. **NICHOLAS BENTLEY**

There are two different kinds of people. There are those who, when they get to the bottom of a page in a magazine which reads 'Continued on page 136', turn to page 136 to continue, and those who angrily turn to some other article. **MILES KINGTON**

There are three things we journalists are told never to criticise: The Queen Mother, Desert Orchid and Liverpool. **QUENTIN LETTS**

Being a columnist is an odd occupation. It's strange when people hate you. Especially when you haven't even been married to them. **TONY PARSONS**

The pay was bad, as it too often is where a paper has ideals. **ARNOLD BENNETT**

—*The Daily Mirror* is read by the people who think they run the country. *The Guardian* is read by people who think they *ought* to run the country. *The Times* is read by the people who actually *do* run the country. *The Daily Mail* is read by the wives of the people who run the country. *The Financial Times* is read by people who own the country. *The Morning Star* is read by people who think the country ought to be run by *another* country. *The Daily Telegraph* is read by the people who think it is.
—And *Sun* readers don't care *who* runs the country – as long as she's got big tits. **JIM HACKER AND BERNARD WOOLLEY,** *YES, PRIME MINISTER*

Can you imagine lying in bed on a Sunday morning with the love of your life, a cup of tea and a bacon sandwich, and all you had to read was the *Socialist Worker*?
                                                                    DEREK JAMESON

Many journalists have fallen for the conspiracy theory of government. I do assure you that they would produce more accurate work if they adhered to the cock-up theory.
                                                                    BERNARD INGHAM

Journalists belong in the gutter because that is where the ruling classes throw their guilty secrets.
                                                                    GERALD PRIESTLAND

The state of public affairs is not inviting, and I rejoice that we take in no daily paper.
                                        DR ARNOLD, HEADMASTER OF RUGBY SCHOOL

Other people's troubles is mostly what folks read the paper for, and it's twice the pleasure when it's the trouble of a man they know.
                                                                    HAROLD BRIGHOUSE

News is what someone wants to suppress; anything else is just advertising.
                                                                    LORD NORTHCLIFFE

Journalism largely consists in saying 'Lord Jones Dead' to people who never knew he was alive.
                                                                    G.K. CHESTERTON

I sold my story to a tabloid to buy a water-sprinkling system for my house in Ibiza.
                            LADY PENELOPE AITKEN, MOTHER OF JONATHAN

There's a lot to be said for not being known to the readers of the *Daily Mirror*.
                                                                    ANTHONY BURGESS

If a man cannot get to sleep over a back number of a weekly paper there is no use his trying to go to sleep at all.
                                                                    GEORGE A. BIRMINGHAM

GOSSIP

Any amusing deaths lately? **SIR MAURICE BOWRA**

Human nature is so well disposed towards those who are in interesting situations, that a young person, who either marries or dies, is sure to be kindly spoken of. **JANE AUSTEN**

I confess I prefer people to say horrid things about me only behind my back. Especially if they're true. **W. SOMERSET MAUGHAM**

Mr Richard Harvey is going to be married; but as it is a great secret and only known to half the neighbourhood, you must not mention it.

JANE AUSTEN

The fact has reached the provincial pulpits. **OSCAR WILDE**

It's not in the village pub that slander flows most free,
But in the virtuous shop and club where women swill their tea. **A.P. HERBERT**

She always tells stories in the present vindictive. **TOM PEARCE**

There is only one thing in the world worse than being talked about, and that is not being talked about. **OSCAR WILDE**

WORDPLAY

I stooped to pick a buttercup. Why people leave buttocks lying around, I've no idea. **STEPHEN FRY**

The most indolent women have been seen running to catch a boss.

JILLY COOPER

—I know.
—I know you know.
—I know you know I know.
—I know you know I know you know.
—I know.   **CHARLES AND FIONA,** *ROUND THE HORNE*

The quality of Mersey is not strained.   **PUNCH MAGAZINE**

Sir, you have tasted two whole worms: you have hissed all my mystery
lectures and been caught fighting a liar in the quad; you will leave
Oxford by the next town drain.   **REVD WILLIAM SPOONER**

He said, 'I'm going to chop off the bottom of one of your trouser legs and
put it in a library.' I thought, 'That's a turn-up for the books.'   **TIM VINE**

Let us drink a toast to the queer old dean.   **REVD WILLIAM SPOONER**

A pun is not bound by the laws which limit nicer wit. It is a pistol let off
at the ear; not a feather to tickle the intellect.   **CHARLES LAMB**

DEFINITIONS

Countryside: the killing of Piers Morgan.   **STEPHEN FRY**

Civilisation is the distance man has placed between himself and his
excreta.   **BRIAN ALDISS**

A cynic is a man who knows the price of everything, and the value of
nothing.   **OSCAR WILDE**

Litter: any object left lying about which is too small to be offensive. The
word is never applied to petrol-stations, advertisements, bungalows etc.

                                                       J.B. MORTON

Dickensian: Adjective used to describe (a) snow at Christmas, (b) very long novels.

J.B. MORTON

Dubai: Debbie from Birmingham.

GRAEME GARDEN

An economist is someone who, if you have forgotten your telephone number, will estimate it for you.

FRANK MORTON

Honolulu: to give an MBE to a Scottish singer.

BARRY CRYER

Insurance is a cross between betting and philosophy.

PAUL JENNINGS

Labour: Tory.

JEREMY HARDY

Library: the room where the murders take place.

J.B. MORTON

No exit: a sign indicating the most convenient way out of a building.

J.B. MORTON

Originality is undetected plagiarism.

DEAN INGE

INSULTS, PUT DOWNS AND COMEBACKS

If there's a worse insult I don't know it. I have just been told by my friend Gladys that she'd trust her husband to spend an evening alone with me.

MARJORIE PROOPS

I expect to pass through this world but once and therefore if there is anybody I want to kick in the crotch I had better kick them in the crotch now, for I do not expect to pass this way again.

MAURICE BOWRA

It seldom pays to be rude. It never pays to be half-rude.

NORMAN DOUGLAS

I saw Mr Gladstone in the street last night. I waited and waited but no cab ran over him.
ELIZA SAVAGE

I'll ruin you! You'll never waitress in Torquay again!
BASIL FAWLTY TO POLLY, *FAWLTY TOWERS*

You want to lower your blood pressure? Slit your wrists, love.

BECKY FAIRHURST, *WIFE SWAP*

If I had to choose between him and a cockroach as a companion for a walking-tour, the cockroach would have had it by a short head.
P.G. WODEHOUSE

You're hit writers – one letter short, but still. **CLIVE ANDERSON TO THE BEE GEES**

He should have his balls snipped off and fastened to his nose with a safety pin.
NOËL COWARD

At the moment I am debarred from the pleasure of putting her in her place by the fact that she has not got one.
EDITH SITWELL

—I've suffering the tortures of the damned.
—Already?
GEORGE ARLISS AND NOËL COWARD

—Could you tell me the way to the House of Commons loo?
—First left, go along the corridor. You'll see a door marked Gentlemen, but don't let that deter you.
J.H. THOMAS, MP AND F.E. SMITH, MP

—Hello, we are Jehovah's Witnesses.
—I am Jehovah. How are we doing?
JEHOVAH'S WITNESSES AND GEORGE BERNARD SHAW

—I'm lending Nancy Mitford my villa in France so she can finish a book.
—Oh really. What's she reading? **FRIEND AND DAME EDITH EVANS**

—I don't know whether you'll die on the gallows or of the pox.
—That depends, my lord, on whether I embrace your principles or your mistress. **LORD SANDWICH AND JOHN WILKES**

—Which do you think is my best side?
—My dear, you're sitting on it.

MARY ANDERSON, ACTRESS, AND ALFRED HITCHCOCK

—Would you sleep with me for a million pounds?
—For a million pounds, yes, I would.
—Would you sleep with me for a fiver?
—Winston, really! What do you take me for?
—Madam, we have already established what you are – now we are just negotiating the price. **WINSTON CHURCHILL AND BESSIE BRADDOCK**

The only consolation I can find in your immediate presence is your ultimate absence. **SHELAGH DELANEY**

—If I were your wife, I'd put poison in your coffee.
—If I were your husband, I'd drink it. **NANCY ASTOR AND WINSTON CHURCHILL**

—Mr Churchill, I care neither for your politics nor your moustache.
—Do not distress yourself, madam, you are unlikely to come into contact with either. **UNIDENTIFIED WOMAN AND WINSTON CHURCHILL**

—Is Ringo Starr the best drummer in the world?
—He's not even the best drummer in The Beatles. **REPORTER AND JOHN LENNON**

—Do you have any regrets in life?
—It's me sitting in this house with £50 million in the bank, not you.

JOURNALIST AND LORD JEFFREY ARCHER

Winston Churchill was relieving himself in the urinal of the House of Commons when Aneurin Bevan entered. Winston turned his back on the staunch socialist and his snub did not go unnoticed. 'Don't be shy, Winston,' said Bevan, 'we've all got the same thing.' 'I know you socialists,' replied Winston. 'As soon as you see something big and successful you want to nationalise it.'

JOHN HARPER

—Two tickets reserved for you for the first night of my new play. Bring a friend. If you have one.

—Cannot make first night. Will come second night. If you have one.

GEORGE BERNARD SHAW AND WINSTON CHURCHILL

—Winston, you're drunk.

—Bessie, you're ugly. But tomorrow I shall be sober.

BESSIE BRADDOCK AND WINSTON CHURCHILL

SILENCE

I believe in the discipline of silence and could talk for hours about it.

GEORGE BERNARD SHAW

He knew the precise psychological moment when to say nothing.

OSCAR WILDE

Silence is the correct answer to an unasked question.   **ARMANDO IANNUCCI**

I left the room with silent dignity, but caught my foot in the mat.

GEORGE AND WEEDON GROSSMITH, *THE DIARY OF A NOBODY*

POLITICS AND SOCIETY

POWER

If you lead a country like Britain, a strong country, a country which has taken a lead in world affairs in good times and in bad, a country that is always reliable, then you have to have a touch of iron about you.

MARGARET THATCHER

Power is like a woman you want to stay in bed with forever.

PATRICK ANDERSON

Powerful men often succeed through the help of their wives. Powerful women only succeed in spite of their husbands. **LINDA LEE-POTTER**

Power is sweet, and when you are a little clerk you love its sweetness quite as much as if you were an emperor, and maybe you love it a good deal more. **OUIDA**

I was allowed to ring the school bell for five minutes until everyone was in assembly. It was the beginning of power. **JEFFREY ARCHER**

The only people I've ever given working orders to have been occasional charwomen, and mostly I've told them not to bother, that I'll do it myself.

PATRICK CAMPBELL

SOCIETY

Society is based on the assumption that everyone is alike and no one is alive. **HUGH KINGSMILL**

I have a total irreverence for anything connected with society, except that which makes the road safer, the beer stronger, the old men and women warmer in the winter, and happier in the summer. **BRENDAN BEHAN**

Say what you like about Genghis Khan but, when he was around, old ladies could safely walk the streets of Mongolia at night.　　**JO BRAND**

Whose fault is it we have a blame culture?　　**WILLIAM CHAPMAN**

The Welfare State may be the Farewell State.　　**NANCY ASTOR**

Does anyone doubt that if chewing gum manufacturers were made responsible for cleaning up the mess consumers of their product make on our streets, within a year they would have developed a gum that would break down in sunlight?　　**RICHARD QUIN**

Scientists have invented something for getting chewing gum off the pavement. It's called a shoe.　　**NICK PERCIVAL**

Is it fair to say that there'd be less litter in Britain if blind people were given pointed sticks?　　**ADAM BLOOM**

—Road cleaning, I shall pay. Street lighting, I shall pay. Ground rent, I shall pay. But when it comes to the drain in front of my house, I shall not. Because it is blocked up and overflowing.
—I shall make a note of that.
—You will do more than that Mr Squires. You will have a plumber on my doorstep at nine o'clock tomorrow morning with a plunger in his hand, or you will not get a penny.
—Just who do think you are Mrs Leadbetter?
—I am the silent majority.
　　MARGOT LEADBETTER AND MR SQUIRES, COUNCIL OFFICIAL, *THE GOOD LIFE*

POLITICS AND GOVERNMENT

Politics is the art of making the inevitable seem planned.　　**QUENTIN CRISP**

Politics is a blood sport.   **ANEURIN BEVAN**

—The trouble with England is it's being governed by cunts.
—Quite frankly, old man, there're an awful lot of cunts in England,
and they deserve representation.   **REX HARRISON AND UNIDENTIFIED MP**

We have a system of government with the engine of a lawnmower and the
brakes of a Rolls-Royce.   **JONATHAN LYNN**

Britain is a place where anyone can become Prime Minister as long as
you've got a degree and aren't black.   **TOM BAKER, NARRATOR, *LITTLE BRITAIN***

There's as much chance of my becoming Prime Minister as there is of
finding Elvis on Mars, or my being decapitated by a frisbee or
reincarnated as an olive.   **BORIS JOHNSON**

The main essentials of a Prime Minister are sleep and a sense of history.
                                                           HAROLD WILSON

Above any other position of eminence, that of Prime Minister is filled
by fluke.   **ENOCH POWELL**

Definition of a politician:
He is asked to stand, he wants to sit,
he is expected to lie.   **WINSTON CHURCHILL**

To reach the top a politician has to conform to the popular image of the
bookie or the clergyman.   **MALCOLM MUGGERIDGE**

The Opposition are the opposition in exile, the Civil Service are the
opposition in residence.   **JIM HACKER, *YES, MINISTER***

—I think the Prime Minister wants to govern Britain.
—Well stop him, Bernard!

BERNARD WOOLLEY AND SIR HUMPHREY APPLEBY, *YES, PRIME MINISTER*

Civil servants – no longer servants, no longer civil.   **WINSTON CHURCHILL**

British people have a Socialist mind and a Conservative heart. **ALBERT FINNEY**

Socialism is government of the duds, by the duds and for the duds.

WINSTON CHURCHILL

Present policies are leading us to the status of a banana republic that has run out of bananas.   **RICHARD MARSH**

The only way to get anything done in a democracy is to take someone out to lunch.   **ANTHONY ARMSTRONG**

Democracy is the worst system devised by wit of man, except for all the others.   **WINSTON CHURCHILL**

You're just like me, dear. Always with the Don't Knows. Someone ought to form a party around us.   **WILLIAM DOUGLAS-HOME**

I've always thought a 'Stuff 'Em All' party would poll a lot of votes.

DAVID PENHALIGON

Reform! Reform! Aren't things bad enough already?   **MR JUSTICE ASTBURY**

I want my campaign to be a good clean fight and therefore will not be alluding to the alleged homosexuality of my opponent.

MR JUSTICE MELFORD STEVENSON

'There's a Muslim paedophile living under your child's bed.'
Vote Conservative.
FRANKIE BOYLE

—Vote for you? I'd rather vote for the Devil!
—But in case your friend is not running, may I count on your support?
CONSTITUENCY MEMBER AND WINSTON CHURCHILL

Vote for you? I'd sooner stick my genitals in a pan of boiling chip fat.

VICTOR MELDREW, *ONE FOOT IN THE GRAVE*

It's not the voting that's democracy, it's the counting.
TOM STOPPARD

The dreadful truth is that when people come to see their MP they have run out of better ideas.
BORIS JOHNSON

Lord, make my words sweet and reasonable; some day I may have to eat them.
PADDY ASHDOWN

Political ability is the ability to foretell what is going to happen tomorrow, next week, next month and next year. And to have the ability afterwards to explain why it didn't happen.
WINSTON CHURCHILL

I could never be a politician. I couldn't bear to be right all the time.
PETER USTINOV

I am humble enough to recognise that I have made mistakes, but politically astute enough to know that I have forgotten what they are.
MICHAEL HESELTINE

Render any politician down and there's enough fat to fry an egg.
SPIKE MILLIGAN

The whole art of political speech is to put nothing into it. It is much more difficult than it sounds. **HILAIRE BELLOC**

A decision is a decision only if it is the decision you want. If not it's just a temporary setback. **SIR HUMPHREY APPLEBY,** *YES, MINISTER*

The problem with committing political suicide is that you live to regret it. **WINSTON CHURCHILL**

'The truth' in politics means any statement that cannot be proved false. **SIR HUMPHREY APPLEBY,** *YES, PRIME MINISTER*

If there was 20 ways of telling the truth and only one way of telling a lie, the Government would find it out. It's in the nature of governments to tell lies. **GEORGE BERNARD SHAW**

If he can't ignore facts, he's no business to be a politician.

SIR HUMPHREY APPLEBY, *YES, PRIME MINISTER*

Here are the seven responses a politician is not allowed to give to a question: 1. I don't know; 2. I don't care; 3. I won't say; 4. There's nothing I can do about it; 5. It's not my responsibility; 6. Mind your own business; 7. No comment. **MATTHEW PARRIS**

All political parties die at last of swallowing their own lies. **JOHN ARBUTHNOT**

He was always bold, clear, concise, cultured, forceful, graceful, classical, eloquent and wrong. **IAN MACKAY ON DEAN INGE**

No one likes Cripps. He does not allow it. **ALAIN VERNEY**

—Ministers should never know more than they need to know. Then they can't tell anyone. Like secret agents, they could be captured and tortured.
—You mean by terrorists?
—By the BBC. **SIR HUMPHREY APPLEBY AND BERNARD WOOLLEY,** *YES, MINISTER*

There are far too many men in politics and not enough elsewhere.
HERMIONE GINGOLD

We should always tell the Press, freely and frankly, anything that they can easily find out. **SIR HUMPHREY APPLEBY,** *YES, PRIME MINISTER*

Karl Marx sought to replace natural antagonisms by class antagonisms.
H.G. WELLS

Karl Marx wasn't a Marxist all the time. He got drunk in the Tottenham Court Road. **MICHAEL FOOT**

I haven't read Karl Marx. I get stuck on that footnote on page two. HAROLD WILSON

Beatrix Potter's *Tale of Ginger and Pickles* is easier to read on the flaws of capitalism than Karl Marx's *Das Kapital*. **BARBARA TRAPIDO**

You know what loyalty means to a cabinet minister? It means that his fear of losing his job is slightly bigger than his hope of pinching mine.
JIM HACKER (PRIME MINISTER), *YES, PRIME MINISTER*

It was as dark as the inside of a Cabinet Minister. **JOYCE CARY**

When he was Foreign Secretary, Lord Rosebery hummed 'Rule Britannia' as he read the contents of his red boxes. Somehow, one can't imagine Jack Straw doing that. **HUGH MASSINGBERD**

The great nations have always acted like gangsters and the small nations like prostitutes. **STANLEY KUBRICK**

As Foreign Secretary, Sir Alec Douglas-Home was determined to reduce the amount of paperwork. One day, a private secretary sent him a two-inch-thick report on Icelandic fisheries, with a note: 'The Secretary of State may care to read this over the weekend.' Sir Alec returned it with his own note: 'A kindly thought, but erroneous.' **RICHARD PEARSON**

An ambassador is an honest man sent abroad to lie for his country. SIR HENRY WOTTON

I've often thought we should breathalyse MPs not when they're driving but when they're legislating. **JIM HACKER, YES, PRIME MINISTER**

There are three things in life not worth running for: a bus, a woman and a new economic panacea. If you wait long enough another one will come along. **DEREK HEATHCOTE AMORY**

If you are working class, being an MP is the job your parents always wanted for you. It's clean, indoor work and there is no heavy lifting. **DIANE ABBOTT MP**

The reason there are so few female politicians is that it is too much trouble to put make-up on two faces. **MAUREEN MURPHY**

There are 11 bars in the House of Commons, no crèche and no shop. It would be an ideal place for a small Waitrose. It could replace the rifle range. **BARBARA FOLLETT MP**

In the last Parliament, the House of Commons had more MPs called John than all the women MPs put together. **TESSA JOWELL**

Most of the duties of the members of the House of Commons could be
better performed by a fairly intelligent poodle-dog. **H.L. LECKY**

Like many successful politicians, he had the face of a rather gross
schoolboy. **ANTHONY POWELL**

It's gay bar culture. They may love mincing around but I'm not going on
TV in a shell suit with wet-look hair. **ALAN CLARK**

Being an MP feeds your vanity and starves your self-respect.

MATTHEW PARRIS

There are no true friends in politics. We are all sharks circling, and
waiting for traces of blood to appear in the water. **ALAN CLARK**

Lord Birkenhead was an outstanding Lord Chancellor who distributed the
ecclesiastical patronage in his gift on the basis of the cricketing skills of
the clerics concerned. **PIERS BRENDON**

Clement Attlee brings to the fierce struggle of politics the tepid enthusiasm
of a lazy summer afternoon at a cricket match. **ANEURIN BEVIN**

He handles political crises with all the confidence of a man dialling his
own telephone number. **JOHN BELL**

He has the sagacity of the elephant as well as its form. BENJAMIN DISRAELI ON GEORGE WARD HUNT

Gladstone's jokes are no laughing matter. **LORD DERBY**

He could persuade most people of most things, and himself of anything.

DEAN INGE ON MR GLADSTONE

William Pitt was stiff with everyone but the ladies.
PERCY BYSSHE SHELLEY

If a traveller were informed that a man like Lord John Russell was leader of the House of Commons, he might begin to comprehend how the Egyptians worshipped an insect.
BENJAMIN DISRAELI

Ramsey MacDonald has, more than any other man, the gift of compressing the largest number of words into the smallest amount of thought.
WINSTON CHURCHILL

For people who have risen to the top of their profession by their gift of the gab, even the randier MPs' seduction routines would look clumsy in a Gateshead nightclub.
SUSANNAH JOWITT

Politics is a field where the choice lies constantly between two blunders.
JOHN MORLEY

He knows nothing and he thinks he knows everything. That points clearly to a political career.
GEORGE BERNARD SHAW

Two words often used to describe Robin Cook: ginger and rogers.
RONNIE CORBETT, *HAVE I GOT NEWS FOR YOU*

What do I think of William Hague? Unredeemable trainspotting vacuity overlaid by the gloss of management theory.
JOHN REDWOOD

David Mellor behaved like an ostrich and put his head in the sand, thereby exposing his thinking parts.
GEORGE CARMAN QC

When Ann Widdecombe reads out the Ten Commandments at Westminster Cathedral it sounds as though she has written them herself.
FATHER MICHAEL SEED

If we could get the common sense revolution to stand up and walk around it would look like Ann Widdecombe.   **WILLIAM HAGUE**

Ann Widdecombe is the best example of the use of bosom as a theatrical prop since Barbara Windsor.   *THE TIMES*

The Tories' main problem is that they don't have anyone you'd want to go to bed with. **ANNE ROBINSON**

Despite her Oxford education, her high-flying career, her media celebrity, Edwina Currie still behaves like a pushy provincial hair-saloniste queening it over her fellow passengers on a Saga cruise to Tenerife.

LYNN BARBER

The Conservative Establishment has always treated women as nannies, grannies and fannies.   **TERESA GORMAN, TORY MP**

—Do you have any skeletons in your cupboard?
—Dear boy, I can hardly close the door.   **ALAN CLARK**

Boris Johnson's naturally peroxide blond hair seems to be on back to front; his suit is a vast, filthy shapeless thing that has room in its seat for at least two floating voters... Off his crotch hangs a blob of gloop that looks like an amalgam of egg white and cobweb.   **A.A. GILL**

Boris Johnson is without doubt the very worst putative politician I've ever seen in action. He is utterly, chronically useless – and I can't think of a higher compliment.   **A.A. GILL, BEFORE JOHNSON'S ELECTION AS AN MP, MAY 2001**

David Blunkett: Satan's bearded folk singer.   **LINDA SMITH**

I am much happier now that I have joined the majority of people in this country who don't give a damn about politics. **CHRISTINE HAMILTON**

Seeing John Major govern the country is like watching Edward Scissorhands try to make balloon animals. **SIMON HOGGART**

Alan Clark was The Keeper of the Wooden Spoon: he loved to stir things up. **SIMON HOGGART**

Mo Mowlam is an only slightly effeminate Geordie trucker. **LYNDA LEE POTTER**

John Prescott, a fine and conscientious ship's steward, I'm sure. But how can the ability to mix a decent gin and tonic qualify someone to run the nation's housing? **JEREMY CLARKSON**

Burly and greasy-haired, John Prescott looks rather like one of those plain-talking policemen who, during the late 1970s, were always being photographed on yachting holidays with villains somewhere in the Mediterranean. **CRAIG BROWN**

There are three reasons why Michael Portillo will never win a race to become leader of the Tory Party: weed, women and woofters. **UNIDENTIFIED MP QUOTED IN** *THE TIMES*

Adultery may be acceptable to the Tory party, but buggery certainly isn't.

TIM RENTON

Tony Blair's done more U-turns than a dodgy plumber. **IAIN DUNCAN SMITH**

They call him Teflon Tony because nothing sticks to him. **WILL SELF**

I don't make predictions. I never have and I never will.   **TONY BLAIR**

Tony Blair has a smile like an ageing collie.   **JAN MORRIS**

Oh, look, there's Cherie Blair! That remind me, I must post a letter.

HUGH DENNIS

I was relieved when Blair's baby was born at the Chelsea and Westminster Hospital. I had thought he would be born in a manger.   **LEO ABSE**

Tony Blair reckons he can get us by sounding like Hugh Grant delivering a Richard Curtis script, with the electorate looking vulnerable in a furry hood and snow falling softly in the background.   **LIBBY PURVES**

New Labour does not do candour, and Mr Blair will find humility when the hippopotamus finds grace.   **MATTHEW PARRIS**

To stay in No. 10 most Prime Ministers would eat their own grandmothers.

NEW SOCIETY

Sometimes the strain of being Prime Minister is so awful, you have to resort to Jane Austen.   **HAROLD MACMILLAN**

The Liberal Democrats' manifesto promises muesli, eggie soldiers and 'sorting things out over a nice cup of tea'.   *DEAD RINGERS*

We could go for marriage, an affair or casual sex.   PADDY ASHDOWN TO TONY BLAIR ON A LIB/LAB PACT

I have spent much of my life fighting the Germans and fighting the politicians. It is much easier to fight the Germans.

FIELD MARSHAL VISCOUNT MONTGOMERY

MARGARET THATCHER

Neil, the bathroom's free! Unlike the country under the Thatcherite junta.

RICK, *THE YOUNG ONES*

Mama Doc.

DENIS HEALEY

A bargain basement Boadicea.

DENIS HEALEY

Voting for Margaret Thatcher was like buying a Vera Lynn LP, getting it home and finding 'Never Mind the Bollocks' inside the red, white and blue sleeve.

JULIE BURCHILL

She cannot see an institution without hitting it with her handbag.

JULIAN CRITCHLEY

The Prime Minister tells us she has given the French President a piece of her mind, not a gift I would receive with alacrity.

DENIS HEALEY

I admire her, but it's like sitting next to electricity.

ROBERT RUNCIE

I often compare Margaret Thatcher with Florence Nightingale...a lady with a lamp. Unfortunately, it is a blowlamp.

DENIS HEALEY

Margaret Thatcher is a strong personality but with the unmistakable air of the supermarket about her.

MALCOLM MUGGERIDGE

—If Mrs Thatcher were run over by a bus...
—It wouldn't dare.

QUESTIONER AND LORD CARRINGTON

Britain under Margaret Thatcher was a cross between Singapore and Telford.

PETER COOK

THATCHER ON THATCHER

I think, historically, the term 'Thatcherism' will be seen as a compliment.

In politics, if you want anything said, ask a man; if you want anything done, ask a woman.

Any woman who understands the problems of running a home will be nearer to understanding the problems of running a country.

I am extraordinarily patient provided I get my own way in the end.

I always cheer up immensely if a political attack is particularly wounding because I think, well, if they attack me personally, it means they have not a single political argument left.

If it is once again one against 48, then I am sorry for the 48.

THE HOUSE OF LORDS

The House of Lords is good evidence of life after death. **BARON SOPER**

Lord Russell was the first man since Guy Fawkes to enter the Houses of Parliament with an honest intention. **HEATHCOTE WILLIAMS**

I have been in favour of Lords reform almost since I have been there, because any House which has me in it really needs its head examined.

EARL OF ONSLOW

I will be sad if I either look up or down after my death and don't see my son fast asleep on the same benches on which I have slept. **EARL OF ONSLOW**

The bright ones are supposed to speak; the others are supposed to support them. That's how it works.

THE EARL OF ROMNEY WHO SPENT 25 YEARS IN THE HOUSE OF LORDS WITHOUT SPEAKING

People seem to think we are a lot of effete old codgers, sleeping on the red benches and waking only to cause the Government unnecessary problems.

LORD FELDMAN OF FROGNAL

The House of Lords is a model for how to care for the elderly. **FRANK FIELD**

When I gave my big speech on the Lords, the longest letter I received was from a lady who wanted to know where I had bought my blouse.

BARONESS JAY

A footnote to a ministerial brief was mistakenly read out in the House of Lords. It read: 'This is a rotten argument, but it should be good enough for their lordships on a hot summer afternoon.' **LORD HOME**

This man I thought had been a Lord among wits; but, I find, he is only a wit among Lords. **SAMUEL JOHNSON ON LORD CHESTERFIELD**

I don't go to the House of Lords any more. I did go once but a bishop stole my umbrella. **LORD BERNERS**

When I'm sitting on the Woolsack in the House of Lords I amuse myself by saying 'Bollocks' *sotto voce* to the bishops. **LORD HAILSHAM**

WINSTON CHURCHILL

When I am abroad, I always make it a rule never to criticise or attack the government of my own country. I make up for lost time when I come home.

It is hard, if not impossible, to snub a beautiful woman – they remain beautiful and the rebuke recoils.

No lover ever studied every whim of his mistress as I did those of President Roosevelt.

Charles de Gaulle looked like a female llama surprised in her bath.

Vladimir Lenin: His sympathies cold and wide as the Arctic Ocean; his hatreds tight as the hangman's noose. His purpose to save the world: his method to blow it up.

The inherent vice of capitalism is the unequal sharing of blessings; the inherent virtue of socialism is the equal sharing of miseries.

DIPLOMACY AND ESPIONAGE

I give confidential briefings; *you* leak; *he* has been charged under Section 2a of the Official Secrets Act.   **BERNARD WOOLLEY, YES, PRIME MINISTER**

Homosexual, are you? We have to ask. Silly, really, as of course no one says yes. With Oxford it's drugs, with Cambridge it's boys.

RECRUITING INTERVIEWER FOR MI6

Malcolm Muggeridge was the worst spy I ever recruited. He once claimed that through his own efficient intelligence network he had effected the sinking of a German U-boat in the Mediterranean. Impossible. It must have been a very large fish. Probably a tuna.   **GRAHAM GREENE**

Progress in the Foreign Service is either vaginal or rectal. You marry the boss's daughter or you crawl up his bottom. **NICHOLAS MONSARRAT**

In Guy Burgess's rooms were gramophone records of all descriptions (he particularly enjoyed the horror of 'laughing songs')... In the plugless bath the water was kept in by the suction supplied by an old tennis ball enshrouded in an old tennis sock that had not recently made contact with soap and water destined for itself alone. **ARTHUR MARSHALL**

—Me, a German spy? I'm as British as Queen Victoria!
—So your father's German, you're half German, and you married a German! **CAPTAIN DARLING AND CAPTAIN BLACKADDER, *BLACKADDER GOES FORTH***

The really interesting thing about James Bond is that he would be what I call the ideal defector. Because if the money was better, the booze freer and women easier over there in Moscow, he'd be off like a shot. Bond, you see, is the ultimate prostitute. **JOHN LE CARRÉ**

The spy who came in for a cardie.

MIKE COLEMAN ON 85-YEAR-OLD SPY MELITA NORWOOD

EUROPE

This 'going into Europe' will not turn out to be the thrilling mutual exchange supposed. It is more like nine middle-aged couples with failing marriages meeting in a darkened bedroom in a Brussels hotel for a group grope. **E.P. THOMSON**

We went in to screw the French by splitting them off from the Germans. The French went in to protect their inefficient farmers from commercial competition. The Germans went in to cleanse themselves of genocide and apply for readmission to the human race.

SIR HUMPHREY APPLEBY, *YES, MINISTER*

The last time Britain went into Europe with any degree of success was on 6 June 1944.   *DAILY EXPRESS*, 1980

Europe is a place teeming with ill-intentioned persons.   **MARGARET THATCHER**

Britain is the grit in the European oyster.   **JOHN MAJOR**

Whereas in England all is permitted that is not expressly prohibited, it has been said that in Germany all is prohibited unless expressly permitted and in France all is permitted that is expressly prohibited. In the European Common Market no-one knows what is permitted and it all costs more.

ROBERT MEGARRY

As for the European Parliament – this place needs a laxative.   **BOB GELDOF**

Up Yours, Delors   **HEADLINE**, *THE SUN*

CLUB

Every Englishman is convinced of one thing: that to be an Englishman is to belong to the most exclusive club there is.   **OSCAR WILDE**

Clubs – those mausoleums of inactive masculinity are places for men who prefer armchairs to women.   **V.S. PRITCHETT**

Lord Glasgow, having flung a waiter through the window of his club, brusquely ordered: 'Put him on the bill.'   **ANTHONY LEJEUNE**

London clubs remain insistent on keeping people out, long after they have stopped wanting to come in.   **ANTHONY SAMPSON**

The Greek God, Zeus, performed acts with swans and heifers that would debar him from every London club except the Garrick or possibly the Naval and Military.   **STEPHEN FRY**

To attract attention in the dining-room of the Senior Conservative Club between the hours of one and two-thirty, you have to be a mutton chop, not an earl.

P.G. WODEHOUSE

The essence of an English club is that we would prefer a silver salt cellar that doesn't work to a plastic one that does.

CECIL HORTON

Members of the Garrick don't mind women being allowed in; they just don't want their wives to be allowed in.

ALAN CLARK

He frequented a particular brothel and would leave his manservant to give indication where he could be found by answering calls, 'Mr Neville-Willing has gone to his club.'

HUGO VICKERS

If more women did Women's Institute, there'd be half the need for hallucinogenic drugs.

CHRIS HARPER, *CALENDAR GIRLS*

Jo Brand offered to appear on our new W.I. calendar as Ms December – standing behind a bungalow.

TRICIA STEWART

As regards the sign in the gents which says 'Wet Paint' – this is not an instruction.

COLIN CROMPTON, *WHEELTAPPERS AND SHUNTERS SOCIAL CLUB*

The first prize in the raffle is a diving suit – no, it's a divan suite.

COLIN CROMPTON, *WHEELTAPPERS AND SHUNTERS SOCIAL CLUB*

You are not a proper member of an Irish club until you become barred.

MICHAEL DAVITT

LAW AND LAWYERS

The one great principle of English law is to make business for itself.

CHARLES DICKENS

Lawyers and tarts are the two oldest professions in the world. And we aim to please. **JOHN MORTIMER**

He did not care to speak ill of any man behind his back, but he believed the gentleman was an 'attorney'. **SAMUEL JOHNSON**

There are unquestionably today more good lawyers in Great Britain than there are good waiters – due to no other cause than the less exacting requirements of the Bar. **WILLIAM MUMFORD**

A British lawyer would like to think of himself as part of that mysterious entity called The Law; an American lawyer would like a swimming pool and two houses. **SIMON HOGGART**

Lawyers enjoy a little mystery, you know. Why, if everybody came forward and told the truth, the whole truth, and nothing but the truth straight out, we should all retire to the workhouse. **DOROTHY L. SAYERS**

Occasionally a lawyer sends you a legal document covered in kisses, and you really think you're getting somewhere until he tells you he only wants you to sign your name in three places. **JILLY COOPER**

In law, nothing is certain but the expense. **SAMUEL BUTLER**

The Lord Chief Justice of England recently said that the greater part of his judicial time was spent investigating collisions between propelled vehicles, each on its own side of the road, each sounding its horn and each stationary. **PHILIP GUEDELLA**

CRIME AND PUNISHMENT

Where once the village post office, a mug of Horlicks, Bing Crosby songs and a Kenneth More film were the only things the average Britain had to fear, nowadays every alleyway can conceal a threat, every encounter a violent confrontation.

STEPHEN FRY

I read in the paper that the discovery of a woman's body in a suitcase is being treated as 'suspicious' by the police. Nice to see the spirit of Sherlock Holmes lives on.

SYDNEY WILKINS

Police probe Leeds girl's snatch. Can you help?

'CRIMETIME' PRESENTER, *PHOENIX NIGHTS*

—Is there a butler?
—I didn't see one.
—Pity, would have saved us lots of time.

INSPECTOR MORSE AND SGT LEWIS, *HAPPY FAMILIES*

A suspected burglar was caught after making so much noise on 70-year-old Jean Collop's cottage roof in Cornwall that she woke up and felled him with a garden gnome.

THE GUARDIAN

Stealing a rhinoceros should not be attempted lightly.

A.E. HERBERT

Is Jack Duckworth light-fingered? Put is this way – they say the midwife that delivered him is still looking for the scissors.

BET LYNCH, *CORONATION STREET*

When you speak of the Great Train Robbery, this, in fact, involved no loss of train. It's merely what I like to call the contents of the train which were pilfered. We haven't lost a train since 1946, the year of the great snows. We mislaid a small one.

PETER COOK

Police revealed that a woman arrested for shoplifting had a whole salami in her knickers. When asked why, she said it was because she was missing her Italian boyfriend. **MANCHESTER EVENING NEWS**

A wheelchair-bound pensioner went berserk with his colostomy bag after spending all day on the green, sitting in his wheelchair and drinking a mixture of Crème de Menthe and a medicine known as 'Night Nurse'. The court later heard that the man had a history of colostomy terrorism, including incidents outside an off-licence and an estate agent's.

PRIVATE EYE MAGAZINE

If you are ever attacked in the street do not shout 'Help!', shout 'Fire!'. People adore fires and always come rushing. Nobody will come if you shout help. **JEAN TRUMPINGTON**

If you're being chased by a police dog, try not to go through a tunnel, then onto a little seesaw, then jump through a hoop of fire. They're trained for that. **MILTON JONES**

Ma always told me she used to keep half a brick in her handbag, just in case. **MICHAEL BENTINE**

A broad definition of crime in England is any lower-class activity that is displeasing to the upper classes. **ANTHONY JAY**

Guns don't kill people, people kill people, and monkeys do too – if they have a gun. **EDDIE IZZARD**

I have a revolver, and I will glass my enemies in the face but, as an Englishman, I draw the line at a knife. **ARTHUR HARDING**

To deal with violence in this country we need more Jane Austen's *Persuasion* and less Quentin Tarantino's *Kill Bill*.

CLIVE WOLDFENDALE, DEPUTY CHIEF CONSTABLE

I would like to see a return to the good old-fashioned policemen: 16 stone and 6 feet 4 inches tall. **JAMES HORSFALL**

Thieves respect property; they merely wish it to become their property.

G.K. CHESTERTON

'Senseless' is a word usually applied to vandalism, but when one grasps the simple proposition that vandals obviously enjoy breaking things, the vandalism is no more senseless than playing tennis. **AUBERON WAUGH**

Almost all crime is due to the repressed desire for aesthetic expression.

EVELYN WAUGH

People are a bit down on ASBOs but you have to remember these are the only qualifications some kids are ever going to get.

LINDA SMITH ON ANTI-SOCIAL BEHAVIOUR ORDERS

—Desire, greed, lust. We're all in prison for different reasons, aren't we?
—With respect, Godber, we're all here for the same reason: we got caught.

LENNIE GODBER AND NORMAN STANLEY FLETCHER, *PORRIDGE*

It is a fairly unique position: to have been in charge of prison funding and then to have been an inmate. I wish I'd been more generous.

JONATHAN AITKEN

Nobody ever commits a crime without doing something stupid.

OSCAR WILDE

Anyone who has ever been to an English public school will always feel comparatively at home in prison. It is the people brought up in the gay intimacy of the slums who find prison so soul-destroying.

EVELYN WAUGH

Crime is terribly revealing. Try and vary your methods as you will, your tastes, your habits, your attitude of mind, and your soul is revealed by your actions.

AGATHA CHRISTIE

MURDER

There are only about 20 murders committed a year in London and not all are serious – some are just husbands killing their wives.

G.H. HATHERILL

I shot an arrow in the air; she fell to earth in Berkeley Square.

LOUIS MAZZINI, *KIND HEARTS AND CORONETS*

I had not forgotten or forgiven the boredom of the sermon of young Henry's, and I decided to promote the Reverend Lord Henry D'Ascoyne to next place on the list.

LOUIS MAZZINI, *KIND HEARTS AND CORONETS*

She can kill a man at ten paces with one blow of her tongue.

BASIL FAWLTY, *FAWLTY TOWERS*

Almost everyone who has committed a murder knows that the business has its tragic side.

ROBERT LYND

One of my friends went on a murder weekend. Now he's doing life for it.

JACK DEE

Every murderer is probably somebody's old friend.

AGATHA CHRISTIE

I specialise in murders of quiet, domestic interest.

AGATHA CHRISTIE

Television has brought murder back into the home – where it belongs.

ALFRED HITCHCOCK

JUSTICE

British justice is the best in the world, and anyone who disagrees is either a gay, a woman, or a mental. **TOM BAKER, NARRATOR, *LITTLE BRITAIN***

In England, Justice is open to all, like the Ritz hotel. **JAMES MATHEW**

Sentence first, verdict afterwards.

LEWIS CARROLL, *ALICE'S ADVENTURES IN WONDERLAND*

The quality of mercy is not strained,
But I can recommend the cabbage. **BARRY CRYER**

To escape jury duty in England, wear a bowler hat and carry a rolled-up copy of the *Daily Telegraph*. **JOHN MORTIMER**

I have come to regard the law-courts not as a cathedral but rather as a casino. **RICHARD INGRAMS**

Whether you're an honest man or whether you're a thief
Depends on whose solicitor has given me my brief. **W.S. GILBERT**

'First rule in murder, old love: never ask the customer if they did it, in case they tell you.' **HORACE RUMPOLE, *RUMPOLE OF THE BAILEY*, JOHN MORTIMER**

Michael Jackson would have been found guilty if he'd been black. **JO BRAND**

It's impossible to obtain a conviction for sodomy from an English jury. Half of them don't believe that it can physically be done, and the other half are doing it. **WINSTON CHURCHILL**

Justice is being allowed to do whatever I like. Injustice is whatever prevents me doing it. **SAMUEL BUTLER**

CAPITAL PUNISHMENT

The Death Penalty – is it enough? **MRS MERTON**

Depend upon it, Sir, when a man knows he is to be hanged in a fortnight, it concentrates his mind wonderfully. **SAMUEL JOHNSON**

I'm totally against capital punishment myself, except for really serious crimes like plumbers who promise to show up at 9.00 a.m. and don't appear until the following Tuesday when they leave a note saying, 'We called to unblock your pipes, but you were out.' **KENNY EVERETT**

There is no satisfaction in hanging a man who does not object to it. **GEORGE BERNARD SHAW**

I went out to Charing Cross, to see Major-general Harrison hanged, drawn, and quartered; which was done there, he looking as cheerful as any man could do in that condition. **SAMUEL PEPYS**

I hanged John Reginald Christie, the Monster of Rillington Place, in less time than it took the ash to fall off a cigar I had left half-smoked in my room at Pentonville. **ALBERT PIERREPOINT, BRITAIN'S LEADING HANGMAN**

Chief hangman Albert Pierrepoint met trouble only once in all the hundreds of executions he carried out, and that was with a spy. 'He was not an Englishman,' Pierrepoint said. *DAILY HERALD*

Even my lamented master never had the privilege of hanging a duke.
What a finale to a lifetime in the public service! I intend to retire.
After using the silken rope, never again be content with the hemp.

HANGMAN, *KIND HEARTS AND CORONETS*

WAR

Tweedledum and Tweedledee
Agreed to have a battle;
For Tweedledum said Tweedledee
Had spoiled his nice new rattle. **LEWIS CARROLL,** *THROUGH THE LOOKING GLASS*

I have never understood this liking for war. It panders to instincts
already well catered for within the scope of any respectable domestic
establishment. **ALAN BENNETT**

Oh, my dear fellow, the noise...and the people! **CAPTAIN STRAHAN**

Make Tea, Not War! **BRITISH GRAFFITI**

The whole art of war consists of getting at what is on the other side of
the hill, or, in other words, in learning what we do not know from what
we do. **DUKE OF WELLINGTON**

Soldiering is the coward's art of attacking mercilessly when you are
strong, and keeping out of harm's way when you are weak. This is the
whole secret of successful fighting. Get your enemy at a disadvantage; and
never, on any account, fight him on equal terms. **GEORGE BERNARD SHAW**

Other nations use 'force'; we Britons alone use 'Might'. **EVELYN WAUGH**

Oh damn! One measly civil war in the entire history of England and I'm
on the wrong bloody side! **EDMUND BLACKADDER,** *THE CAVALIER YEARS*

The professional military mind is by necessity an inferior and unimaginative mind; no man of high intellectual quality would willingly imprison his gifts in such a calling. **H.G. WELLS**

Whenever a massacre of Armenians is reported from Asia Minor, everyone assumes that it has been carried out 'under orders' from somewhere or another; no one seems to think that there are people who might like to kill their neighbours now and then. **SAKI**

If Kitchener was not a great man, he was, at least, a great poster.

MARGOT ASQUITH

—Granddad, you mean to say you were gun-running during the Spanish Civil War?
—Well, that was the best time to do it.

DEL BOY AND GRANDDAD, *ONLY FOOLS AND HORSES*

The craziest war ever was the War of Jenkins' Ear since there was nobody else it would fit. **MIKE HARDING**

The best defence against the atom bomb is not to be there when it goes off. **BRITISH ARMY JOURNAL, 1949**

A war hasn't been fought this badly since Olaf the Hairy, high chief of all the Vikings, accidentally ordered 80,000 battle helmets with the horns on the inside. **CAPTAIN BLACKADDER,** *BLACKADDER GOES FORTH*

—Mrs Thatcher showed guts during the Falklands War.
—It's a pity others had to leave theirs on the ground at Goose Green to prove it. **HECKLER AND NEIL KINNOCK**

During the Falklands War, British soldiers nicknamed the Islanders 'Bennies', after Benny, the gormless but likeable moron in the TV soap opera, *Crossroads*. When the Ministry of Defence banned the term the soldiers called them 'Stills', as in, 'Still Bennies'. **BERNARD CLARKE**

I think Iraq and Iran had a war simply because their names are so similar they kept getting each other's post. PAUL MERTON

Saddam Hussein is not fit to have a finger on the nuclear trigger. And once we stop to think, nor is anyone else. **MICHAEL FOOT**

The belief in the possibility of a short decisive war appears to be one of the most ancient and dangerous of human illusions. **ROBERT LYND**

As soon as you know an H-bomb is on the way, run out and paint your windows with a mixture of whitewash and curdled milk to deflect dangerous rays. Soak your curtains and upholstery with a solution of borax and starch to prevent fire. **LECTURER IN CIVIL DEFENCE,** *REYNOLDS NEWS*

There is only one thing worse than fighting with allies – and that is fighting without them. **WINSTON CHURCHILL**

The snowdrop is more powerful than the Panzer. **BEVERLEY NICHOLS**

Rather hoped I'd get through the whole show, go back to work at Pratt and Sons, keep wicket for the Croydon Gentlemen, marry Doris. Made a note in my diary on the way here. Simply says: 'Bugger'.

CAPTAIN DARLING, *BLACKADDER GOES FORTH*

THE ARMY, NAVY AND AIR FORCE

At the army medical the doctor said, 'Take all your clothes off.' I said, 'Shouldn't you take me out to dinner first?'
SPIKE MILLIGAN

He only went into the army to put his moustache to good purpose.
ALAN BENNETT

Would you mind awfully falling into three lovely lines?
SERGEANT WILSON, *DAD'S ARMY*

I am the very model of a modern major general,
I've information vegetable, animal and mineral.
W.S. GILBERT, *PIRATES OF PENZANCE*

In enterprise of martial kind,
When there was any fighting,
He led his regiment from behind –
He found it less exciting.
W.S. GILBERT, *THE GONDOLIERS*

The further away you remove the English soldier from the risk of injury, the higher you pay him.
IAN HAY

Generals detest generals on their own side far more than they dislike the enemy.
PETER USTINOV

Donald Neville-Willing was sent to Cairo with the Ambulance Field Service. He was interviewed by General 'Jumbo' Wilson, who granted him a commission after inspecting his fingers when drinking a cup of tea. 'Good Boy! You don't hold your *pinkie* out.'
HUGH MASSINGBERD

In the army there is never any reason for anything.
PHILIP KING

When you come back with the information, Captain Darling will pump you thoroughly in the debriefing room.

GENERAL MELCHETT, *BLACKADDER GOES FORTH*

There's not much makeup in the army, is there? No. They only have that night-time look, and that's a bit slapdash isn't it? **EDDIE IZZARD**

Many years ago, my son, a young subaltern in the army, was told that the best way to avoid wrath on losing equipment was to send a message: 'Regret the loss of six water-bottles down a ravine.' After several weeks had elapsed a further message should be sent saying: 'Referring to my earlier message, for water-bottles read tanks.' **PATRICIA CAMPBELL**

'Tis more blessed to ask for forgiveness than to ask for permission.

MILITARY SAYING

The best confidential report I ever heard of was also the shortest. It ran: Personally I would not breed from this officer.

MAJOR GENERAL R.J. COLLINS

Even in the age of nuclear warfare the best training for an officer is to ride a horse. It brings out the best qualities in a chap.

ARMY CAPTAIN, *NEWS CHRONICLE*

The British army works like this: if you hang a man and he dies, keep hanging him until he gets used to it.

SPIKE MILLIGAN

The navy was gin, sodomy and the lass – quite an attractive career – but not for me on two counts. **GEORGE GALLOWAY**

You need reasonably good sight to be in the Navy, but as a pilot, once you've flown a bit you can guess the way.   **PRINCE ANDREW, THE DUKE OF YORK**

'Can you bowl the chinaman?' the Group Captain said. For non-cricketers, that meant, could I bowl a difficult-to-play spinner, called either the googly or the chinaman. 'Five times out of six,' I replied truthfully. 'Splendid! Absolutely first class! We must have you in the RAF.' At that wonderful moment, I realised that I could have been Adolf Hitler's illegitimate son but, so long as I could bowl the chinaman five times out of six, I was apparently needed by the Royal Air Force.

MICHAEL BENTINE

J.L. Carr entered the RAF to be as far as possible from killing. He applied to work in intelligence and was allotted to painting coal white to stop it being stolen.   **SIMON JENKINS**

Crikey, sir. I'm looking forward to today. Up diddly up, down diddly down, whoops, poop, twiddly dee – decent scrap with the fiendish Red Baron – bit of a jolly old crash landing behind enemy lines – capture, torture, escape, and then back home in time for tea and medals.

LIEUTENANT GEORGE, *BLACKADDER GOES FORTH*

COURAGE

—Well, Captain, I've got to admire your balls.
—Perhaps later.

CORPORAL PERKINS AND CAPTAIN BLACKADDER, *BLACKADDER GOES FORTH*

Courage is rightly esteemed the first of human qualities because it is the quality that guarantees all others.   **WINSTON CHURCHILL**

The important thing when you are going to do something brave is to have someone on hand to witness it.   **MICHAEL HOWARD**

A hero is one who is afraid to run away.   **ENGLISH PROVERB**

'I'm very brave generally,' he went on in a low voice: 'only today I happen to have a headache.'   **LEWIS CARROLL, *THROUGH THE LOOKING GLASS***

Pluck is not so common nowadays as genius.   **OSCAR WILDE**

I never thought much of the courage of a lion-tamer. Inside the cage he is at least safe from people.   **GEORGE BERNARD SHAW**

The nation had the lion's heart. I had the luck to give the roar.   **WINSTON CHURCHILL**

WORLD WAR II

Sir, –It may be of interest to record that, in walking through St James' Park today, I noticed a grey wagtail running about on the now temporarily dry bed of the lake, near the dam below the bridge, and occasionally picking small insects out of the cracks in the dam...   **NEVILLE CHAMBERLAIN, LETTER TO *THE TIMES*, 24 JAN 1933**

(SIX DAYS LATER ADOLF HITLER BECAME CHANCELLOR OF GERMANY)

In 1933, Hitler held his first Nuremberg rally (not a driving event), not to be confused with the later Nuremberg Trials (not a riding event).   **JO BRAND**

I don't think there'll be a war. The Führer doesn't want his new buildings bombed.   **UNITY MITFORD**

All the same, Sir, I should put some of the colonies in your wife's name.   **CHIEF RABBI, TO GEORGE VI**

They don't like it up 'em.   **CORPORAL JONES, *DAD'S ARMY***

It was September 3, 1939. Father and I were watching Mother digging our air raid shelter as the last minutes of peace were ticking away. 'She's a great little woman,' said Father. 'And getting smaller all the time,' I added.

SPIKE MILLIGAN

If it were not for the war, this war would suit me down to the ground.

DOROTHY L. SAYERS

On the Friday morning when Hitler invaded Poland, I chanced to be in the Long Room at Lord's... Balloon barrages hung over Lord's. As I watched, a beautifully preserved member of Lord's, spats and rolled umbrella, stood near me inspecting the game. We did not speak of course; we had not been introduced. Suddenly two workmen entered the Long Room in green aprons and carrying a bag. They took down the bust of W.G. Grace, put it into the bag, and departed with it. The noble lord at my side watched their every movement; then he turned to me. 'Did you see, sir?' he asked. I told him I had seen. 'That means war,' he said.

NEVILLE CARDUS

We ought to have declared war on Germany the moment Mr Hitler's police stole Einstein's violin.

GEORGE BERNARD SHAW

When World War II broke out Don Bradman was given 21 lines in *Who's Who* – only 8 fewer than the more topical Hitler, and 17 more than Stalin.

R.S. WHITINGTON

When Chamberlain resigned as Prime Minister in 1940, Lord Halifax rather than Churchill was his preferred replacement. But on the key afternoon when the decision was taken, Halifax chose to go to the dentist. If Halifax had had better teeth, we might have lost the war.

ALAN BENNETT

The most pathetic thing about Adolf Hitler was his passionate desire to be approved of by English gentlemen. **DAILY TELEGRAPH**

If the fellow's going to raise his right arm so much, he really ought to go to a decent tailor. **HORACE BROWN**

That strange feeling we had in the war. Have you found anything in your lives since to equal it in strength? A sort of splendid carelessness it was, holding us together. **NOËL COWARD**

The war was terrifying and exhilarating at the same time. There was a lot of love, a lot of laughter, a lot of waiting for news, a lot of grieving. And, my goodness, everyone drank. **MARY WESLEY**

—I met my husband during an air raid. The bombs were raining down and I saw his face lit by an incendiary. He threw me on my face and said, 'Look out, here comes a big one!'
—I suppose there wasn't much time for chatting in those days.

MRS SLOCOMBE AND MR LUCAS, *ARE YOU BEING SERVED?*

The Battle of Crete was like German opera. Too long and too loud. EVELYN WAUGH

—I could have sworn the Nazis would never break through the Maginot line.
—They didn't...They went round the side.
—I see... they what?! That's a typical shabby Nazi trick. You see the sort of people we're up against, Wilson.
—Most unreliable, sir. **CAPTAIN MAINWARING AND SERGEANT WILSON,** *DAD'S ARMY*

Oh I do wish that Captain Mainwaring would let my sister Dolly knit him a suit of armour. **PRIVATE GODFREY,** *DAD'S ARMY*

Official advice as to what action to take in a gas attack: put both your hands in your pockets and if you carry an umbrella, put it up.

STAUNTON FULHAM

She came downstairs carrying her gas mask and a neat little suitcase, in which she had packed her knitting, *Pride and Prejudice*, some biscuits, and a precious bar of milk chocolate.

BARBARA PYM

Wednesday 1 July 1942: Lost sunglasses. Tobruk fallen!

KENNETH WILLIAMS, DIARY ENTRY

If you dropped a live grenade prematurely, they urged you not to wait or apologise or to cry a mocking 'Butterfingers' but to dart behind a buttress.

ARTHUR MARSHALL

When you've made gravy under gunfire you can do anything.

PERCY SUGDEN, CATERING CORPS, *CORONATION STREET*

Virginia and I did a tour of hospitals during the war. We were a little surprised to hear ourselves announced as 'two well-known artistes who have flown out from home to entertain men in bed'.

JOYCE GRENFELL

The commandant at Preston thanked me for organising the military hospital show. I said, 'We don't want thanking – after all these lads did for us at Dunkirk.' 'Oh, none of them have been further than under the pier at Blackpool,' he replied. 'This is a V.D. hospital.'

ARTHUR ASKEY

Overpaid, overfed, oversexed, and over here.

TOMMY TRINDER ON AMERICAN FORCES

In defeat unbeatable; in victory unbearable.

WINSTON CHURCHILL ON FIELD MARSHAL VISCOUNT MONTGOMERY

A German prisoner of war was sent each week to tend my garden. He always seemed a nice friendly chap, but when the crocuses came up in the lawn in February, 1946, they spelt out 'Heil Hitler'.　　**IRENE GRAHAM**

As I was saying when I was interrupted...

**WILLIAM CONNOR RESUMING HIS COLUMN IN THE *DAILY MIRROR*
AFTER FOUR YEARS' ACTIVE SERVICE IN WORLD WAR II**

Don't mention the war! I mentioned it once, but I think I got away with it.　　**BASIL FAWLTY, *FAWLTY TOWERS***

BUSINESS

Put the key of despair into the lock of apathy. Turn the knob of mediocrity slowly and open the gates of despondency – welcome to a day in the average office.　　**DAVID BRENT, *THE OFFICE***

I have grown to my desk, as it were, and the wood has entered into my soul.　　**CHARLES LAMB**

I yield to no one in my admiration for the office as a social centre, but it's no place actually to get any work done.　　**KATHARINE WHITEHORN**

Three things in life are certain: death, taxes, and more meetings.　　**SIMON JENKINS**

I'm going to start at the bottom and work my way down.　　**P.G. WODEHOUSE**

Happy is the man with a wife to tell him what to do and a secretary to do it.　　**LORD STORMONT MANCROFT**

I find it rather easy to portray a businessman. Being bland, rather cruel and incompetent comes naturally to me.　　**JOHN CLEESE**

I like your qualifications. You have the makings of a first-class underling.

HECTOR BREEZE

The difference between a supermarket trolley and a non-executive director is that, while both hold a vast quantity of food and drink, only the trolley has a mind of its own.

T.P. BLENKIN

Reps – travelling salesmen – all wearing striped shirts and soaked in cheap after-shave but still with dirty fingernails. They are in a purgatory for those halfway between lager lout and yuppie.

JEFFREY BERNARD

When it comes to labour relations, the two sides of industry (management and workforce) have traditionally always regarded each other in Britain with the greatest possible loathing, mistrust and contempt. They are both absolutely right.

AUBERON WAUGH

Economics is the systematic complication of the simple truths of housekeeping.

PHILIP HOWARD

You never expected justice from a company, did you? They have neither a soul to lose, nor a body to kick.

REVD SYDNEY SMITH

ADVERTISING

I've written books on advertising – cheque books. I hope one day you get to run a company that has a turnover the same as I've pissed up the wall on advertising.

SIR ALAN SUGAR

Death – Bit of a Worry Isn't It?

ADVERT OUTSIDE A CHURCH

The poster of Jesus is modelled on Che Guevara with the slogan, 'Meek, Mild, As If.' We want people to realise that Jesus is not a meek, mild wimp in a white nightie.

REVD TOM AMBROSE

Half the money my company has spent on advertising was wasted.
The problem is to find out which half.   LORD LEVERHULME

You can tell the ideals of a nation by its advertisements.   NORMAN DOUGLAS

Bowens's Beer Makes You Drunk.   KINGSLEY AMIS

MONEY

Imagine six apartments
It isn't hard to do
One is full of fur coats
The other's full of shoes.

ELTON JOHN, MESSAGE IN 40TH BIRTHDAY CARD TO JOHN LENNON

Elton John admitted to spending $57 million in 20 months. 'I am not a
nest-egg person,' he said.   ADVOCATE MAGAZINE

Pop stars earn only two kinds of money: not as much as you think,
and more than you could ever dream of.   BOB GELDOF

There's a famous essay written on the subject of poverty by an Eton
pupil: 'The father was poor. The mother was poor. The children were
poor. The butler was poor. The maid was poor. The gardener was poor.
The chauffeur was poor.'   ALICE CONNOR

The insolence of wealth will creep out.   SAMUEL JOHNSON

The rich are the scum of the earth in every country.   G.K. CHESTERTON

The man with a toothache thinks everyone happy whose teeth are sound.
The poverty-stricken man makes the same mistake about the rich man.

GEORGE BERNARD SHAW

The British have a curious attitude toward wealth: they desire it for themselves but wish to deny it to others. And so, not surprisingly, there are very few methods of acquiring wealth of which they approve. Among them is gambling.   **THEODORE DALRYMPLE**

There are few things in this world more reassuring than an unhappy lottery winner.

TONY PARSONS

When I see people queuing for lottery tickets in the post office, I feel like saying to them, 'Fond of Aïda are you?'   **MELANIE JOHNSON**

Poor Little Rich Girl   **NOËL COWARD, SONG TITLE**

—Remember, you're a person of Gold Credit Card status.
—But I don't have a Gold Credit Card!
—That's only because you haven't got enough money.

HYACINTH AND RICHARD BUCKET, *KEEPING UP APPEARANCES*

He's got a wonderful head for money. There's a long slit on the top.

DAVID FROST

Hymn numbers can be helpful in memorising PIN numbers. Numbers 7 and 490 in the English Hymnal helped me to remember a PIN I once had. 'Lo! He comes, the King of Love,' I would say as I tapped in my PIN; and out He would come with £100 or whatever sum I had requested.

STANLEY EVANS

Nobody will persuade me there is no money about when I see so much spent on gambling, foreign travel, glossy magazines, and plastic gnomes in every front garden.   **FREDERICK SEEBOHM, CHAIRMAN, BARCLAYS BANK**

People say I wasted my money. I say 90 per cent went on women, fast cars and booze. The rest I wasted. **GEORGE BEST**

To be clever enough to get all that money, one must be stupid enough to want it. **G.K. CHESTERTON**

I don't want money. It is only people who pay their bills who want money and I never pay mine. **OSCAR WILDE**

Commenting on a complaint from a Mr Arthur Purdey about a large gas bill, a spokesman for North West Gas said, 'We agree it was rather high for the time of year. It's possible Mr Purdey has been charged for the gas used up during the explosion that destroyed his house.' *THE DAILY TELEGRAPH*

A judge said that all his experience both as Counsel and Judge had been spent sorting out the difficulties of people who, upon the recommendation of people they did not know, signed documents which they did not read, to buy goods they did not need, with money they had not got. **GILBERT HARDING**

All decent people live beyond their incomes nowadays, and those who aren't respectable live beyond other people's. A few gifted individuals manage to do both. **SAKI**

Michael Bentine is confined to bed with a severe overdraft. **SPIKE MILLIGAN**

I'm overdrawn at the bank. I won't say how much, but if you saw it written down, you'd think it was a sex chatline number. **JULIE BURCHILL**

It takes as much imagination to create debt as it does to create income. **LEONARD ORR**

My bank manager went for a heart transplant, but they couldn't find a stone the right size.
                                                                DAVE ALLEN

Having money is rather like being a blonde. It is more fun but not vital.
                                                                MARY QUANT

Never economise on luxuries.
                                                                ANGELA THIRKELL

The real tragedy of the poor is that they can afford nothing but self-denial. Beautiful sins, like beautiful things, are the privilege of the rich.
                                                                OSCAR WILDE

Come away; poverty's catching.
                                                                APHRA BEHN

If Harold Wilson ever went to school without any boots it was because he was too big for them.
                                                                IVOR BULMER-THOMAS

The value of money is that with it we can tell any man to go to the devil. It is the sixth sense which enables you to enjoy the other five.
                                                                W. SOMERSET MAUGHAM

People don't resent having nothing nearly as much as having too little.

IVY COMPTON-BURNETT

Robin Hood is my hero. Have I robbed the rich and given to the poor? Well, half of that.
                                                                LEE HURST

There are few sorrows, however poignant, in which a good income is of no avail.
                                                                L.P. SMITH

He was so mean he only breathed in.
                                                                BOB MONKHOUSE

I bought an account book. I have it still. It contains just one entry: 'Account book – 1s 6d.'   **ARTHUR MARSHALL**

What do you spend your money on? You've got no car, no hobbies. You cut your own hair, you buy all your clothes at Tim's Trouser Warehouse. You buy five pairs of socks for a pound. I bet Terry Waite spent more than you in his hostage years.   **DOROTHY,** *MEN BEHAVING BADLY*

I've just heard the best definition for English meanness. A friend has a weekend cottage in the country, with a bit of a garden. He hangs up bird feeders because he likes the sound and the flutter. Before he leaves on Sunday, he takes them down and puts them in the shed.   **A.A. GILL**

Many speak the truth when they say that they despise riches, but they mean the riches possessed by others.   **CHARLES CALEB COLTON**

TAX

All money nowadays seems to be produced with a natural homing instinct for the Treasury.   **PRINCE PHILIP**

—What does £336,000 in a suitcase look like, Mr Dodd?
—The notes are very light, m'lud.
JUDGE AND KEN DODD DURING COURT CASE FOR TAX EVASION

For a nation to try to tax itself into prosperity is like a man standing in a bucket and trying to lift himself up by the handle.   **WINSTON CHURCHILL**

I had a very successful business lunch with my accountant. He paid the bill and I managed to snatch the receipt.   **KEN DODD**

—We're your actual accountants. He's chartered and I'm certified.
SANDY, *ROUND THE HORNE*

Self-assessment? They pinched that idea from me you know.   **KEN DODD**

Next to being shot at and missed, nothing is really quite as satisfying as an income tax refund.   **F. J. RAYMOND**

I contact Alun Owen in Eire and ask him what the tax advantages would be if I became domiciled in Dublin. 'None,' he says. 'What you save on tax you spend on drink.'   **SPIKE MILLIGAN**

If you live in a council flat...next to a river...but are not blind...WHAT?

BERNARD BLACK FILLING IN HIS TAX-RETURN FORM, *BLACK BOOKS*

'You don't know a way of doing down the income-tax people, do you Bertie?' 'Sorry, no. I doubt even Jeeves does.'   **P.G. WODEHOUSE**

CHARITY

It's hard to get donations for a charity for drug addicts but *please* give. Remember, if they're in treatment, they're not nicking your car.

DAVINA MCCALL

Please give as if the person next to you were watching you.

REVD V. LINES TO HIS CONGREGATION

Like Christmas or bent sex, it's better to give than to receive.   **JIMMY CARR**

There are two different kinds of people. There are people who always feel sorry for buskers and put something in their hat and there are those who look into the hat and think: 'By gum, I wish I was making that sort of money.'   **MILES KINGTON**

All this talk about famine makes you a bit peckish, doesn't it?   **JO BRAND**

—You never give to charity.
—I do. I buy poppies.
—You bought a poppy in 1989. You make me iron it every year.

GARY AND DOROTHY, *MEN BEHAVING BADLY*

The fishy glitter in his eye became intensified. He looked like a halibut which had been asked by another halibut to lend it a couple of quid till next Wednesday.

P.G. WODEHOUSE

No matter how much you give a homeless person for a cup of tea, you never get it.

JIMMY CARR

After a taxi-ride Tommy Cooper would slip something into the top pocket of the driver and say, 'Have a drink on me.' When the taxi-driver looked in his pocket he'd find it was a tea bag.

BOB MONKHOUSE

Starving Africans – it is a serious problem. But then again, they don't get our winters.

JIMMY CARR

I saw an ad for a charity, which said: 'Little Zuki has to walk 15 miles each day just to fetch water.' I couldn't help thinking: she should move.

JIMMY CARR

I am not entirely uncharitable. I can't, for example, walk past a Big Issue seller without averting my gaze and picking up my speed. And as for Children in Need and that Pudsey Bear, I don't exactly hate him, but I still wouldn't mind having a go at poking that other eye out.

DEBORAH ROSS

People who mean well – always a poisonous class.

E.V. LUCAS

You and your mother are always trying to help lame dogs over stiles – even if they're not lame and don't want to go.   NOËL COWARD, *THE VORTEX*

She's the sort of woman who lives for others – you can always tell the others by their hunted expression.   **C.S. LEWIS**

Philanthropy has become simply the refuge of people who wish to annoy their fellow-creatures.   **OSCAR WILDE**

The Queen supports foxhunting so having her as the patron of the RSPCA is like having a paedophile as the patron of the NSPCC.   **ANGELA WALDER**

There has been a decrease in support for landmine clearance since the death of Diana, Princess of Wales. Landmine clearance was supposed to be the issue to unite mankind for the new century, but that was when leaders could be seen with Diana.
        KEN RUTHERFORD, LANDMINES SURVIVORS NETWORK

He is one of those wise philanthropists who, in a time of famine, would vote for nothing but a supply of toothpicks.   **DOUGLAS JERROLD**

There is often a great deal of spleen at the bottom of benevolence.
        WILLIAM HAZLITT

Blessed is he who expects nothing, for he shall not be disappointed.
        JONATHAN SWIFT

SCIENCE AND TECHNOLOGY

SCIENCE

Given apples and motion, the English produced Isaac Newton, the Swiss, William Tell. **MALCOLM SCOTT**

I believe that the souls of five hundred Sir Isaac Newtons would go to the making up of a Shakespeare or a Milton. **SAMUEL TAYLOR COLERIDGE**

Even if I could be Shakespeare, I think I should still choose to be Faraday. **ALDOUS HUXLEY**

Why does the universe go to all the bother of existing? **STEPHEN HAWKING**

The idea that life was put together by a random shuffling of constituent molecules can be shown as ridiculous and improbable as the proposition that a tornado blowing through a junk-yard might assemble a Boeing 747 from the materials therein. **SIR FRED HOYLE**

The universe is not only stranger than we imagine, it is stranger than we can imagine. **J.B.S. HALDANE**

Television, and radar and atomic energy are so far beyond my comprehension that my brain shudders at the thought of them and scurries for cover like a primitive tribesman confronted for the first time with a Dunhill cigarette lighter. **NOËL COWARD**

When I am in the company of scientists, I feel like a shabby curate who has strayed by mistake into a drawing room full of dukes. **W.H. AUDEN**

All science is either physics or stamp collecting. **ERNEST RUTHERFORD**

Most people are now of the opinion that Mr and Mrs Einstein should never have given little Albert that chemistry set. **MIKE HARDING**

Science is simply common sense at its best.   THOMAS HUXLEY

You can analyse a glass of water and you're left with a lot of chemical components, but nothing you can drink.   J.B.S. HALDANE

There comes a time when every scientist, even God, has to write off an experiment.   P.D. JAMES

Every body continues in its state of rest or uniform motion in a straight line, except insofar as it doesn't.   SIR ARTHUR EDDINGTON

The great tragedy of science: the slaying of a beautiful hypothesis by an ugly fact.   THOMAS HUXLEY

Flying is simple. You just throw yourself at the ground and miss.   DOUGLAS ADAMS

Pavlov's cat: Day one: rang bell – cats answered the door. Day two: cats said they had eaten. Day three: cats stole the battery. Day four: cats rang the bell, I ate the food.   EDDIE IZZARD

Science is but an exchange of ignorance for that which is another kind of ignorance.   LORD BYRON

I almost think it is the ultimate destiny of science to exterminate the human race.   THOMAS LOVE PEACOCK

SPACE

One small step for man...a taxi ride for Ronnie Corbett.   BARRY CRYER

I got a bit of moon rock once. When I broke it open it had MOON written all through it.   KEN DODD

Space...is big. Really big. You just wouldn't believe how vastly hugely mind-boggling big it is. I mean, you may think it's a long way down the road to the chemist, but that's just peanuts to space.   **DOUGLAS ADAMS**

I have never really understood what we hope to gain by sending eight people whizzing around the world for 90 days at a cost of $35,000 per hour per person.   **AUBERON WAUGH**

Outer space is no place for a person of breeding.   **LADY VIOLET BONHAM CARTER**

My ambition is to host a TV chat show with Neil Armstrong and never mention the moon.   **ARDAL O'HANLON**

I thought I saw a UFO once but turned out I just rubbed my eyes too hard.   **PETE GRIGSON**

We'd all be doing exactly the same things we are doing today if Galileo had never made his telescope.   **GEORGE A. BIRMINGHAM**

COMPUTER

The goal of computer science is to build something that will last until you've finished building it.   **DOUGLAS ADAMS**

I think computer viruses should count as life. I think it says something about human nature that the only form of life we have created so far is purely destructive. We've created life in our own image.   **STEPHEN HAWKING**

Personally, I rather look forward to a computer program winning the world chess championship. Humanity needs a lesson in humility.   **RICHARD DAWKINS**

Reading computer manuals without the hardware is as frustrating as reading sex manuals without the software.   **ARTHUR C. CLARKE**

TECHNOLOGY

Any sufficiently advanced technology is indistinguishable from magic.

ARTHUR C. CLARKE

Mechanical things are made, in the main, so that they will go wrong.

MIKE HARDING

Nowhere does Parkinson's Law operate so efficiently as in the house: mechanical gadgets don't cut down the time spent, they just mean you wash sweaters after you've worn them once instead of scraping the food blob off with your fingernail. **JILLY COOPER**

None of the modern machines, none of the modern paraphernalia have any power except over the people who choose to use them.

G.K. CHESTERTON

The thing with high tech is that you always end up using scissors.

DAVID HOCKNEY

MATHEMATICS

Is a right-angled triangle likely to have a square on its hypotenuse – I mean, in real life? **H.F. ELLIS**

Mathematics may be defined as the subject in which we never know what we are talking about, nor whether what we are saying is true.

BERTRAND RUSSELL

—What is two and two?
—Are you buying or selling? **SMALL CHILD AND LEW GRADE**

I'm very well acquainted too with matters mathematical,
I understand equations both the simple and quadratical,
About binomial theorem I'm teeming with a lot o' news –
With many cheerful facts about the square of the hypotenuse.

W.S. GILBERT, *THE PIRATES OF PENZANCE*

Other than when playing darts, I become confused at the mere mention of figures.

NEIL KINNOCK

Double decker buses for widths; football pitches for length; Nelson's Columns for heights.

STANDARD BRITISH UNITS OF MEASUREMENT

INVENTIONS

Every revolutionary idea seems to evoke three stages of reaction. They may be summed up by the phrases: (1) It's completely impossible. (2) It's possible, but it's not worth doing. (3) I said it was a good idea all along.

ARTHUR C. CLARKE

The moment fire was invented, men didn't say, 'Hey, let's cook!'
They said, 'Great! now we can see naked women in the dark.'

STEVE TAYLOR, *COUPLING*

A common mistake people make, when trying to design something completely foolproof, is to underestimate the ingenuity of complete fools.

DOUGLAS ADAMS

Sirs, I have tested your machine. It adds a new terror to life and makes death a long-felt want.

HERBERT BEERBOHM TREE ABOUT THE GRAMOPHONE

I don't think necessity is the mother of invention. Invention, in my opinion, arises directly from idleness, possibly also from laziness – to save oneself trouble.

AGATHA CHRISTIE

I don't operate rationally. I think just like a woman.

JAMES DYSON, INVENTOR OF DYSON VACUUM CLEANER

Dr Strabismus (Whom God Preserve) of Utrecht, is working hard on
about 1,450 more inventions. These include…false teeth for swordfish,
a revolving wheel-barrow, a screw for screwing screws into other screws,
a plush sausage-sharpener and a chivet for screaming radishes.   **J.B. MORTON**

TRANSPORT – GENERAL

If God had meant us to walk everywhere, he wouldn't have given
us Little Chefs.   **REVEREND BERNICE WOODALL**, *THE LEAGUE OF GENTLEMEN*

The bicycle is the most civilised conveyance known to man. Other forms
of transport grow daily more nightmarish. Only the bicycle remains pure
in heart.   **IRIS MURDOCH**

Every time you went over a stone or a rut the saddle nipped you. It was
like riding on an irritable lobster.   **JEROME K. JEROME**

For sheer pleasure few methods of progression, one comes gradually to
realise, can compare with the perambulator. The motion is agreeable,
the range of vision extensive and one has always before one's eyes the
rewarding spectacle of a grown-up maintaining prolonged physical
exertion.   **OSBERT LANCASTER**

His name was Ernie, and he drove the fastest milk cart in the west.

BENNY HILL

London's big red Routemaster bus is the greatest icon of Britain. Like
Britain itself, everyone tries to squeeze on board for a free ride and it ends
up going nowhere.   **BBC NEWS ONLINE**

CAR

Alex Issigonis didn't believe in styling. The Mini just took the shape of what was inside – the style of the car was just a skin. He designed it for charladies and district nurses.

GILLIAN BARDSLEY

It is a fearful thing to contemplate that, when you are driving along the road, a heavy horse may at any moment drop from the sky on top of you.

MR JUSTICE VAISEY

The salesman who sold me the car told me I'd get a lot of pleasure out of it. He was right. It was a pleasure to get out of it.

LES DAWSON

The only part of the car that didn't make a noise when in motion was the hooter.

DENIS NORDEN

Start! Start, you vicious bastard! Oh my God! I'm warning you, if you don't start...I'll count to three: one, two, three – right, that does it! I'm going to give you a damn good thrashing!

BASIL FAWLTY TO HIS CAR, *FAWLTY TOWERS*

The mechanic said that if it had been a horse he'd have had to shoot her.

BASIL BOOTHROYD

I've always felt it was the car which went down to the showroom to choose the man, not the other way round, and Volvos like to pick a dentist who is going to send his son to a not quite first-rate public school.

ROBERT ROBINSON

One enjoys the cheek of a car company that can take a panelled sitting-room, propel it down the road at over 100mph and still make as little noise as a skilled fly fisherman eating his packed lunch.

JOHN WHISTON ON ROLLS-ROYCE

The VW Beetle has such a completely pathetic heater that on cold days you'd be better off setting fire to your hair. **RICHARD PORTER**

The car's a GTI. If you rearrange the number plates you have yourself a personalised number plate. **DEL BOY TROTTER,** *ONLY FOOLS AND HORSES*

Why, oh why, does Rolls-Royce, brightest diamond in the crown of British technological achievement, have to name its latest product 'Camargue' after an area of French marshland? Have we no British bogs to commemorate? **RALPH SHELDON**

At 60 miles an hour the loudest noise in this new Rolls-Royce comes from the electric clock. **DAVID OGILVY, ADVERTISEMENT**

The policy of the Government is not to reduce the speed of motor cars, but to increase the speed of pedestrians. **A.P. HERBERT**

I've found a way to make my wife drive more carefully. I told her that if she has an accident, the newspapers would print her age. **JAN MURRAY**

Nissan QX. It exists. So does dog dirt but I don't want it outside my house.

JEREMY CLARKSON

To park your car for an hour in Soho costs more than the minimum wage. There are people working in McDonald's in Soho who can look out of the window and see parking meters earning more than they do. **SIMON EVANS**

Dearest Warden. Front tooth broken off: look like 81-year-old pirate, so at dentist 19a. Very old – very lame – no metras [sic]. **LADY DIANA COOPER, NOTE SHE LEFT ON HER CAR WINDSCREEN**

Like minor poets, traffic wardens feel that anything they've written –
like the date or the first two digits of your number plate, are too
precious to cross out.

CLEMENT FREUD

Speed cameras are fatuous instruments of oppression designed to
exercise power and impose subservience purely for its own sake.

AUBERON WAUGH

A short time after my release from being held hostage in the Lebanon,
I travelled to Ireland. On arrival at Dublin airport, I got into a taxi.
The taxi-driver looked at me and said, 'You're that John McCarthy,
aren't you?' I said I was. He nodded, thought for a moment, then said:
'Wouldn't you be more comfortable in the boot?'

JOHN MCCARTHY

AEROPLANE

There's nothing like an airport for bringing you down to earth.

RICHARD GORDON

Could you ask our captain to go a little faster and land a little earlier?
My husband would tip him handsomely.

HYACINTH BUCKET AT THE CHECK-IN DESK, *KEEPING UP APPEARANCES*

It was a pretty little plane rather like a cottage all blue and white with
plush curtains. No nonsense about fasten your safety belt – and no safety
belt either.

NANCY MITFORD

Nothing is so uninteresting to look at as clouds from the inside.

RICHARD GORDON

An airport is a free-range womb.

BRIGID BROPHY

TRAIN

This train will call at Garforth, East Garforth, Micklefield and Ulleskelf, due to arrive in York, whenever.

ANNOUNCEMENT ON A MANCHESTER TO YORK TRAIN

How can we take seriously a film like *Brief Encounter,* which relies on the absurd notion of punctual railway trains? **DESMOND BOND**

Euston, we have a problem. **ALEX MASON**

Twenty-two minutes late: badger ate a junction box at New Malden.

REGGIE PERRIN, *THE FALL AND RISE OF REGINALD PERRIN*

A tedious railway journey was made in a train that seemed to stop every few minutes to admire the scenery. **BALAAM**

It is better to travel hopefully than to arrive, Robert Louis Stevenson assures us. I doubt if he had to sit an hour outside Didcot station while British Rail, reluctant to admit that in winter our weather tends to be wintry, struggled to unfreeze the points. **LORD MANCROFT**

To rely on a train in Blair's Britain is to engage in a crapshoot with the devil. **BORIS JOHNSON**

It was the wrong kind of snow. **TERRY WORRALL, BRITISH RAIL**

An Arctic seal is to be transported free of charge in a wooden crate in an unheated carriage of a Virgin train. Is this a one-off or is the entire fleet to be upgraded to this standard? **TONY MOORE**

Twenty-two minutes late: escaped puma, Chessington North.

REGGIE PERRIN, *THE FALL AND RISE OF REGINALD PERRIN*

Today the automated voice at National Train Inquiries apologised for the delay in answering, due to 'adverse weather conditions'. Leaves on the telephone line? **CHARLES HEDGCOCK**

The trouble with many British Rail passengers is that they think the railways are being run for their benefit. **JEREMY CLARKSON**

Unfortunately for you lot, we are now stuck behind a broken train. We'll be here for a quite a while but I don't care, I'm now on overtime. **LONDON TUBE TRAIN ANNOUNCEMENT**

I cannot get rid of a secret conviction that the aim of railway trains is to give me the slip. **A.G. GARDINER**

The only way of catching a train I ever discovered is to miss the train before. **G. K. CHESTERTON**

The best etiquette for getting off a crowded train against a crowd of people forcing their way on is to shout, 'Excuse me, I think I'm going to be sick.' **FRAN COLLINS**

I think the full tide of human existence is at Charing Cross. **SAMUEL JOHNSON**

Sir, Saturday morning, although recurring at regular and well-foreseen intervals, always seems to take this railway by surprise. **W.S. GILBERT, LETTER OF COMPLAINT TO THE STATION-MASTER AT BAKER STREET**

If any one of London's railway stations deserves to be a shrine, it's Paddington. Its departure board reads like a romantic novel, as it flicks its way through Oxford, Bath, the Cotswolds and the very heart of England. **MARK WALLINGTON**

Train crew displacement.

THAMESLINK EUPHEMISM FOR ITS FAILURE TO PROVIDE A DRIVER

Paddington Station is two very different places depending on whether you are arriving or departing.   **GEOFFREY MADAN**

Once there had been an exit on this side of the station, but it had been discovered that the only people who benefited were passengers.

KINGSLEY AMIS

Do engine-drivers, I wonder, eternally wish they were small boys?

FLANN O'BRIEN

Railways and the Church have their critics, but both are the best ways of getting a man to his ultimate destination.   **REVD W. AWDRY**

UNIVERSAL LAWS

I have discovered a law which states that the information you particularly need is on the only piece of paper you cannot find.   **JANE IONS**

Why is it that when I have a cup of tea in one hand and a plate of sticky cakes in the other, I invariably want to sneeze.   **LAMBERT JEFFRIES**

An unwatched pot boils immediately.   **H.F. ELLIS**

A watched postman never delivers.   **OLIVER PRITCHETT**

The greatest duffer at the game is the most enthusiastic.   **R.A. FITZGERALD**

The major difference between a thing that might go wrong and a thing that cannot possibly go wrong, is that when a thing that cannot possibly go wrong goes wrong it usually turns out to be impossible to get at or repair.   **DOUGLAS ADAMS**

The rule is, jam tomorrow and jam yesterday – but never jam today.

LEWIS CARROLL

The golden rule is that there are no golden rules.   **GEORGE BERNARD SHAW**

In five years it will be against the law to smoke or drink and the food shops will stock nothing but muesli. It will also be against the law to die; I am not quite sure how they will punish people for that but they will, they will.   **JEFFREY BERNARD, 1994**

There is only one immutable law in life – in a gentleman's toilet, incoming traffic has the right of way.   **HUGH LEONARD**

BODY, MIND
AND SOUL

APPEARANCE – GENERAL

Well, how are you? Much the same as usual, I see – hair arranged with a pitchfork and dress with a view to ventilation.   **RHODA BROUGHTON**

It was one of those British faces that, once seen, are never remembered.

OSCAR WILDE

All human faces are divided into buttons, birds and horses.   **JOYCE GRENFELL**

If Noël Coward's face suggested an old boot it was unquestionably hand made.   **KENNETH TYNAN**

His face looked as if it were pressed against a window, except there was no window.   **REBECCA WEST**

He had but one eye, and the popular prejudice runs in favour of two.

CHARLES DICKENS

He looked like an extra from a crowd scene by Hieronymus Bosch.

KENNETH TYNAN

She looked a million dollars, even if in well-used notes.   **ANGELA CARTER**

Naked, I had a body that invited burial.   **SPIKE MILLIGAN**

We tolerate shapes in human beings that would horrify us if we saw them in a horse.   **DEAN INGE**

It is only shallow people who do not judge by appearances.   **OSCAR WILDE**

Let us be grateful to the mirror for revealing to us our appearance only.

SAMUEL BUTLER

PLASTIC SURGERY

Have I had plastic surgery? Don't be daft. A bloody estimate would cost me about ten grand.
MICHAEL PARKINSON

Never mind a face lift, I need Lourdes.
PAUL O'GRADY

Jackie Stallone says she's never had plastic surgery. Really? Well I hope she got the number of the bus that hit her.
PAUL O'GRADY

Did you see her boob job? You don't wanna drive around in an old Transit just because it's got new headlamps.
RIPLEY HOLDEN, BLACKPOOL

Posh is just one operation behind me.
JORDAN

There are perks to being flat-chested. I can pass for 14 in a blackout.
JENNY ECLAIR

HAIR

My hair is a bit like the Tory Party. There is nothing you can do with it.
TONY BLAIR

My hair's got a life of its own. Last week, I found it in the kitchen making itself an omelette.
PAUL MERTON

Do you know a shop where they cut your hair properly? I keep on having my hair cut but it keeps on growing again.
G.K. CHESTERTON

It is now 5 o'clock. We have our haircutter below stairs, William is reading *The Leech-Gatherer* to him.
DOROTHY WORDSWORTH

I tried to have a trendy haircut and ended up looking like a lesbian on the tennis circuit.   **HUGH GRANT**

Peter Stringfellow has the hair of a 19-year-old – usually stuck between his teeth.   **JONATHAN ROSS**

His hair looked like an explosion in a pubic hair factory.

JONATHAN MILLER ON PAUL JOHNSON

My dandruff's just been signed up for the title role in *White Christmas*.

BOB MONKHOUSE

TEETH

Oh, I wish I'd looked after me teeth,
And spotted the dangers beneath…   **PAM AYRES**

My teeth are all my own. I've just finished paying for them.   **KEN DODD**

I didn't know my uncle had a denture until it came out in conversation.

BOB MONKHOUSE

Mr Craven's always been on the side of progress: he had false teeth, when he was 27.   **ALAN BENNETT**

He had faced death in many forms but he had never faced a dentist. The thought of dentists gave him just the same sick horror as the thought of Socialism.   **H.G. WELLS**

Evelyn Waugh famously once said: 'All this fuss about sleeping together. For physical pleasure I'd sooner go to the dentist any day.' Well, in my part of Wales, it's now easier to find someone to sleep with than it is to find a dentist.   **PATRICK HANNAN**

My father kept several pairs of false teeth, one set in a jar marked
'Best Pair', another marked 'Next Best' and a third marked 'Not Bad'.

DAVID HOCKNEY

BEAUTY AND UGLINESS

There are charms made only for distant admiration. No spectacle is
nobler than a blaze.

SAMUEL JOHNSON

Of all the world's vistas, the one that cannot be surpassed is the female
posterior.

JOHN B. KEANE

The buttocks are the most aesthetically pleasing part of the body
because they are non-functional. Although they conceal an essential
orifice, these pointless globes are as near as the human form can ever
come to abstract art.

KENNETH TYNAN

There was a young lady of Exeter
So pretty that men craned their nexetter.
One was even so brave
As to take out and wave
The distinguishing mark of his sexetter.

ANON

Back Beauty: A woman who appears to be attractive from behind, but
when seen from the front is a bit of a horse. Back beauties form a staple
joke in Benny Hill's oeuvre.

VIZ

I'm not saying my wife's ugly but she went to see that film, *The Elephant
Man*, and the audience thought he was making a personal appearance.

LES DAWSON

Why did I marry a plain girl? My dear, buggers can't be choosers.

MAURICE BOWRA

Single bagger: a lady so ugly she needs a bag on the head.
Double bagger: a lady so ugly that she needs a bag on her head and so do you in case hers falls off.   **BRITISH ARMY SLANG**

There is no cosmetic for beauty like happiness.   **LADY BLESSINGTON**

Nothing gives a brighter glow to the complexion, or makes the eye of a beautiful woman sparkle so intensely, as triumph over another.

LADY CAROLINE LAMB

It has been said that a pretty face is a passport. But it's not, it's a visa, and it runs out fast.   **JULIE BURCHILL**

It can hardly be a coincidence that no language on earth has ever produced the expression 'as pretty as an airport'.   **DOUGLAS ADAMS**

Beauty is only sin deep.   **SAKI**

Remember always that the least plain sister is the family beauty.

GEORGE BERNARD SHAW

FASHION AND DRESS

Some people are born with a sense of how to clothe themselves, others acquire it, others look as if their clothes had been thrust upon them.   **SAKI**

Fashion is what you adopt when you don't know who you are.

QUENTIN CRISP

Mr Jones, landlord of the 300-year-old Rose and Crown, said: 'One Belgian tried to strangle me. I didn't mind him at my throat, but I took exception to a drunken foreigner grabbing my 1st Airborne Division tie.'

DAILY MIRROR

I once saw in a French journal, under a drawing of a bonnet, the words: 'With this style the mouth is worn slightly open.'   **OSCAR WILDE**

I never cared for fashion much, amusing little seams and witty little pleats: it was the girls I liked.   **DAVID BAILEY**

I hold that gentleman to be the best-dressed whose dress no one observes.   **ANTHONY TROLLOPE**

Contrary to popular belief, English women do not wear tweed nightgowns.   **HERMIONE GINGOLD**

Mrs Blount appeared...with the same broad face, diamond bandeau, white shoes, pink husband, and fat neck.   **JANE AUSTEN**

To dismiss the English style by saying that the key is understatement is to overlook an air of nonchalance which is habitual and comes from an innate sense of security.   **HARDY AMIES**

Your English style will no doubt put all other gentlemen to bed. I speak figuratively of course.   **JOHN GIELGUD**

I did not feel my best when the helicopter made an emergency landing on a mountain in Peru, but I did not let it show. I kept clutching my red Hermès bag, which matched my hat and red jacket.   **PRINCESS MICHAEL OF KENT**

The tie is, equally with the shine on a man's shoes, the clearest indication of his character. Never trust a man whose tie is habitually an inch below his collar.   **THOMAS JAGGER**

—What do ties matter, Jeeves, at a time like this?
—There is no time, sir, at which ties do not matter.   **P.G. WODEHOUSE**

With an evening coat and a white tie, anybody, even a stockbroker, can gain a reputation for being civilised.   **OSCAR WILDE**

Fashion is like God, man cannot see into its holy of holies and live. **SAMUEL BUTLER**

You can never rival a millionaire if he has even the faintest inclination towards smartness. His valet wears his suits for the first three days so that they never look new, and confiscates them after three months so that they never look old.   **EVELYN WAUGH**

The sense of being well-dressed gives a feeling of inward tranquillity which religion is powerless to bestow.   **C.F. FORBES**

When Spring comes around, I merely write my tailor, send him a small sample of dandruff, and tell him to match it exactly.   **OLIVER HERFORD**

My tailor always says, 'Trousers should shiver on the shoe but not break'.   **ARNOLD BENNETT**

Bow-ties: are you a gay professor? Then take it off.   **DAVID QUANTICK**

One good reason for wearing a bow-tie is that it lasts four times as long as an ordinary tie.   **ROBIN DAY**

What is elegance? Soap and water.   **CECIL BEATON**

How on earth did Gandhi manage to walk so far in flip-flops? I can't last ten minutes in mine.   **MRS MERTON**

So I went down my local ice-cream shop, and said, 'I want to buy an ice-cream.' He said, 'Hundreds and thousands?' I said, 'We'll start with one.' He said 'Knickerbocker glory?' I said 'I do get a certain amount of freedom in these trousers, yes.'   **TOMMY COOPER**

When you buy a V-necked sweater there's a V of material missing. You know what they do with that? They send it to Ann Summers and she makes those fancy pants.   **HARRY HILL**

She wore far too much rouge last night and not quite enough clothes. That is always a sign of despair in a woman.   **OSCAR WILDE**

I dined yesterday at Deane... Mrs Powlett was at once expensively and nakedly dress'd.   **JANE AUSTEN**

Father told me that if I ever met a lady in a dress like yours, I must look her straight in the eyes.   **PRINCE CHARLES**

I could never be a nudist. I could never decide what not to wear. JENNIFER COOMBS

Never forget that what looks good on an 18-year-old fashion model in the catalogue is not necessarily right for a 66-year-old bookie's clerk from Chorley with elephantitus in her left knee.   **MRS MERTON**

Budgie smugglers: Extremely tight gentleman's bathing trunks.   **VIZ**

At Marks and Spencer's I bought a peach coloured vest and trollies to match with insertions of lace. Disgraceful I know but I can't help choosing my underwear with a view to it being seen.   **BARBARA PYM**

The way I buy my clothes is like this: if it's shiny, I buy it.   **GRAHAM NORTON**

—Why do you have no underwear, Lord Flasheart?
—Because the pants haven't been built yet that'll take the job on!

CAPTAIN BLACKADDER AND LORD FLASHEART, *BLACKADDER GOES FORTH*

Winston Churchill's pale pink underclothes were made in very finely woven silk…and he spent £80 on them. He told me 'the garments are essential to my well-being…The delicate skin on one small part of my anatomy demands the finest covering.'   **VIOLET BONHAM CARTER**

I was shown round Tutankhamun's tomb in the 1920s. There was all this wonderful pink on the walls and the artefacts. I was so impressed that I vowed to wear it for the rest of my life.   **DAME BARBARA CARTLAND**

The best-dressed woman is one whose clothes wouldn't look too strange in the country.   **HARDY AMIES**

We really like dowdiness in England. It's absolutely incurable in us, I believe.   **PETER SHAFFER**

Life nowadays is dominated and complicated by the remorseless Zip. Is there anything more deadly than a Zip that turns nasty on you?   **AGATHA CHRISTIE**

Yes, I do wear spectacles, but only for reading and seeing things. **RONNIE BARKER**

Jeeves lugged my purple socks out of the drawer as if he were a vegetarian fishing a caterpillar out of his salad.   **P.G. WODEHOUSE**

I daresay you know these Folk Dance people. They tie bells to their trousers and dance old rustic dances showing that it takes all sorts to make a world.   **P.G. WODEHOUSE**

There is invariably something queer about women who wear ankle socks.

ALAN BENNETT

The Joy of Socks

WENDY COPE, TITLE OF POEM

As a Morris Dancer I require a good supply of plain white handkerchiefs
with good aerodynamic 'float' for the best possible display effect.
Handkerchiefs in the major chain stores seem to be multicoloured...
Luckily, in Tunbridge Wells I found a good old-fashioned draper with
a fine stock of loose hankies.

NEIL MURRAY ON HIS SEARCH FOR THE GREAT BRITISH HANKY

I like clothes – on other people. Somehow, they seem to suffer a sea-
change when they get on me. They look quite promising in the shop;
and not entirely without hope when I get them back into my wardrobe.
But then, when I put them on they tend to deteriorate with a very strange
rapidity and one feels so sorry for them.

JOYCE GRENFELL

I don't own a dress. I wear skirts but I look like a netball teacher.

VICTORIA WOOD

One thing I've learned from *Star Trek* is that men are going to be
wearing simple pullovers for ever. I've also learned, not to my surprise,
that women will continue to sport minis and plenty of décolletage
whatever the stardate.

BERNARD HOLLOWOOD

FOOD AND DRINK

We can do you something pretty bizarre in marzipan...I could let
myself go in Dundee...or I could do something provocative in sponge –
with a fruit filling.

JULIAN, *ROUND THE HORNE*

A good fish finger butty is hard to beat.

JAMIE OLIVER

I would walk miles for a bacon sandwich.   **DIANA, PRINCESS OF WALES**

A man who is sick of chips is tired of life.   **CILLA BROWN,** *CORONATION STREET*

Samantha's going to spend the evening licking the nuts off a large Neapolitan.

HUMPHREY LYTTELTON

Good apple pies are a considerable part of our domestic happiness.

JANE AUSTEN

Who can resist the smell of a mature woman's macaroons?

MRS OVERALL, *ACORN ANTIQUES*

My favourite food, Guinness. It's the only food that doesn't have to be cooked or kept in the refrigerator.   **QUENTIN CRISP**

As accurately as I can calculate, between the ages of 10 and 70,
I have eaten 44 waggon-loads of food more than was good for me.

REVD SYDNEY SMITH

Digestion is the great secret of life.   **REVD SYDNEY SMITH**

He who does not mind his belly, will hardly mind anything else.

SAMUEL JOHNSON

A man's own dinner is to himself so important that he cannot bring himself to believe that it is a matter utterly indifferent to anyone else.

ANTHONY TROLLOPE

If the British can survive their meals, they can survive anything.

GEORGE BERNARD SHAW

Any of us would kill a cow rather than not have beef.   **SAMUEL JOHNSON**

Into these bowls Mrs Squeers poured a brown composition which looked like diluted pincushions without the covers.

CHARLES DICKENS, *NICHOLAS NICKLEBY*

I love fish and chips. I keep salt and vinegar in the glove compartment of my white Rolls-Royce so I can enjoy my meal on my way home from a show.   **LARRY GRAYSON**

Oh, the superb wretchedness of English food. How many foreigners has it daunted, and what a subtle glow of nationality one feels in ordering a dish that one knows will be bad and being able to eat it.

CYRIL CONNOLLY

Whilst in Normandy last summer, I found Bisto gravy powder in a hardware shop on the same shelf as colouring for tile grout.   **M.J. TANNER**

You can't make a silk purse out of a sow's ear but there's nothing to stop you making a lovely pork pie.   **HUMPHREY LYTTELTON**

What is a roofless cathedral compared to a well-built pie?

SIR MORGAN O'DOHERTY

Sandwich recipe: take two bits of bread. Put them together. Now eat it.

VICTORIA WOOD

My Heath Robinson Pasta only needs one saucepan, a tin of spinach, some nests of vermicelli, olive oil, shavings of mild English cheddar, nuggets of garlic and boiling water. Shove everything in, and cook for eight minutes, stirring occasionally.   **JOHN BAYLEY**

I love the *philosophy* of a sandwich. It typifies my attitude to life. It's all there, it's fun, it looks good, and you don't have to wash up afterwards.

MOLLY PARKIN

Thursday at school was Sausage Morning and even as far off as Tuesday I began to be filled with a vague joy at the prospect.   **GRAHAM ROBERTSON**

Mrs Boller, your sausage rolls have come and they are absolutely lovely! Almost as much sausage as roll.   **JOYCE GRENFELL**

—These cucumbers are hot, Victoria.
—They're courgettes, David.   **DAVID AND VICTORIA BECKHAM,** *DEAD RINGERS*

As a vegetable, cabbage has original sin, and needs improvement... Cabbage also has a nasty history of being good for you.   **JANE GRIGSON**

Only a nation that thought of food as an extension of engineering could have invented brown sauce. You can clean silver with it. It doesn't go with anything. It's a culinary assassin, an olfactory blackout. And it's got tamarinds in it: ''ere guv, we've got these weird little fruits from out east. What will we do with them?' 'Chuck 'em in the brown sauce.'   **A.A. GILL**

It is not true that I never eat vegetables. I once ate a pea. **BEAU BRUMMELL**

I went to the supermarket and bought some HP sauce. I've got to pay six pence a week over three months.   **SIMON BLIGH**

Here's something new to do with pineapple chunks: one evening, if you're rather bored and haven't got much to do, why not try putting the pieces together again.   **KENNETH WILLIAMS**

Custard powder has been one of our minor national tragedies.   **JANE GRIGSON**

—Fruit cocktail and squirty cream?
—No juice for me, mam.   **BARBARA AND DENISE ROYLE,** *THE ROYLE FAMILY*

Oh bring back the roly-poly pudding,
Bread and butter pudding...Spotted Dick!   **PAM AYRES**

—What's long and thin, covered in skin; red in parts, and goes in tarts? —Rhubarb.
RIDDLE

I always spell plumb-pudding so – I think it sounds fatter and more suetty.
CHARLES LAMB

English puddings are eaten to keep out the cold.   **LEN DEIGHTON**

If Lord Berners' mood was pink, lunch might consist of beet soup, lobster, tomatoes, strawberries, with pigeons flying about outside dyed pink to match.   **ANON**

I never see any home cooking. All I get is fancy stuff.   **PRINCE PHILIP**

Lady Desborough's food is fussy and over-elaborate. You know the kind of thing – the salad was decorated with the Lord's Prayer in beetroot.
MARGOT ASQUITH

Things taste better in small houses.   **QUEEN VICTORIA**

My cook gets £80 a year and gives me a kipper. Sullivan's cook gets £500 a year and gives him the same thing in French.   **W.S. GILBERT**

All millionaires love a baked apple. **RONALD FIRBANK**

My New Year's Resolution: I'm going to start making Cup-a-Soup in a bowl instead of a cup because it will seem more of a meal that way.

NATALIE COOK

We English don't have a lot to be proud of but we can be proud of our mustard. On the continent mustard is used to bring out the flavour of meat, but English mustard really makes your nose bleed. **JACK DEE**

The French cook; we open tins.

JOHN GALSWORTHY

The cook was a good cook, as cooks go; and as cooks go she went. **SAKI**

—Have you had your tea?
—Yeah.
—What d'ya have?
—Dairylea on toast...I made it myself.

BARBARA AND DENISE ROYLE, *THE ROYLE FAMILY*

We may find in the long run that tinned food is a deadlier weapon than the machine-gun. **GEORGE ORWELL, 1937**

I thought my mother was a bad cook, but at least her gravy used to move about a bit. **TONY HANCOCK**

The nearest her cooking comes to the poetic is, perhaps, in her baked jam roll, which I have always found to be an emotion best recollected in tranquillity. **JOHN MORTIMER,** *RUMPOLE OF THE BAILEY*

I went to a Cordon Bleu cookery school quite unable to boil an egg, and came out with Homard Thermidor and Crêpes Suzette at my fingertips. I was still unable to boil an egg, however. **MONICA DICKENS**

Too many cooks, in baking rock cakes, get misled by the word 'rock'.

P.G. WODEHOUSE

Samantha is an expert cook and is often to be seen at the nearby inn, enjoying some of the local pork in cider.

HUMPHREY LYTTELTON

Marmite has given me a very useful phrase to describe certain people. I call thcm 'Marmite people' – very little goes a long way.

CLARE RAYNER

The advantage of Irish stew is that you get rid of such a lot of things.

JEROME K. JEROME

He never touches water: it goes to his head at once.

OSCAR WILDE

Darling, You Shouldn't Have Gone To So Much Trouble

ALICE THOMAS ELLIS, COOKERY BOOK TITLE

I've got Gordon Ramsay's new cook book, *Take Two Eggs and Fuck Off*.

JACK DEE

Oysters are considered to be an aphrodisiac. Not true. A few weeks ago I had twelve and only eight of them worked.

CLEMENT FREUD

Cooking is a minor art. I can't imagine a hilarious soufflé, or a deeply moving stew.

KENNETH TYNAN

And now with some pleasure I find that it's seven; and must cook dinner. Haddock and sausage meat. I think it is true that one gains a certain hold on sausage and haddock by writing them down.

VIRGINIA WOOLF

A woman should never be seen eating or drinking, unless it be lobster salad and champagne, the only truly feminine viands. **LORD BYRON**

And she made him a feast at his earnest wish
Of eggs and buttercups fried with fish.

EDWARD LEAR, *THE POBBLE WHO HAS NO TOES*

A picnic is the Englishman's grand gesture, his final defiance flung in the face of fate. No climate in the world is less propitious to picnics than the climate of England, yet with a recklessness which is almost sublime the English rush out of doors to eat a meal on every possible and impossible occasion. **GEORGINA BATTISCOMBE**

Looking across the gathering, I was struck by the delightfully disorganised chaos that seems to attend the British picnic – tweed clad figures arising from a sea of paper and plastic. Everyone jovial with an *esprit* a bit like that which unites refugees. **SIR ROY STRONG**

Things Not to be Forgotten at a Picnic: A stick of horseradish, a bottle of mint-sauce well-corked, a bottle of salad-dressing, a bottle of vinegar, made mustard, pepper, salt, good oil, and pounded sugar. If it can be managed, take a little ice...also teacups and saucers, three or four teapots, some lump sugar, and milk, if this last-named article cannot be obtained in the neighbourhood. Take three corkscrews. **ISABELLA BEETON**

Picnic: A meal of tinned food eaten in a motor-car by the roadside.

J.B. MORTON

Korean food is great. It's the dog's bollocks. **JIMMY CARR**

Vindaloo is a great British dish. It's the staple diet of more than 90 per cent of Britain's colonic masochists. **JONATHAN MEADES**

—I've got some Indian takeaway for my dinner.
—Then will you kindly eat it in the kitchen with the extractor fan full on. The last time, this upholstery reeked of vindaloo for over a week.

JERRY AND MARGOT LEADBETTER, *THE GOOD LIFE*

If you eat a lot of spicy food you can damage your sense of taste. I was in India last year and found myself listening to a lot of Michael Bolton.

JIMMY CARR

I bit the head off a live bat the other night. It tasted like a Crunchie wrapped in chamois leather.

OZZY OSBOURNE

My favourite sexual fantasy is smearing my naked body with chocolate and cream and being left in a room on my own to eat it.

JO BRAND

No one has yet had the star-defying audacity to hint at a separation between bread and cheese.

G.K. CHESTERTON

I knew a cannibal who had been influenced by Catholic missionaries. On Fridays he ate only fisherman.

TOMMY COOPER

VEGETARIAN

Tell me, have you eaten that or are you going to?

J.M. BARRIE TO GEORGE BERNARD SHAW WITH A PLATEFUL OF GREENS

A mind of the calibre of mine cannot derive its nutriment from cows.

GEORGE BERNARD SHAW

I won't eat anything that has intelligent life, but I'd gladly eat a politician.

MARTY FELDMAN

Carbonated Spring Water. Suitable for vegetarians.

LABEL ON BOTTLE

Vegetarianism is harmless enough, though it is apt to fill a man with wind and self-righteousness. **SIR ROBERT HUTCHINSON**

Hardcore vegans won't drive through towns with 'ham' in the name.

BILL BAILEY

My funeral will not be followed by mourning coaches but by herds of oxen, sheep, swine, flocks of poultry, and a small travelling aquarium of live fish, all wearing white scarves in honour of the man who perished rather than eat his fellow creatures. It will be, with the exception of the procession into Noah's Ark, the most remarkable thing of the kind ever seen. **GEORGE BERNARD SHAW**

RESTAURANT

The idea for 'The Frog and Peach' came to me in the bath... I suddenly thought, as I was scrubbing my back with a loofah, I thought, 'Where can a young couple, who are having an evening out, not too much money, and they want to have a decent meal, you know, a decent frog and a nice bit of peach, where can they go and get it?' And answer came there none. And so I had this idea of starting a restaurant specialising in these frogs' legs and peaches, and on this premise I built this restaurant. **PETER COOK**

There are two different kinds of people. There are those who will gladly choose a new and interesting-sounding dish on a menu, and those who, afraid of anything unfamiliar, will persuade someone else at the table to choose it, so that they can have a taste. **MILES KINGTON**

You should try everything once except incest and steak tartar.

PHILIP HOWARD

—What's the chicken like?
—It doesn't like anything. It's dead. **SPIKE MILLIGAN**

—There's only two other dishes on the menu really. There's frog à la pêche, which is a frog done in Cointreau with a peach stuffed in its mouth. And then, of course, pêche à la frog, which is really not much to write home about...

—I suppose this sort of menu could, in fact, appeal to the French?

PETER COOK AND DUDLEY MOORE

Tough? Tough? It's the toughest chicken I've ever known. It's asked me for a fight in the car park twice. **DEL BOY TROTTER, ONLY FOOLS AND HORSES**

—It's nouvelle cuisine.
—You don't get much.
—But it's very well presented.
—So is *Blue Peter.* **ERIC GARTSIDE AND SHELLEY UNWIN, CORONATION STREET**

The anchovy starter was the worst thing I've eaten since I inadvertently swallowed a large flying insect while laughing open-mouthed in Greece.

SUE TOWNSEND

'Turbot, Sir,' said the waiter, placing before me two fishbones, two eyeballs, and a bit of black mackintosh. **THOMAS EARLE WELBY**

There are people chefs hate more than food critics, namely, those who ask for their steak well done. ANGUS DEAYTON

The bread ate as if it had been made by a manic depressive creative therapy class. **A.A. GILL**

'This coffee tastes like mud,' I said. 'I'm not surprised,' the waitress said, 'it was only ground this morning.' **LES DAWSON**

Well, that soup might be a big event in a day in the life of Ivan Denisovich but it didn't do much for me.   **RUSSELL HARTY**

The vol-au-vent is the single nastiest thing ever invented as a food that doesn't involve an initiation ceremony. This one was like eating a ripe camel's conjunctive eye socket.   **A.A. GILL**

Charles took me to dine at Boulestins. Oysters, red mullet grilled with a slip of banana laid along it like a medieval wife on a tomb.

SYLVIA TOWNSEND WARNER

Salad, I can't bear salad. It grows while you're eating it, you know. You start one side of your plate and by the time you've got to the other, there's a fresh crop of lettuce taken root and sprouted up. **ALAN AYCKBOURN**

The waiter should bring in a small dish of olives exactly as if he were carrying John the Baptist's head on a platter.   **PAUL EDWARDS**

—Is there anywhere they do French food?
—Yes, France, I believe. They seem to like it there.

MR JOHNSON AND BASIL FAWLTY, *FAWLTY TOWERS*

When I ask for a watercress sandwich, I do not mean a loaf with a field in the middle of it. OSCAR WILDE

'Would you like the wine list,' the waiter would ask. 'Not really,' Dad would say, and one had to be quick in order to stop Mam explaining about his duodenal ulcer. Mind you, what wine was there that would go with spaghetti on toast? 'Which is really all we want at this time in the evening.'

ALAN BENNETT

A garçon entered with an enormous omelettc soufflé...all puff, by Jove!
A regular humbug – a balloon pudding in short! I won't eat such stuff....
I like the solids; – will trouble you for some of that cheese, sir, and don't
let it taste of the knife.

R.S. SURTEES

You ponce in here expecting to be waited on hand and foot while I'm trying to run a hotel here!

BASIL FAWLTY, *FAWLTY TOWERS*

Great restaurants are, of course, nothing but mouth-brothels. There is no
point in going to them if one intends to keep one's belt buckled.

FREDERIC RAPHAEL

Our studenty waitress took so long to fetch our fizzy water that it
would have been quicker to fly to Switzerland and fill a flask from an
Alpine spring.

MATTHEW NORMAN

What looked like a sea mine in miniature was the most disgusting thing
I've put in my mouth since I ate earthworms at school.

MATTHEW FORT

Black Forest Gâteau and apple pie: both would have worried gypsy caterers
at a Troggs concert in Norwich.

A.A. GILL

The taste and texture of the pease pudding reminded me of occasions
when I have accidentally inhaled while emptying the Dyson.

GILES COREN

Memo to meek diners: bellow for better service. My best method,
which I use a great deal, is to raise my napkin in the air, arm outstretched
above the head, and wave it around slowly. That always gets them.

MICHAEL WINNER

The snails had their horns and were curled up and wrinkled like frost-bitten snotty noses boiled to death in their beds. But the taste was miraculous.

A.A. GILL

The lighting in a restaurant should be dark enough to be discreet, light enough for a short-sighted person to read a menu, and not quite so light as to let people read the prices without looking most carefully.   **CLEMENT FREUD**

Never dine in a restaurant where the speciality of the house is the Heimlich manoeuvre.

VICTOR LEWIS-SMITH

The name Big Mac is generally supposed to have come about because it is a big McDonald's burger, but in fact it was named after a big raincoat whose taste it so closely resembles.

JO BRAND

I wouldn't go in a fast-food outlet even to use the toilet.   **JONNY WILKINSON**

The secret of a restaurant is sharp knives.

GEORGE ORWELL

BREAKFAST

There are two different kinds of people. There are those who lay the table for breakfast the night before, and those who lay the table as they are actually eating breakfast.

MILES KINGTON

[*matter-of-factly, to Jessie, over breakfast*] You're nude in *The Telegraph*, dear. Can you pass the bacon.

RICHARD, *CALENDAR GIRLS*

What? Sunday morning in an English family and no sausages? God bless my soul, what's the world coming to?

DOROTHY L. SAYERS

He that but looketh on a plate of ham and eggs to lust after it, hath already committed breakfast with it in his heart.

C.S. LEWIS

The British are better at breakfast and umbrellas. **REGINALD JACKSON**

To eat well in England, you should have breakfast three times a day.

W. SOMERSET MAUGHAM

Tourists tend to enjoy the traditional English breakfasts because they don't eat such things often at home. If they did, they would die.

LONELY PLANET GUIDE TO BRITAIN

Eating an egg is always an adventure. **OSCAR WILDE**

My boiled eggs are FANTASTIC, FABULOUS. Sometimes as hard as a 100 carat diamond, or again as soft as a feather bed, or running like a cooling stream, they can also burst like fireworks from their shells and take on the rubbery look of a baby octopus. **NANCY MITFORD**

Yesterday morning my wife asked me to make love to her in the kitchen. When I asked why, she said the egg timer had broken and she wanted a soft boiled egg. **DAVID BRINHAM**

The hymn *Onward Christian Soldiers* sung to the right tune and in a not-too-brisk tempo, makes a very good egg-timer. If you put the egg into boiling water and sing all five verses and chorus, the egg will be just right when you come to Amen. **DAILY TELEGRAPH**

The wife was up. I could hear her scraping the toast. **LES DAWSON**

He thought of toast in a Gothic Revival toast-rack like the nave of some miniature cathedral. **DENTON WELCH**

I always drink champagne for breakfast. Doesn't everyone? **NOËL COWARD**

In England people actually try to be brilliant at breakfast. That is so dreadful of them! Only dull people are brilliant at breakfast.   **OSCAR WILDE**

She was definitely the sort of girl who puts her hand over her husband's eyes, as he is crawling into breakfast with a morning head, and says: 'Guess who?'   **P.G. WODEHOUSE**

Thirsting for conversation, Cocklecarrot sought to kindle his wife's imagination by saying at breakfast, 'My love, hasn't E.D. Wivens fallen down the manhole again yet?'   **J.B. MORTON**

My wife and I tried two or three times in the last few years to have breakfast together, but it was so disagreeable we had to stop.

WINSTON CHURCHILL

For breakfast, at present, and as a rule, I take nothing but a cup of tea and the newspapers; and equally, as a rule, I can't get through either of them.   **GEORGE AUGUSTUS SALA**

TEA

—I spy with my little eye something beginning with 'T'.
—Breakfast. My breakfast always begins with tea.

BLACKADDER AND BALDRICK, *BLACKADDER II*

The best thing to do, when you've got a dead body and it's your husband's on the kitchen floor, and you don't know what to do about it, is to make yourself a good strong cup of tea.   **ANTHONY BURGESS**

Ma always said that without tea the British would have lost both world wars.   **MICHAEL BENTINE**

Milk and then just as it comes dear?   **SIR JOHN BETJEMAN**

When I was released from death row in Malaysia, I stood under the shower for what seemed like an hour and since then I have been drinking endless cups of tea.   **DAVID CHELL**

William Gladstone invariably filled his hot water bottle with tea, which he drank the next morning.   **LAWRENCE WRIGHT**

Is it me or is *EastEnders* sponsored by the tea marketing board?   JONATHAN ROSS

The pleasures of afternoon tea run like a trickle of honey through English literature from Rupert Brooke's wistful lines on the Old Vicarage at Grantchester to Miss Marple, calmly dissecting a case over tea-cakes at a seaside hotel.   **STAN HEY**

As an example of the undeviating tea-table habits of the house of Harrington, General Lincoln Stanhope once told me that, after an absence of several years in India, he made his reappearance at Harrington House, and found the family, as he had left them on his departure, drinking tea in the long gallery. On his presenting himself, his father's only observation and speech of welcome to him was, 'Hallo, Linky, my dear boy! Delighted to see you. Have a cup of tea?'   **REES HOWELL GRONOW**

Our trouble is that we drink too much tea. I see in this the slow revenge of the Orient, which has diverted the Yellow River down our throats.

J.B. PRIESTLEY

Whatever the vagaries of fashion in English tea-drinking, one institution remains inviolable and rock-solid: the early morning cuppa prepares the Englishman for the day ahead...Traditionally, and quite properly made by the man of the house.   **GODFREY SMITH**

American-style iced tea is the perfect drink for a hot, sunny day. It's never really caught on in the UK, probably because the last time we had a hot, sunny day was back in 1957.

TOM HOLT

FAT

—Just look at the size of your stomach! What would you say if that was on a woman?
—Half an hour ago, it was.

NANCY ASTOR AND LORD CASTLEROSSE

Floating in his pool, he was just the reverse of an iceberg – 90 per cent of him was visible.

PETER USTINOV

His waistcoat swelled like the sail of a racing yacht.

P.G. WODEHOUSE

I am asked to deny once again the rumour that Lady Cabstanleigh is to be floodlit.

J.B. MORTON

I'm anorexic actually. Anorexic people look in the mirror and think they look fat, and so do I.

JO BRAND

DIET AND EXERCISE

You know what Rik Waller's body fat was? Sixty per cent. I looked that up. That is the same per cent fat as a pork scratching.

RICKY GERVAIS

Sex for breakfast, sex for dinner, sex for tea, and sex for supper...
Have you never heard of it? It's called the F-plan.

SHIRLEY VALENTINE

I went to a party in a large white sheet – as Alaska.

JO BRAND

I yearn to be like one of those women you see photographed on yoga pamphlets, on the tip of a jetty, possibly not in Margate: 'Daz-white lycra; lotus position; face and palms upturned to the sun' who look so serene and unpolluted that, I suspect, should you cut them they will bleed Evian.

DEBORAH ROSS

To lose two pounds of body fat you would have to walk from London to Dover and then swim the Channel. **RICHARD GORDON**

My dream was to have a wedding reception in a marquee, not to be wearing a marquee. MANDY RUFFLES, SLIMMER OF THE YEAR, 2001

I'm not fat. I'm three laxatives away from being Posh Spice.

MARIA MOOGAN, *VON TRAPPED*

If I had been around when Rubens was painting, I would have been revered as a fabulous model. Kate Moss? She would have been the paintbrush. **DAWN FRENCH**

No one ever made a success in the world without a large bottom.

ADAM SEDGWICK

It's easy to distract fat people. A piece of cake. **CHRIS ADDISON**

My doctor recommends I take a daily walk on an empty stomach. Whose?

REVD SYDNEY SMITH

The mere pursuit of health always leads to something unhealthy. Physical pleasure must not be made the direct object of obedience; it must be enjoyed, not worshipped. **G.K. CHESTERTON**

I like long walks, especially when they are taken by people who annoy me.

NOËL COWARD

My idea of going for a walk is sitting on a gate.   **W. SOMERSET MAUGHAM**

My only encounter with exercise is when I once jogged to the ashtray.

WILL SELF

The only exercise I take is walking behind the coffins of friends who took exercise.   **PETER O'TOOLE**

It's put-downs not press-ups that keep a man on his toes.   **JEFFREY BERNARD**

Free your mind, and your bottom will follow.   **SARAH FERGUSON**

I have never been able to sacrifice my appetite on the altar of appearance.

ROBERT MORLEY

Porridge fills the Englishman up, prunes clear him out.   **E.M. FORSTER**

Don't dig your grave with your own knife and fork.   **ENGLISH PROVERB**

I would rather eat a cream cake than take Prozac.   CLARISSA DICKSON-WRIGHT

The Japanese eat very little fat and suffer fewer heart attacks than the British or Americans. The French eat a lot of fat and also have fewer heart attacks than the British or Americans. The Japanese drink very little red wine and suffer fewer heart attacks than the British or Americans. The Italians drink excessive amounts of red wine and also suffer fewer heart attacks than the British or Americans. Conclusion: Eat and drink what you like. What kills you is speaking English.   **MICHAEL FITZPATRICK**

Everything I eat has been proved by some doctor or other to be a deadly poison, and everything I don't eat has been proved to be indispensable for life.　　**GEORGE BERNARD SHAW**

HEALTH AND MEDICINE

I haven't felt myself all day.　　**LARRY GRAYSON**

I do have to be careful about my health because I have a grumbling ovary, which once flared up in the middle of *The Gondoliers*.　　**KITTY, *VICTORIA WOOD***

Fifteen years ago, Britain was a great country in which to have a heart attack in the street.　　**JOHN LE CARRÉ**

Everyone goes into an aeroplane or a hospital wondering if they'll ever get out of either again alive.　　**RICHARD GORDON**

—My brother-in-law tells me that Peckham General is the filthiest hospital in the country.
—What does your brother-in-law know about it?
—He's the head cleaner.　　**GRIFF RHYS JONES AND MEL SMITH**

No bloody mini-bar!
　　PATSY STONE CHECKING INTO HER HOSPITAL ROOM, *ABSOLUTELY FABULOUS*

I hastened over to the Orthopaedic Ward, hoping to find the man who knew more about surgical procedures than anyone else in the hospital. Luckily he was still in his Porter's Cubicle.　　**DENIS NORDEN**

—How are you feeling?
—I'm dying but otherwise I'm in perfect health.　　**FRIEND AND EDITH SITWELL**

Barium: purée of tombstone.　　**JONATHAN MILLER**

After the hospital food, a Barium meal is a treat. It goes in like liquid clay and comes out like a 62-piece earthenware tea-set. If you've got constipation, well, then you've got an early Henry Moore on your hands.

GRIFF RHYS JONES

Half the patients who get up in the middle of the night and think they are dying are suffering from wind.

FRANCES BRETT YOUNG

Besides death, constipation is the big fear in hospitals.

ROBERT McCRUM

I had never seen Sister close to before. This unexpected proximity had the effect of being in a rowing-boat under the bows of the Queen Mary.

RICHARD GORDON

—Come, come, Matron, surely you've seen a temperature taken like this before?
—Yes, Colonel, but never with a daffodil.

WILFRED HYDE-WHITE AND MATRON, CARRY ON NURSE

In hospitals there is no time off for good behaviour.

JOSEPHINE TEY

To nab a nurse for a bedpan outside regulation hours is an art compared with which catching a waiter's eye in a busy restaurant is simple.

RICHARD GORDON

When I was a nurse, my favourite assignment was the anorexic ward. Sometimes I ate as many as 17 dinners.

JO BRAND

How to tell the difference between a cold and flu: if there's a £50 note in the middle of a field and you can reach it, you haven't got flu.

DIANA WAINMAN

The modern sympathy with invalids is morbid. Illness of any kind is hardly a thing to be encouraged in others.   **OSCAR WILDE**

His chief allergies include nephews, Scottish traditional songs and male secretaries.   **P.G. WODEHOUSE**

Do I examine myself for testicular cancer? I do. But I do it on the train.
                                                                           ARTHUR SMITH

If you have an artificial leg make it unnoticeable by wearing long trousers.
                                                                     O. CRAIG, VIZ, TOP TIP

An independent healthcare regulator: Ofsick? What about Oftrolley?
                                                                       MICHAEL MOUNSEY

If you want a cure for a cold, put on two pullovers, take up a baton, poker or pencil, tune the radio to a symphony concert, stand on a chair, and conduct like mad for an hour or so and the cold will have vanished. It never fails. You know why conductors live so long? Because we perspire so much.   **SIR JOHN BARBIROLLI**

Mothers have colds; fathers have flu.

                                                                          A.J. WILCOCK

I have kleptomania, but when it gets bad, I take something for it. **KEN DODD**

A doctor is the only man without a guaranteed cure for a cold.
                                                                        DOMINIC CLEARY

—Doctor, Doctor, I can't stop singing 'The Green Green Grass of Home'.
—Sounds like Tom Jones syndrome.
—Is it common?
—Well, it's not unusual.   **TOMMY COOPER**

Bloke walks into the doctor's and says, 'Doctor, doctor, I've got a cricket ball stuck up my bum.' The doctor says, 'How's that?' and he replies, 'Don't you start!'

TOMMY COOPER

I went to the doctor and he said, 'You've got hypochondria.' I said, 'Not that as well!'

TIM VINE

—Do you find you can't finish the crossword like you used to, nasty taste in the mouth in the mornings, can't stop thinking about sex, wake up with a sweat in the mornings, keep falling asleep during 'Play For Today'?
—That's extraordinary, Doc! That's exactly how I've been feeling.
—So have I. I wonder what it is?

DOC MORRISSEY AND REGGIE PERRIN, *THE FALL AND RISE OF REGINALD PERRIN*

An apple a day keeps the doctor away, but in my experience so does an air rifle, top bedroom window.

HARRY HILL

One finger professionally, gentlemen; two fingers socially.

GYNAECOLOGISTS' CREED

I never could stand doctors. Well, they've got to find something wrong, haven't they? It's only professional.

JOYCE CARY

I wonder what an osteopath does if a patient suddenly comes apart in his hands?

P.G. WODEHOUSE

Lord Dawson was not a good doctor. King George V told me that he would never have died, had he had another doctor.

MARGOT ASQUITH

A doctor who isn't a hypochondriac is as rare as a teetotal pub-keeper.

RICHARD GORDON

I don't believer the kindliest of men ever learned about the death of his doctor without a feeling of smugness.

RICHARD GORDON

In a few moments I shall ask you to remove your clothes in their entirety...
I shall be as far from desire as a plumber uncovering a manhole.

ALAN BENNETT

MADNESS AND THERAPY

'Do you know if there was any insanity in her family?' 'Insanity?...
Her father lives in West Kensington, but I believe he's sane on all other
subjects.'

SAKI

They called me mad, and I called them mad, and damn them, they
outvoted me.

NATHANIEL LEE

Madmen are always serious; they go mad from lack of humour.

G.K. CHESTERTON

Five exclamation marks, the sure sign of an insane mind.

TERRY PRATCHETT

Poets do not go mad; but chess players do.

G.K. CHESTERTON

I didn't have a nervous breakdown. I was clinically fed up for two years.

ALAN PARTRIDGE

It is a common delusion that you make things better by talking about them.

ROSE MACAULAY

Noble deeds and hot baths are the best cure for depression.

DODIE SMITH

In moments of considerable strain I tend to take bread-and-butter
pudding. There is something about the blandness of soggy bread, the
crispness of the golden outer crust and the unadulterated pleasure of
lightly set custard that makes the world seem a better place to live.

CLEMENT FREUD

Audrey carried in the *Daily Telegraph*. Mother turned with avidity to the Deaths. When other helpers fail and comforts flee, when the senses decay and the mind moves in narrower and narrower circles, when the grasshopper is a burden and the postman brings no letters, and even the Royal Family is no longer quite what it was, an obituary column stands fast.   **SYLVIA TOWNSEND WARNER**

The trouble with tranquillisers is that you find yourself being nice to people you don't like.   **MARK BUSHMAN**

Depression is the most extreme form of vanity.   **JULIE BURCHILL**

If you feel depressed or let down, my advice is to roast a chicken.
                                                    DELIA SMITH

She were agoraphobic till they had that chip pan fire and then she were first out the house.   **KEN,** *EARLY DOORS*

One should only see a psychiatrist out of boredom.   **MURIEL SPARK**

Psychoanalysis is confession without absolution.   **G.K. CHESTERTON**

I have been discharged from the Mental Institute and I'm back at my old job in a solicitor's office. I work there as a teapot.   **LES DAWSON**

These days we have to call mental asylums 'care homes'. It's madness gone politically correct.   **ARMANDO IANNUCCI**

There is a pleasure in madness, which none but madmen know.
                                                    WILLIAM HAZLITT

DRUGS

I was horrified to find the other week that my second son is taking drugs. My very best ones too. **BOB MONKHOUSE**

I've never had a problem with drugs. I've had problems with the police. **KEITH RICHARDS**

In the 1960s people took acid to make the world weird. Now the world's weird and people take Prozac to make it normal. **DAMON ALBARN**

Taking LSD is like going to Stratford-on-Avon: you only need to go there once. **JOHN PEEL**

I once took marijuana but felt no effects as I was on coke at the time. **BOB MONKHOUSE**

My Barbie is a Crack Whore **SLOGAN ON CHARLOTTE CHURCH'S T-SHIRT**

I took some MC^2. It's great – just like E. **PHIL KAY**

In one week, Colin Farrell is said to have done 20 Es, 4 grams of coke, 6 of speed, half an ounce of hash, 3 bottles of Jack Daniels, 12 bottles of red wine, 60 pints, and 40 fags a day. Sounds like Harvest Festival at The Priory. **JONATHAN ROSS**

What's my view on drugs? I've forgotten my view on drugs. **BORIS JOHNSON, MP, CAMPAIGNING IN THE 2005 ELECTION**

I'm on so many pills, I'll need a childproof lid on my coffin. **PAUL O'GRADY**

I don't do drugs. If I want a rush I just get out of a chair when I'm not expecting it. **DYLAN MORAN**

I was in a nightclub with my producer, John Walters, when a famous rock star who shall be nameless walked up to me and said, 'Hey, man, come to the concert on Saturday.' He winked and pressed something into my hand. 'Take these,' he said. In the dark club, I looked into my hands and saw he'd given me some pink pills. I'm scared of things like that so I decided to just throw them away there and then. Ages later, I met the rock star again. I told him that I'd enjoyed the concert but I'd not taken the pink pills he'd given me. 'Good thing,' he said, 'they were earplugs.'

JOHN PEEL

Soon after my grandmother's death we were amused to find among the odds and ends in her dressing-table drawer a bottle labelled 'Might be Aspirin.'

JEAN GIBBS

I *can* drink, and bear a good deal of wine: but it don't exhilarate – it makes me savage and suspicious. Laudanum has a similar effect...but the thing that gives me the highest spirits (it seems absurd, but true), is a dose of *salts*.

LORD BYRON

My Lords, I regret to say that this is a drug to which all the evidence shows the House of Lords is seriously addicted; and the drug in question is tea.

BARONESS WOOTON

ALCOHOL

Come on, Manny. You can find work and sort your life out anytime. The pub closes in five hours.

BERNARD BLACK, *BLACK BOOKS*

What two ideas are more inseparable than Beer and Britannia?

REVD SYDNEY SMITH

I can't stand light. I hate weather. My idea of heaven is moving from one smoke-filled room to another.

PETER O'TOOLE

Right, here's the plan. First, we go in there and get wrecked, then we eat a pork pie, then we drop some Surmontil-50s each. That way we'll miss out on Monday and come up smiling Tuesday morning.

WITHNAIL, *WITHNAIL AND I*

Two fat blokes in a pub, one says to the other 'Your round.' The other one says, 'So are you, you fat bastard.'

TOMMY COOPER

On the chest of a barmaid in Sale
Were tattooed the prices of ale,
And on her behind,
For the sake of the blind,
Was the same information in Braille.

ANON

The Boy's First Pint was about as close as middle-class, middle-century, middle England ever got to the bar mitzvah.

JONATHAN MEADES

A tavern chair is the home of human felicity.

SAMUEL JOHNSON

I have stood in a bar in Lambourn and been offered, in the space of five minutes, a poached salmon, a leg of a horse, a free trip to Chantilly, marriage, a large unsolicited loan, ten tips for a ten-horse race, two second-hand cars, a fight, and the copyright to a dying jockey's life story.

JEFFREY BERNARD

I only take a drink on two occasions – when I'm thirsty and when I'm not.

BRENDAN BEHAN

Artists are renowned for being binge drinkers. Have you ever had a bottle of binge?

PAUL MERTON TO TRACEY EMIN

Ah, Seven Up – Snow White's favourite drink.

DAVE ALLEN

If all else fails, he will drink ink.

ANON ON RICHARD PORSON, ENGLISH SCHOLAR

—Sweetie, what are you drinking?
—Oh this? Chanel No. 5.

EDINA MONSOON AND PATSY STONE, *ABSOLUTELY FABULOUS*

'I love a Martini,' said Mabel,
'I only have two at the most.
After three I am under the table,
After four, I am under the host.'

ANON

Cocktails have all the disagreeability without the utility of a disinfectant.

SHANE LESLIE

He handed me a tumbler containing what I tried, with some success, not to think of as a urine sample from one gravely ill.

KINGSLEY AMIS

Gin is a dangerous drink. It's clear and innocuous looking. You also have to be 45, female and sitting on the stairs.

DYLAN MORAN

Champagne has the taste of an apple peeled with a steel knife.

ALDOUS HUXLEY

—Raspberries...myrtles...heather...honeysuckle...I'm getting melons, with marram grass...
—Personally, I prefer my wine to taste of grapes.

JONATHAN MEADES

I was called out of a wine-tasting to a non-existent phone call. When I returned I lifted my glass, smelled and said, 'My God, this is foul, it smells like piss.' A voice from the back called out, 'We know, but *whose*?'

T.P. WHELEHAN

At a recent wine-tasting a man inhaled deeply and proclaimed, 'I'm getting Brazilian woman.'

JONATHAN MEADES

Compromises are for relationships, not wine.

SIR ROBERT SCOTT CAYWOOD

The juice of the grape is the liquid quintessence of concentrated sunbeams.

THOMAS LOVE PEACOCK

This is the sulphurous urination of some aged horse.

D.H. LAWRENCE ON SPANISH WINE

Wine should be stored in a cool, dry place. The glove compartment of a Jaguar or an abandoned washing machine are my personal favourites.

RICHARD SMITH

One of the disadvantages of wine is that it makes a man mistake words for thoughts.

SAMUEL JOHNSON

Never drink claret in an East wind. Never sit on a hard chair after drinking port.

REVD H.J. BIDDER

Harry Lauder always drank from a bottle in a paper bag; it gave him an air of respectability.

SPIKE MILLIGAN

We don't know much about the human conscience, except that it is soluble in alcohol.

JOHN MORTIMER

All I can say is that I have taken more out of alcohol than alcohol has taken out of me.

WINSTON CHURCHILL

Malt does more than Milton can,
To justify God's ways to man.

A.E. HOUSMAN

I never turned to drink. It seemed to turn to me.

BRENDAN BEHAN

I haven't touched a drop of alcohol since the invention of the funnel.

MALACHY MCCOURT

The only proper intoxication is conversation.

WINSTON CHURCHILL

Too young to die. Too drunk to live.   **RENEE MCCALL ON BRENDAN BEHAN**

I am sparkling; *you* are unusually talkative; *he* is drunk.   *NEW STATESMAN*

Try opening your eyes. It's like when you were young and you used to take the cellophane wrapper from a Quality Street toffee and hold it over your eyes.   **STEPHEN FRY**

His mouth had been used as a latrine by some small creature of the night, and then as its mausoleum.   **KINGSLEY AMIS,** *LUCKY JIM*

—So, you got drunk again last night. Why was that?
—Because I was sober.   **ARDAL O'HANLON**

I often sit back and think, 'I wish I'd done that,' and find out, after my hangover has worn off, that I already have.   **RICHARD HARRIS**

I once woke up in a drawer at the bottom of a wardrobe. That was fairly frightening. Try opening a drawer from the inside. It's quite tricky.

JEFFREY BERNARD

Sir, – The publishers, Michael Joseph, have asked me to write my autobiography and I'd be grateful if you could give me any information about my whereabouts and behaviour between 1960 and 1974.

JEFFREY BERNARD, LETTER IN THE *NEW STATESMAN*, 1975

Dear Mr Bernard, – I read with interest your letter asking for information as to your whereabouts and behaviour between the years 1960–74. On a certain evening in September 1969 you rang my mother to inform her that you were going to murder her only son. If you would like further information I can put you in touch with many people who have enjoyed similar bizarre experiences in your company. Yours sincerely.

MICHAEL J. MOLLOY, EDITOR OF THE *DAILY MIRROR*, 1975

I hear the Duke of Ancaster has left a legacy to a very small man that was his companion, and who, when he was drunk, he used to fling at the heads of the company, as others fling a bottle. **HORACE WALPOLE**

There is a certain social barrier between the drunk and the sober which is very difficult to bridge. Especially on a narrow stairway. **MICHAEL FRAYN**

An alcoholic is someone who drinks more than their doctor. **BARRY CRYER**

I once asked an alcoholic doctor how did he first know he was an alcoholic and he told me, 'When I sprayed vaginal deodorant on a man's face'. **JEFFREY BERNARD**

It took a lot of bottle for him to own up to his alcoholism. **IAN WRIGHT**

I couldn't go to AA meetings. I couldn't drive. I was too drunk. **FRANK SKINNER**

People say, 'Now you've given up the booze at least you can remember what you did last night.' I say, 'Yeah, nothing.' **FRANK SKINNER**

What is the point of warning young people about the evils of alcohol? They know them already and can see them every day in the streets or in the House of Commons. I should imagine there are a few grog blossoms in the House of Lords too. **JEFFREY BERNARD**

I am a teetotaller because my family has already paid its debt to the distilling industry so munificently as to leave me no further obligation. **GEORGE BERNARD SHAW**

I am a strict teetotaller. I never take anything between drinks. **JAMES JOYCE**

SMOKING

—You got a light, mac?
—No, but I got a dark brown overcoat.   **VIVIAN STANSHALL**

If God had intended men to smoke he'd have put chimneys in their heads.
                                                          J.B. PRIESTLEY

If it's good enough for beagles, it's good enough for me.   **RICHARD LITTLEJOHN**

Did you know that by the time he'd turned 80, Winston Churchill had
coronary thrombosis, three attacks of pneumonia, a hernia, two strokes
and something called senile itch? All the same, though often setting fire to
himself, he still managed to enjoy a cigar.   **BERYL BAINBRIDGE**

A good cigar is as great a comfort to a man as a good cry is to a woman.
                                                    SIR EDWARD BULWER LYTTON

—Name a major disease associated with smoking.
—Premature death.   **GCSE EXAM ANSWER**

There are various ways to give up smoking – nicotine patches, nicotine
gum. My auntie used to pour a gallon of petrol over herself every
morning.   **PAUL MERTON**

Give up smoking by sticking one cigarette from each new pack up a fat
friend's arse, filter first, then replacing it in the box. The possibility of
putting that one in your mouth will put you off smoking any of them.
                                                          VIZ, TOP TIP

One MP said, 'Smoking shouldn't be banned. It's the only thing single
parents on estates have left to enjoy.' That's not true. What about joy-
riding and incest?   **ANGUS DEAYTON, *HAVE I GOT NEWS FOR YOU***

Since giving up smoking, I have no urge to take up the habit again, but I now talk to myself – mostly about Winston Churchill – sing hymns out loud while in the queue at the bank, and find it extremely difficult to construct a worthwhile sentence. **BERYL BAINBRIDGE**

Ciggie-loving Marie Ellis was laid to rest yesterday – after living to 105 despite smoking nearly half a million fags. She was cremated clutching a packet of her favourite Benson & Hedges with flowers in the shape of a cigarette laid on top of her coffin. Staff and residents from the nursing home sent her off with a chorus of *Smoke Gets In Your Eyes*. **THE SUN**

SLEEP

One of the most adventurous things left is to go to bed, for no one can lay a hand on our dreams. **E.V. LUCAS**

You eat, in dreams, the custard of the day. **ALEXANDER POPE**

An eight-hour peep show of infantile erotica. **J.G. BALLARD**

I dreamt last night I was chopping up carrots with the Grim Reaper: dicing with death. **TIM VINE**

My most frequent dream is that I am back at school, trying to construe difficult passages from Greek authors unknown to me. **A.A. MILNE**

I dreamt that I was making a speech in the House of Lords. I woke up, and by Jove I was! **DUKE OF DEVONSHIRE**

I am sure that it was only because Michelangelo was engaged in the ancient and honourable occupation of lying in bed that he ever realised how the roof of the Sistine Chapel might be made into an awful imitation of a divine drama that could only be acted in the heavens. **G.K. CHESTERTON**

How can I sleep? Every time I nod off, I have this hideous dream that I'm imprisoned in a lunatic asylum and Arthur Askey is singing underneath the window. **VICTOR MELDREW,** *ONE FOOT IN THE GRAVE*

Have you noticed there is never any third act in a nightmare? They bring you to a climax of terror and then leave you there. They are the work of poor dramatists. **SIR MAX BEERBOHM**

I did not sleep. I never do when I am over-happy, under-happy, or in bed with a strange man. **EDNA O'BRIEN**

As a cricket fan, I find that the most effective way of encouraging sleep is to imagine that I am a bowler faced with Trevor Bailey. I shuffle up, bowl, Bailey blocks, the ball returns down the pitch to me, I collect it, return to my run-up point, bowl, Bailey blocks. Before the over is completed I am asleep. **TIM BIDDISCOMBE**

A lady was awoken in the night with the disagreeable sense of not being alone in the room, and soon felt a thud upon her bed. There was no doubt that someone was moving to and fro in the room, and that hands were constantly moving over her bed. She was so dreadfully frightened that at last she fainted. When she came to herself, it was broad daylight, and she found that the butler had walked in his sleep and had laid the table for 14 upon her bed. **AUGUSTUS HARE**

Time for my afternoon nap. If God rings, tell Him I'm not in.
NOËL COWARD TO HIS PERSONAL ASSISTANT, COLE LESLEY

AGE AND YOUTH

There's a fascination frantic
In a ruin that's romantic;
Do you think you are sufficiently decayed? **W.S. GILBERT,** *THE MIKADO*

Every morning, when you are 93, you wake up and say to yourself, 'What, again?'

BEN TRAVERS

Time's wingèd chariot is starting to goose me.

NOËL COWARD

If you live to be 90 in England and can still eat a boiled egg they think you deserve the Nobel Prize.

ALAN BENNETT

'You are old, Father William,' the young man said,
'And your hair has become very white;
And yet you incessantly stand on your head –
Do you think, at your age, it is right?'

LEWIS CARROLL, *YOU ARE OLD, FATHER WILLIAM*

People always live for ever when there is any annuity to be paid to them.

JANE AUSTEN

Mrs Prentle, of 2 The Villas, Horsepot, celebrated her 143rd birthday yesterday, surrounded by her 398 children. Though still vigorous, Mrs Prentle persists in calling herself the oldest Etonian, and thinks that she rowed for Eton against the MCC in 1812, with Tchaikovsky as cox. Mrs Prentle has never seen a train.

J.B. MORTON

We are happier in many ways when we are old than when we were young. The young sow wild oats, the old grow sage.

WINSTON CHURCHILL

Middle age is when you look at the rain teeming down and say: 'That'll be good for the garden.'

GRACE MARSHALL

Middle age is that time in life when children and parents cause equal amounts of worry.

ROMY HALLIWELL

Anthony Powell lamented that 'growing old is like being increasingly penalised for a crime you haven't committed'. Now, well into my nineties, I prefer to regard each passing year as an extension of bail, despite the offences I have committed.

ALAN KING-HAMILTON

Young people make a lot of noise, and I don't really understand what they say. But I do admire them for being able to pee on the street.

ALAN BENNETT

One should never make one's debut in a scandal. One should reserve that to give interest to one's old age.

OSCAR WILDE

Middle-age – by which I mean anything over 20 and under 90.

A.A. MILNE

The middle age of buggers is not to be contemplated without horror.

VIRGINIA WOOLF

It's the menopause. I've got my own climate.

JULIE WALTERS

I've become a pensioner so I've started saving up for my own hospital trolley.

TOM BAKER

I could tell you were a pensioner. You've got one of those half-price haircuts.

KEN DODD

I'm far too old to retire.

ARTHUR LUNN, AGED 90

On a recent train journey, I asked the ticket inspector if he would like to see my senior rail card, to which he replied: 'No, thank you, sir, that won't be necessary.'

GEORGE PRATT

He was 50. It's the age when clergymen first begin to be preoccupied with the underclothing of little schoolgirls in trains, the age when eminent archaeologists start taking a really passionate interest in the Scout movement.

ALDOUS HUXLEY

I'm now at the age where I've got to prove that I'm just as good as I never was.

REX HARRISON

To my extreme mortification, I grow wiser every day.

LADY MARY WORTLEY MONTAGU

I am not so deaf as the man who said family prayers kneeling on the cat.

SIR WILLIAM RIDGEWAY

It is not the hearing that one misses but the over-hearing.

DAVID WRIGHT

I attribute my longevity to constant smoking and marrons glacés.

NOËL COWARD

Faces can lie, but not necks. Look at a horse's teeth and a woman's neck.

HENRY CECIL

One of the two things that men who have lasted for one hundred years always say: either that they have drunk whisky and smoked all their lives, or that neither tobacco nor spirits ever made the slightest appeal to them.

E.V. LUCAS

Moisturisers do work. The rest is pap. There is nothing on God's earth that will take away 30 years of arguing with your husband.

ANITA RODDICK

How foolish to think that one can ever slam the door in the face of age.
Much wiser to be polite and gracious and ask him to lunch in advance.

NOËL COWARD

—One lives and learns, doesn't one?
—That is certainly one of the more prevalent delusions.

NOËL COWARD, *NUDE WITH VIOLIN*

We talked about growing old gracefully
And Elsie who's seventy-four
Said, 'a) it's a question of being sincere,
And b) if you're supple you've nothing to fear.'
Then she swung upside down from a glass chandelier –
I couldn't have liked it more.

NOËL COWARD, *I'VE BEEN TO A MARVELLOUS PARTY*

I'm spending my old age carving at no charge mediaeval effigies in
limestone to replace those knocked from niches during the Reformation.

J.L. CARR

One evil in old age is that you think every little illness is the beginning
of the end. When a man expects to be arrested, every knock at the door is
an alarm.

REVD SYDNEY SMITH

DEATH

—He's been buried alive under a thousand tons of earth.
—Thank heavens he's safe.

SEAGOON AND MINNIE, *THE GOON SHOW*

Death has something to be said for it: There's no need to get out of bed
for it.

KINGSLEY AMIS

—Is he...dead?
—Well, put it this way, I needn't have bothered rinsing out the extra mug.

MISS BERTA AND MRS OVERALL, *ACORN ANTIQUES*

If the guest isn't singing 'Oh What a Beautiful Morning', I don't immediately think, 'Oh there's another snuffed it in the night. Another name in the Fawlty Towers Book of Remembrance.' I mean this is a hotel, not the Burma Railway.

BASIL FAWLTY, *FAWLTY TOWERS*

If I were to choose where to die, it would be in the herbaceous border.

MIRIAM STOPPARD

Very irritating, death.

JOHN MORTIMER

I have been dead for two years, but I don't choose to have it known.

LORD CHESTERFIELD

I am ready to meet my Maker. Whether my Maker is prepared for the great ordeal of meeting me is another matter.

WINSTON CHURCHILL

Let me die eating ortolans to the sound of soft music.

BENJAMIN DISRAELI

I'd like to die on stage in the middle of a good performance and with a full house.

JOHN GIELGUD

I was offered the chance to do a tandem sky dive but I draw the line at that. That's no way to die. Imagine my mother at the funeral and the priest saying, 'He died as he lived: strapped to another man.'

DARA O'BRIAIN

I hope I go like mother. She just sat up, broke wind and died.

ENA SHARPLES, *CORONATION STREET*

He deserves to be preached to death by wild curates.   **REVD SYDNEY SMITH**

My grandmother made dying her life's work.   **HUGH LEONARD**

Crucifixion...it's a slow, horrible death. But at least it gets you out into the open.   **MATTHIAS, *MONTY PYTHON'S LIFE OF BRIAN***

There is nothing quite so good as burial at sea. It's simple, tidy, and not very incriminating.   **ALFRED HITCHCOCK**

When somebody told me that a man once died from excitement at a cricket match and another spectator gnawed the handle off his umbrella in a nervous spasm, it was hardly a shock. It seemed a pleasing way to die.   **JACK POLLARD**

May my last breath be drawn from a pipe and exhaled in a pun.   **CHARLES LAMB**

May you die in bed at 95, shot by a jealous spouse.   **IRISH BLESSING**

On 26 February 1994, J.L. Carr chuckled on hearing that Denis Compton's kneecap had been preserved in a cake tin at Lord's, and died.   **SIMON JENKINS**

John Le Mesurier wishes it to be known that he conked out on November 16th. He sadly misses family and friends.   **JOHN LE MESURIER, SELF-PENNED OBITUARY NOTICE**

My aunt died at precisely 10:47 a.m. and the old grandfather clock stopped precisely at this moment also. It fell on her.   **PAUL MERTON**

I blame myself for my boyfriend's death. I shot him.   **JO BRAND**

On 5 April 1998, following a courageous fight for life, Catherine Thomas, surrounded by family, died at home – and she's bloody annoyed.

OBITUARY NOTICE, *CARDIFF GAZETTE*

It's not pining, it's passed on. This parrot is no more. It's ceased to be. It's expired. It's gone to meet its maker. This is a late parrot. It's a stiff. Bereft of life it rests in peace. It would be pushing up the daisies if you hadn't nailed it to the perch. It's rung down the curtain and joined the choir invisible. It's an ex-parrot.   **JOHN CLEESE,** *MONTY PYTHON'S FLYING CIRCUS*

For most people, death comes at the end of their lives. **GREATER LONDON RADIO PRESENTER**

While other people's deaths are deeply sad, one's own is surely a bit of a joke.   **JAMES CAMERON**

To die will be an awfully big adventure.   **JAMES BARRIE,** *PETER PAN*

Everyone seems to fear dying alone and I have never understood this point of view. Who wants to have to die and be polite at the same time?

QUENTIN CRISP

Some people don't die; they go on a cruise instead.   **JOHN SERGEANT**

To the Bank of Scotland I bequeath my testicles, because it has no balls.

LORD ERSKINE

Too late for fruit, too soon for flowers.   **WALTER DE LA MARE, LAST WORDS**

Be British, boys, be British.   **CAPTAIN EDWARD SMITH OF THE** *TITANIC***, LAST WORDS**

There were no last words. His wife was with him to the end.   **LES DAWSON**

When Mr Overall was dying, he said, 'Well, Boadicea, I shall never have to play another game of travel Scrabble.'   MRS OVERALL, *ACORN ANTIQUES*

Max Miller's last words: 'Oh Mum,' to his wife. There is so much to dread.

JOHN OSBORNE

Stop dying at once, and when you get up, get your bloody hair cut!

LT. COL. ALFRED DANIEL WINTLE TO HIS CRITICALLY ILL BATMAN,
CEDRIC MAYS, WHO OBEYED THE ORDER

SUICIDE

On 14 April 1988 Kenneth Williams made a scene in the Oxford Circus tube station about the cost of repairing his mother's Timex watch: 'Charge was £4 which was after I'd remonstrated about £4.95!!' Then, having saved 95 pence, he walked home to kill himself.   PETER CONRAD

We cannot tear out a single page of our life, but we can throw the whole book in the fire.   GEORGE ELIOT

They're like poems, suicide notes: nearly everyone tries their hand at them some time, with or without the talent.   MARTIN AMIS

—If you want to end it all, drowning – now, there's a way to go.
—I can't swim.
—Well, you don't have to fuckin' swim, you divvy, that's the whole point. God, you're not very keen are you?   DAVE AND LOMPER, *THE FULL MONTY*

Self-decapitation is an extremely difficult, not to say dangerous, thing to attempt.   W.S. GILBERT, *THE MIKADO*

I thought about killing myself but I went on holiday to Belgium instead.

STEPHEN FRY

Dear World, I am leaving because I am bored. I feel I have lived long enough. I am leaving you with your worries in this sweet cesspool. Good luck.　　　　　　　　　　　　**GEORGE SANDERS, SUICIDE NOTE**

I was surprised to find that one of the all-time great cricketers had committed suicide. That, somehow, seems so very unlike the action of a cricketer. You can expect almost anything of a boxer but cricket and suicide seem strange bedfellows. Fielding at silly mid-on for a lousy bowler is just about as near to it as they come, or so I had thought.

JEFFREY BERNARD

There are many who dare not kill themselves for fear of what the neighbours will say.　　　　　　　　　　　　**CYRIL CONNOLLY**

FUNERAL

—So. You're going to Parslow's funeral.
—Yes. Even though it's very unlikely that he'll ever come to mine.

MRS BLEWITT AND ARKWRIGHT, *OPEN ALL HOURS*

In India, if a man dies, the widow flings herself onto the funeral pyre; if a man dies in this country, the woman just drags herself into the kitchen and says, 'Seventy-two baps, Connie, you slice, I'll spread.'　**VICTORIA WOOD**

The funeral cortege will stop outside the pub my parents ran together for many years. I think that is appropriate. My father never went on a long journey without stopping at a pub.　　**BILLY KEANE ON JOHN B. KEANE**

There's nothing like a morning funeral for sharpening the appetite for lunch.　　　　　　　　　　　　**ARTHUR MARSHALL**

In Liverpool, the difference between a funeral and a wedding is one less drunk.　　　　　　　　　　　　**PAUL O'GRADY**

A large group is gathered at the graveside to bid farewell to Harry Tate.
One of the mourners is Charles Coburn, so ancient that he's retired.
As the coffin is being lowered into the grave, one curious sprout leans
over and whispers, 'How old are you, Charlie?' 'I'm 89,' Coburn replies.
'Hardly seems worthwhile you going home,' the young 'un says.

ALFRED HITCHCOCK

Well, thank you, Rector, it was a lovely funeral. We must have one
again sometime. **AUDREY FFORBES-HAMILTON,** *TO THE MANOR BORN*

After being an awed witness of the funeral of King Edward VII, the little
daughter of Lord Kinnoull refused to say her prayers that night: 'God will
be too busy unpacking King Edward,' she said. **LORD RIDDELL**

For sale: Undertaker's overcoat. Slightly worn on one shoulder.

LOOT **MAGAZINE**

EPITAPH

Without you, Heaven would be too dull to bear,
And Hell would not be Hell if you are there.

JOHN SPARROW, EPITAPH FOR MAURICE BOWRA

I want my epitaph to have my name, then 'best before' followed by the
date of my death. **CLEMENT FREUD**

As in life, so in death, lies a bat of renown,
Slain by a lorry (three ton);
His innings is over, his bat is laid down;
To the end a poor judge of a run. **GEORGE McWILLIAM**

If the whole human race lay in one grave, the epitaph on the headstone
might well be, 'It seemed a good idea at the time.' **REBECCA WEST**

Here lies the body
of dear old Dick
who went through life
with a twisted prick.
All his life
was a lifelong hunt
looking for the girl
with the twisted cunt.
When he found one
he dropped down dead,
for the one he found
had a left-hand thread.

ANON

HEAVEN

I want to go to heaven. But if Jeffrey Archer is there I want to go to
Lewisham.

SPIKE MILLIGAN

My heaven will be filled with wonderful young men and dukes.

BARBARA CARTLAND

One thing I shall miss in heaven is gardening. We shan't have weeds in
heaven, shall we?

COMMISSIONER CATHERINE BRAMWELL-BOOTH

I'm definitely not going to heaven. I'm sure it's very white and cold,
sparsely furnished, with maybe a bit of shining chrome here and there.

JEFFREY BERNARD

It is a curious thing that every creed promises a paradise which will be
absolutely uninhabitable for anyone of civilised taste.

EVELYN WAUGH

My mother was worried about whether my father would be wearing
pyjamas or a mackintosh in the afterlife.

GEORGE MELLY

Poor Matt, he's gone to Heaven, no doubt – but he won't like God.

ROBERT LOUIS STEVENSON ON MATTHEW ARNOLD

We have no reliable guarantee that the afterlife will be any less exasperating than this one, have we? **NOËL COWARD**

If there's no room in heaven when I die, I'll accept a West Indian cricket ground. **SIMON HUGHES**

The last dream of bliss: staying in Heaven without God there.

GEOFFREY MADAN

HELL

'Corky,' I said, 'I've been through hell.' 'About the only place I thought you didn't have to go through to get to King's Deverill. And how were they all?' **P.G. WODEHOUSE**

Hell is an all-male black tie dinner of chartered accountants which goes on for eternity. **JOHN MORTIMER**

That's what hell must be like, small chat to the babbling of Lethe about the good old days when we wished we were dead. **SAMUEL BECKETT**

Ah, well, there is just this world and then the next, and then all our troubles will be over with. **MARGOT ASQUITH**

BELIEFS

My mother and I once paid out for a seance in Widnes. We wanted to contact my father because we were going camping and couldn't lay hands on the mallet. **KITTY,** *VICTORIA WOOD*

I was walking along the street when I saw a dead baby ghost on the road. On reflection, it might have been a handkerchief... **MILTON JONES**

Some things have got to be believed to be seen. **RALPH HODGSON**

Spiritualism? I always knew the living talked rot, but it's nothing to the rot talked by the dead. **MARGOT ASQUITH**

How can what an Englishman believes be heresy? It is a contradiction in terms. **GEORGE BERNARD SHAW**

There are some things only intellectuals are crazy enough to believe. **GEORGE ORWELL**

Why, sometimes I've believed as many as six impossible things before breakfast. **LEWIS CARROLL,** *THROUGH THE LOOKING GLASS*

Man can believe the impossible, but man can never believe the improbable. **OSCAR WILDE**

Sometimes I think we're alone in the universe, and sometimes I think we're not. In either case the idea is quite staggering. **ARTHUR C. CLARKE**

PHILOSOPHY

My German engineer was very argumentative and tiresome. He wouldn't admit that it was certain that there was not a rhinoceros in the room. **BERTRAND RUSSELL**

Rousseau fixed the summit of his earthly bliss at living in an orchard with an amiable woman and a cow, and he never attained even that. He did get as far as the orchard, but the woman was not amiable, and she brought her mother with her, and there was no cow. **JEROME K. JEROME**

My husband loved to recount how late one evening he stopped a taxi. As he got in, the driver said: 'You're T.S. Eliot, aren't you? I've got an eye for celebrity. Only the other evening I picked up Bertrand Russell, and I said to him, "Well, Lord Russell, what's it all about?" and, do you know, he couldn't tell me.'

VALERIE ELIOT

My philosophy, like colour television, is all there in black and white.

MONTY PYTHON

If you have sex with Abi Titmuss and there's no one there to video it does she still make a sound?

PETER SERAFINOWICZ

All philosophies, if you ride them home, are nonsense; but some are greater nonsense than others.

SAMUEL BUTLER

I long ago came to the conclusion that nothing has ever been definitely proved about anything.

NOËL COWARD

Nothing matters very much, and very few things matter at all.

ARTHUR JAMES BALFOUR

Philosophy teaches us to bear with equanimity the misfortunes of others.

OSCAR WILDE

For there was never yet philosopher
That could bear the toothache patiently.

WILLIAM SHAKESPEARE

I have tried in my time to be a philosopher, but cheerfulness always kept breaking in.

OLIVER EDWARDS

RELIGION

Religion is really for women and queers. **COLIN HAYCRAFT**

Never make a god of religion. **ARTHUR HELPS**

It is the test of a good religion whether you can joke about it.
G.K. CHESTERTON

Half the rules seemed to forbid things he had never heard of; and the other half forebade things he was doing every day and could not imagine not doing. **C.S. LEWIS**

I'm not a religious woman, but I find if you say no to everything you can hardly tell the difference. **MRS FEATHERSTONE, OPEN ALL HOURS**

Never call a Jew a Jew unless you can be sure of making him lose his temper by doing so. **KINGSLEY AMIS**

I'm not really a practising Jew, but I keep a kosher kitchen just to spite Hitler. **MIRIAM MARGOLYES**

'Jedi Knight' is on the list of religions for the 2001 UK census.
A campaign to get people to write the entry on their census forms has succeeded in the term being included on the list of religions, alongside Church of England, Roman Catholic, Muslim, Buddhist and Hindu.
BBC NEWS WEBSITE

A religious maniac is someone who believes in God. **COLIN HAYCRAFT**

When I was a child I used to think that the Day of Judgement meant that we were all going to judge God, and I still don't see why not.
LORD BERNERS

Christianity might be a good thing if anyone ever tried it.

GEORGE BERNARD SHAW

I expect you know my friend Evelyn Waugh, who, like your Holiness, is a Roman Catholic. **RANDOLPH CHURCHILL DURING AN AUDIENCE WITH THE POPE**

You have no idea how much nastier I would be if I wasn't a Roman Catholic.

EVELYN WAUGH

My husband converted to Catholicism only after he had been assured that dogs could enter Heaven.

MARY WESLEY

Catholics are just Protestants, protesting against Protestantism.

D.H. LAWRENCE

J.L. Carr switched from Methodism to Anglicanism for the architecture.

SIMON JENKINS

There are no atheists in foxholes.

WILLIAM CUMMINGS

Most Englishmen, if forced into analysing their own creeds – which Heaven forbid – are convinced that God is an Englishman, probably educated at Eton.

E.M. DELAFIELD

I'm half Christian and half Muslim so I guess that makes me a Christmus.

GINA YASHERE

Thank the Lord, who, incidentally, is British, for the great things he has brought to this land... Take a Break, Spearmint Rhino and Findus Crispy Pancakes.

TOM BAKER, NARRATOR, *LITTLE BRITAIN*

W.H. Auden didn't love God, he just fancied him.   **STEPHEN SPENDER**

I don't believe in God but I'm very interested in her.   **ARTHUR C. CLARKE**

To put one's trust in God is only a longer way of saying that one will chance it.
SAMUEL BUTLER

Prayer must not be answered: if it is, it ceases to be prayer and becomes correspondence.   **OSCAR WILDE**

My feelings toward Christ are that he was a bloody good bloke even though he wasn't as funny as Margaret Thatcher.   **TERRY JONES**

I have always envisaged death and the Resurrection of the body as like finding your motorcar after a party.   **NANCY MITFORD**

In heaven an angel is nobody in particular.   **GEORGE BERNARD SHAW**

When I was in a convent in Belgium I had to bathe in a bath which was sheeted over to prevent my guardian angel seeing me.   **MARIE TEMPEST**

I've always fancied being a monk – drinking mead, tending gardens and making honey.   **VIC REEVES**

Monica Baldwin's book, *I Leapt Over the Wall*, strengthened my desire not to become a nun.   **NOËL COWARD**

Because of a shortage of bell ringers, parishioners have to imitate ringing. Some people 'ding' and 'dong' in the wrong place, but it's still wonderful.
REVD NORMAN LEA OF ST CATWG'S, VALE OF GLAMORGAN

We were discussing the possibility of making one of our cats Pope recently, and we decided that the fact that she was not Italian, and was female, made the third point, that she was a cat, quite irrelevant.

KATHARINE WHITEHORN

If you drop a Bible from a great height, you can kill a fieldmouse. So maybe the Bible isn't all good. **HARRY HILL**

In the Bible: No one coughs. One person sneezes. Only one woman's age is mentioned (Sarah: 127). **GEOFFREY MADAN**

The total absence of humour from the Bible is one of the most singular things in all literature. **ALFRED NORTH WHITEHEAD**

For most people the Church has become little more than a useful landmark by which to offer directions. **THE ARCHBISHOP OF YORK**

I always put on my thickest greatcoat to go to our church in, as fungi grow in great numbers about the communion table. **EDWARD FITZGERALD**

I went to church on Sunday and the priest threw hot ash at me. I was so incensed.

TIM VINE

Kinglake wanted an inscription on all churches: 'Important If True'.

GEOFFREY MADAN

If English is spoken in heaven, God undoubtedly employs Cranmer as his speechwriter. The angels of the lesser ministries probably use the language of the New English Bible and the Alternative Service Book for internal memos. **PRINCE CHARLES**

Operationally, God is beginning to resemble not a ruler but the last fading smile of a cosmic Cheshire cat.   **SIR JULIAN HUXLEY**

Goodnight, and may your God go with you.   **DAVE ALLEN**

—May the benevolence of the God Shevou bring blessing on your home.
—And on yours.
—And may his wisdom bring success in all your undertakings.
—And in yours.
—And may his radiance light up your life.
—And up yours.   **KENNETH WILLIAMS AND SID JAMES, *CARRY ON UP THE KHYBER***

VICARS AND CLERGYMEN

There are three sexes – men, women and clergymen.   **REVD SYDNEY SMITH**

He has the canonical smirk and the filthy clammy palm of a chaplain.   **WILLIAM WYCHERLEY**

I asked him why he was a priest, and he said if you have to work for anybody an absentee boss is best.   **JEANETTE WINTERSON**

A clergyman who plays cricket and can break both ways is sure to get on in England.   **J.M. BARRIE**

The dear Archdeacon is getting so absent-minded. He read a list of box-holders for the opera as the First Lesson the other Sunday. Fortunately no one noticed the mistake.   **SAKI**

The Reverend Lord Henry was not one of those new-fangled parsons who carry the principles of their vocation uncomfortably into private life.   **LOUIS MAZZINI, *KIND HEARTS AND CORONETS***

Charlie Dimmock's nipples: Term used by vicars to describe the hat-pegs in their chapels.

VIZ

The vicar addressed his congregation: 'I have good news and bad news,' he said. 'The good news is, we have enough money to pay for a new roof on the church. The bad news is, it's still out there in your pockets.'

LEWIS RATHBONE

The vicar's wife has to get on with everyone, but you can take only so much of hearing that the sun shines out of your husband's bum.

SUSAN DEVONSHIRE-JONES, VICAR'S WIFE

The Bishop of Stortford was talking to the local Master of Hounds about the difficulty he had in keeping his vicars off the incense.   **P.G. WODEHOUSE**

Sober as a bishop. Soberer.   **P.G. WODEHOUSE**

The priest is always fascinating to an adulterous generation because they think he knows more ways of committing adultery than anybody else. It's logical. He deals in sin as much as a dustman deals in garbage.

AUBREY MENEN

Never take a reference from a clergyman. They always want to give someone a second chance. **LADY SELBORNE**

The British churchman goes to church as he goes to the bathroom, with the minimum of fuss and no explanation if he can help it.   **RONALD BLYTHE**

Bishops tend to live long lives – apparently the Lord is not all that keen for them to join Him.   **SIR HUMPHREY APPLEBY, *YES, PRIME MINISTER***

Welbourn's Dictionary of Prelates, Parsons, Vergers, Wardens,
Sidesmen, Preachers, Sunday-school Teachers, Hermits, Ecclesiastical
Flowerarrangers, Fifth Monarchy Men and False Prophets

J.L. CARR, BOOK TITLE

How can a bishop marry? How can he flirt? The most he can say is,
'I will see you in the vestry after service.'   REVD SYDNEY SMITH

With heaving breast the Dean undressed
The Bishop's wife to lie on.
She thought it crude done in the nude,
So he kept his old school tie on.   ANON

Headline in *Daily Mirror*: 'Secret Love of Vanished Vicar'
(splendid hymn metre).   BARBARA PYM, DIARY ENTRY, 5 OCTOBER 1956

My attitude to transsexual clergy is that if a man becomes a woman or a
woman becomes a man, if they are priests they remain priests willy-nilly.

RT REVD MICHAEL SCOTT-JOYNT, THE BISHOP OF WINCHESTER

We had to remove from our railway compartment three times to avoid a
clergyman who was looking up my daughter's legs under cover of the
Daily Telegraph.   ALAN BENNETT

He managed to make his escape while Father Thames was being
buttonholed by an elderly woman of the type that always seems to
waylay the clergy in porches and doorways.   BARBARA PYM

ABROAD

ABROAD – GENERAL

The great and recurrent question about abroad is, is it worth getting there?
ROSE MACAULAY

Abroad is utterly bloody and foreigners are fiends.
NANCY MITFORD

Dangerous foreigners begin at Calais and don't stop until you get to Bombay, where they speak English and play cricket.
CLEMENT ATTLEE

How fast and how loud foreigners talk! If is a gift; the British cannot talk so loud or so fast. They have too many centuries of fog in their throats.
ROSE MACAULAY

A gesticulation is any movement made by a foreigner.
J.B. MORTON

An Italian remained silent because it was too cold to take his hands out of his pockets.
GEOFFREY MADAN

The one phrase it is imperative to know in every foreign language is: my friend will pay.
ALAN WHICKER

I don't hold with abroad and think that foreigners speak English when our backs are turned.
QUENTIN CRISP

The only places he likes on the Continent are those in which it's only by an effort of the imagination that you can tell you're not in England.
W. SOMERSET MAUGHAM

How could any English person want to live abroad? Foreigners can't help living abroad because they were born there, but for an English person to go is ridiculous, especially now that sun-ray lamps are readily available.
ADRIAN MOLE

If I were compelled to choose between living in West Bromwich and Florence, I should make straight for West Bromwich.   J.B. PRIESTLEY

I don't want a villa in Spain unless I can see Beachy Head from the bedroom window.   DEREK LUNN

An acre in Middlesex is better than a principality in Utopia. LORD MACAULAY

TRAVEL

McCarthy's First Rule of Travel: 'On Arrival, Buy a Local Paper and Go For a Drink'.   The court cases, property prices and obituaries will tell you more than any guidebook and the drink will help you feel you understand things that are in reality beyond your comprehension.

PETE MCCARTHY

The British tourist is always happy abroad as long as the natives are waiters.   ROBERT MORLEY

I had travelled extensively in Catford, Lewisham and Brockley SE26, but somehow never in Austria.   SPIKE MILLIGAN

I've never travelled…but I daresay you can't judge Egypt by *Aïda*.

RONALD FIRBANK

The best way of seeing Alexandria is to wander aimlessly about. E.M. FORSTER

The Giant's Causeway: worth seeing, yes; but not worth going to see.

SAMUEL JOHNSON

I shall be glad to have seen it – for the same reason Papa gave for being glad to have seen Lisbon – namely, 'that it will be unnecessary ever to see it again.'   WINSTON CHURCHILL

Here we are in the holy land of Israel – a Mecca for tourists.   **DAVID VINE**

She lives in Spain. She likes the majesty and grandeur of the landscape, but she's not keen on the bacon.   **VICTORIA WOOD**

Norway. What a dreadful place. Grieg and £3 for half a pint of lousy lager. You would have to be a millionaire to be an alcoholic there.

JEFFREY BERNARD

Sweden is where they commit suicide and the king rides a bicycle.   **ALAN BENNETT**

Finland is a nation of drunken Captain Birds Eyes.   **A.A. GILL**

Apart from cheese and tulips, the main product of Holland is advocaat, a drink made from lawyers.   **ALAN COREN**

Switzerland has produced the numbered bank account, Ovaltine and Valium.   **PETER FREEDMAN**

The weird mixture of smells which together compose the anthology of a Greek holiday under the pines – petrol, garlic, wine and goat.

LAWRENCE DURRELL

In Italy, the whole country is a theatre and the worst actors are on the stage.   **GEORGE BERNARD SHAW**

The median Italian is a cowardly baritone who consumes 78.3 kilometres of carbohydrates a month and drives about in a car slightly smaller than he is, looking for a divorce.   **ALAN COREN**

I do like Italian graves; they look so much more lived in.   **ELIZABETH BOWEN**

There is, in fact, no law or government at all in Italy; and it is wonderful how well things go on without them. **LORD BYRON**

I've done the elephant. I've done the poverty. I might as well go home. **PHIL TUFNELL ON INDIA**

How do you cope with poverty is the most asked question about India – the best answer comes from Mark Tully, who lives in Delhi: 'I don't have to cope with the poverty; the poor have to cope with the poverty.' **A.A. GILL**

You have no idea what it cost to keep the old man in poverty. **LORD MOUNTBATTEN ON MAHATMA GANDHI**

—What are you most looking forward to after your tour of India? — A dry fart! **PHIL EDMONDS**

Australia! Land of strange, exotic creatures, freaks of evolution, ghastly victims of Mother Nature's vicious whimsy – kangaroo and platypus, potoroo and bandicoot, Richie Benaud... **PETER TINNISWOOD**

Australia. Earth is here so kind, that just tickle her with a hoe and she laughs with a harvest. **DOUGLAS JERROLD**

I find it hard to say what I thought of New Zealand, because when I was there it seemed to be shut. **CLEMENT FREUD**

Can it be true, as some claim, that the Italian for ping-pong is pinka-ponka?

ARTHUR MARSHALL

The Japanese have almost as big a reputation for cruelty as do young children. **DENNIS BLOODWORTH, 1759**

If Freud had lived in Tokyo, we'd never have got analysis. He wouldn't have known where to start. **A.A. GILL**

The russians are roters; americans are swankpots; the french are slack; the germans are unspeakable; the rest are as bad if not worse than the above; the british are brave noble super cheers cheers cheers.

GEOFFREY WILLANS AND RONALD SEARLE

There's only one thing I miss about England. It's the smell of summer in the countryside in Cornwall. **RONALD BIGGS**

I missed England until I got back to Dover in the pouring rain, and asked the dining car attendant on the train for anchovies and toast. 'The anchovies are off, sir,' he said. 'So is the toast.' I must say I felt a little better about my exile then. **EARL OF ST GERMANS**

AMERICA

I love going to America but I couldn't live there. You know why?
Too many Americans. **JONATHAN ROSS**

A lot of people quote the fact that only ten per cent of Americans have a passport. They say it like it's a bad thing. **JIMMY CARR**

Americans don't stand on ceremony. They make no distinction about a man's background, his parentage, his education. They say what they mean...They are irrepressibly good-humoured, ambitious and brimming with self-confidence in any company. Apart from that I've got nothing against them. **TOM STOPPARD**

I do *detest* the Americans. They expect everyone to go to the devil at the same hectic pace as themselves. It takes hundreds of years to do it properly. Look at us. **JOHN LE CARRÉ**

The terrible newly-imported American doctrine that everyone ought to *do* something.   SIR OSBERT SITWELL

I could not, even for a couple of months, live in a country so miserable as to possess no castles.   JOHN RUSKIN

The difference between England and America is this: when we have a world series, we ask other countries to participate.   JOHN CLEESE

Any foreigner visiting the United States can perform an easy magic trick: buy a newspaper and see your own country disappear.   JULIAN BARNES

'How would you like your egg? Easy over, hard over, sunny side up?' 'I'd like it well cooked.' 'Sure, but how would you like it cooked? Easy over, hard over, sunny side up?' It's only breakfast, and I'm already bewildered.   KEITH FLOYD

My dear, it's so uncivilised! Did you know that when tea was first introduced in the American colonies, many housewives mistakenly served the tea leaves with sugar or syrup, after throwing out the water in which they had been boiled.   MARY FIELDS

It's frightening how easy it is to commit murder in America. Just a drink too much. I can see myself doing it. In England, one feels all the social restraints holding one back. But here, anything can happen.   W.H. AUDEN

Actually, American football is somewhat like rugby. But why do they have all those committee meetings?   WINSTON CHURCHILL

Americans should not be allowed to carry guns. They should no longer be allowed to own or carry anything more dangerous in public than a vegetable peeler.   **JOHN CLEESE**

The United States, I believe, are under the impression that they are 20 years in advance of this country; whilst, as a matter of actual verifiable fact, of course, they are just about six hours behind it.   **HAROLD HOBSON**

Los Angeles is awful – like Liverpool with palm trees.   **JOHN LYDON**

Being in New York was like being in heaven, without going to all the bother and expense of dying.   P.G. WODEHOUSE

Americans need to learn to resolve personal issues without using guns, lawyers or therapists.   **JOHN CLEESE**

Perhaps we can at least teach the Americans that there are better things to do with a cigar than Bill Clinton seems to realise.   **AUBERON WAUGH**

An American publisher rejected *Animal Farm* saying, 'It is impossible to sell animal stories in the USA.'   **ANON**

England and America are two countries divided by a common language.   **GEORGE BERNARD SHAW**

American politics: dullness, occasionally relieved by rascality.   **SIR CECIL SPRING RICE**

When I met President Bush he asked me what state Wales was in.   **CHARLOTTE CHURCH**

Anyone wishing to communicate with Americans should do so by c-mail, which has been specifically invented for the purpose, involving neither physical proximity nor speech. **AUBERON WAUGH**

You say 'oregano', we say 'ore-gah-no'. You say 'tomato', we say 'tom-ah-to'. You say 'erb', and we say 'herb' because there's a fucking 'h' at the beginning. **PAUL BETTANY**

Americans should look up 'aluminium' in the Oxford English Dictionary. Check the pronunciation guide. They will be amazed at just how wrongly they have been pronouncing it. **JOHN CLEESE**

Americans have different ways of saying things. They say, 'elevator', we say, 'lift'...they say, 'President', we say, 'stupid psychopathic git'.
ALEXEI SAYLE

In the States, the election has become a so-called watercooler debate, meaning that Americans gather round the watercooler at work and discuss whether it would make a better president than Bush. **ANGUS DEAYTON**

Anyone who is capable of getting themselves made President should on no account be allowed to do the job. **DOUGLAS ADAMS**

American senators take themselves so seriously that they'd wear togas if they thought they could get away with it. **GERARD BAKER**

Irish Americans are about as Irish as black Americans are African.
BOB GELDOF

You can always trust the Americans. In the end they will do the right thing, after they have eliminated all the other possibilities.

WINSTON CHURCHILL

The thing that impresses me most about America is the way parents obey their children.

THE DUKE OF WINDSOR

America invented the dumb broad as the English perfected the gun dog.

JOHN OSBORNE

They're the experts where personality is concerned, the Americans; they've got it down to a fine art.

ALAN BENNETT

Loyd Grossman's impersonation of an American intellectual was about as plausible as Douglas Bader captaining the British synchronised swimming team.

VICTOR LEWIS-SMITH

Americans get nervous abroad. As a result they tend either to travel in groups or bomb Libya.

MILES KINGTON

The American method of fighting is, 'If it moves, shoot it. If it doesn't move, shoot it in case it does.'

I. P. SETH

Please tell us who killed JFK. It's been driving us crazy.

JOHN CLEESE

I believe that the heaviest blow ever dealt at liberty's head will be dealt by the United States in the ultimate failure of its example to the earth.

CHARLES DICKENS

FRANCE

—I was born French, have lived French and will die French.
—Have you no ambition, man? **THE COMTE D'ORSAY AND BENJAMIN DISRAELI**

The Almighty in His infinite wisdom did not see fit to create Frenchmen
in the image of Englishmen. **WINSTON CHURCHILL**

The French are short, blue-vested people who carry their own onions
when cycling abroad, and have a yard which is 3.37 inches longer than
other people's. **ALAN COREN**

Is it possible to wear a beret back to front? **DAVID PERRIL**

Am I the only one who's always tempted to light the little wick on top
of a beret? **PAUL MERTON**

We always have been, we are, and I hope that we always shall be,
detested in France. **DUKE OF WELLINGTON**

So, we land at Boulogne, and I said from the look of those lavatories
there won't be a British consul there. **KITTY,** *VICTORIA WOOD*

—You know, French women don't shave under their arms. There was
this French woman I met and the hair under her arms was so long she
put it in a bun.
—Eww. Those French'll eat anything. **TONY AND GARY,** *MEN BEHAVING BADLY*

France – that country to which lesbianism is what cricket is to England.
QUENTIN CRISP

If the French noblesse had been capable of playing cricket with their
peasants their châteaux would never have been burnt. **G.M.TREVELYAN**

I don't understand the French. These are people with a town called Brest and none of them thinks it's funny.   **AL MURRAY**

The French have a tendency to be very French.   **MATTHEW STURGIS**

Into the face of the young man...there had crept a look of furtive shame, the shifty, hangdog look that announces that an Englishman is about to talk French.   **P.G. WODEHOUSE**

The last time I asked for directions in Paris, I inadvertently gave the man my mother's recipe for baked Alaska.   **JEREMY CLARKSON**

When I bought my villa in the South of France I changed its name from 'La Magnerie' to 'Sea View' – it was easier to pronounce.   **EARL OF ST GERMANS**

Rex Harrison never mastered French. Once, when we ate in Nice, he summoned the *maître d'*: 'Ce bifstek,' he complained, 'est brûlé comme la buggèré.'   **PATRICK GARLAND**

My attitude to France was, I suppose, inherited from my father, who always felt perfectly at home there because he never attempted to talk or make friends with the natives.   **ROBERT MORLEY**

France is the largest country in Europe, a great boon for drunks, who need room to fall.   **ALAN COREN**

The proof that God has a very weird sense of humour is that, having invented the sublime mystery of haute cuisine, he went and gave it to the French.   **A.A. GILL**

Aïoli is the nearest thing the French have to HP sauce.   **JOHN LANCHESTER**

The French favour le cyclisme and have the famous Tour de France and the shorter (but steeper) Tour d'Eiffel. **MATTHEW STURGIS**

That Eiffel Tower's a tragic waste of Meccano. As a result, French boys have nothing to play with except themselves and that's how all the trouble with the French started... **AL MURRAY**

The French are tremendous snobs, despite that rather showy and ostentatious Revolution. **ARTHUR MARSHALL**

France has for centuries blocked our way to Europe. Before the invention of the aeroplane we had to step over it to get anywhere. **ROBERT MORLEY**

Albert Camus was a philosopher, novelist and playwright. Like so many French intellectuals, Camus kept goal for Algeria and died in a car crash. **WILLIAM DONALDSON**

Britain has football hooligans, Germans have neo-Nazis, and France has farmers. **ANON**

The French are a logical people, which is one reason the English dislike them so intensely. The other is that they own France, a country which we have always judged to be much too good for them. **ROBERT MORLEY**

A television reporter asked people in a London street why they thought the two nations were always at loggerheads. 'The trouble with the French,' said one, 'is they can't stand being foreign.' It was a wonderful echo of a London newspaper headline in the 1930s: 'Fog in Channel – continent cut off.' **THOMAS O'DWYER**

The overall impression from the British is that they love France but would prefer it if the French didn't live there.   **JOHN MORTIMER**

What I gained by being in France was, learning to be better satisfied with my own country.   **DR SAMUEL JOHNSON**

GERMANY

—Do you know Germany?
—I flew over it once – but I had an aisle seat.   **FRAN AND JAMES SHELLEY, *SHELLEY***

In prison, I studied German. Indeed, this seems to be the proper place for such study.   **OSCAR WILDE**

The Germans are a cruel race. Their operas last for six hours and they have no word for 'fluffy'.   **EDMUND BLACKADDER, *BLACKADDER GOES FORTH***

Think of the man who first tried German sausage.   **JEROME K. JEROME**

West Germany may beat us at our national sport tonight, but that would be only fair. We beat them twice at theirs.   **VINCENT MULCHRONE**

LIFE, THE UNIVERSE AND EVERYTHING: MISCELLANEOUS

LIFE

'Life is like that, dear,' she would sometimes say, but she would never say what it was that life was like. **RONALD FIRBANK**

What is human life but a game of cricket? **THE DUKE OF DORSET**

Life was planned by a committee while the clever ones had popped out to the lav. **VICTORIA WOOD**

—I believe that life is for living, don't you?
—It's difficult to know what else one could do with it.
NOËL COWARD, NUDE WITH VIOLIN

My talent I put into my writing; my genius I have saved for living. **OSCAR WILDE**

You fall out of your mother's womb, you crawl across open country under fire, and drop into your grave. **QUENTIN CRISP**

I should have liked the kind of life where one ate food flavoured with garlic, but it was not to be. **BARBARA PYM**

I'd like my life to be like a Bruce Springsteen song. Just once. I know I'm not born to run, I know that Seven Sisters' Road is nothing like Thunder Road, but feelings can't be different, can they? **NICK HORNBY**

Life is what happens to you while you're busy making other plans. **JOHN LENNON**

When I look back on all these worries I remember the story of the old man who said on his deathbed that he had had a lot of troubles in his life, most of which never happened. **WINSTON CHURCHILL**

I wouldn't dream of taking life as it comes: it may not be colour-coordinated.

JULIAN CLARY

Life's not fair, is it? Some of us drink champagne in the fast lane, and some of us eat our sandwiches by the loose chippings on the A597.

VICTORIA WOOD

My only regret in life is that I did not drink more champagne.

JOHN MAYNARD KEYNES

My regret in life is that I haven't had enough sex.

SIR JOHN BETJEMAN

As you slide down the bannister of life, may the splinters never point in the wrong direction.

IRISH BLESSING

'What is the meaning of Life, The Universe and Everything?' 'Forty-two,' said Deep Thought, with infinite majesty and calm.

DOUGLAS ADAMS

If you feel that life is one of God's jokes, there is still no reason why we shouldn't make it a *good* joke.

KENNETH WILLIAMS

I can imagine no more comfortable frame of mind for the conduct of life than a humorous resignation.

W. SOMERSET MAUGHAM

THE WORLD

I have recently been all round the world and have formed a very poor opinion of it.

SIR THOMAS BEECHAM

The world is disgracefully managed, one hardly knows to whom to complain.

RONALD FIRBANK

Maybe this world is another planet's hell.

ALDOUS HUXLEY

If the good God had asked me to help Him in making the world, I'd have left uric acid out of it. **E.V. LUCAS**

The world is a dangerous place. Only yesterday I went into Boots and punched someone in the face. **JEREMY LIMB**

It's not so much the world that's got so much worse but news coverage that's got so much better. **G.K. CHESTERTON**

It's a mad world, isn't it? And I can never understand which side of the asylum wall is the inside. **WILLIAM DOUGLAS-HOME**

All the world's queer save thee and me, and even thou art a little queer. **ROBERT OWEN**

And that's the world in a nutshell – an appropriate receptacle. **STAN DUNN**

HISTORY

1066 And All That: A Memorable History of England, Comprising all the Parts you can Remember Including 103 Good Things, 5 Bad Kings and 2 Genuine Dates **W.C. SELLAR AND R.J. YEATMAN, BOOK TITLE**

Ancient Britons, Angles, Saxons, and Danes were all ugly, aggressive men with bad hair, in rough frocks. All I can think about the Dark Ages is that everything must have chafed horribly. **A.A. GILL**

'How wonderful it must have been for the Ancient Britons,' my mother said once, 'when the Romans arrived and they could have a Hot Bath.' **KATHARINE WHITEHORN**

The Emperor Marcus Aurelius was a sort of primitive Bob Hope, given to throwing off wisecracks. **P.G. WODEHOUSE**

Have you ever noticed that all hot-water bottles look like Henry the Eighth?

SIR MAX BEERBOHM

I have, occasionally, remarked that the only entirely creditable incident in English history is the sending of £100 to Beethoven on his deathbed by the London Philharmonic Society; and it is the only one that historians never mention.

GEORGE BERNARD SHAW

Infamy, infamy, they've all got it in for me! **KENNETH WILLIAMS AS CAESAR, *CARRY ON CLEO***

Napoleon seized power with a 'whiff of grapefruit' and many of his famous battles were fought at railway termini (Austerlitz, Waterloo, Trafalgar Square – now Charing Cross). **MATTHEW STURGIS**

Henry VIII, or King Syphilis Gut Bucket Wife Murderer VIII as I prefer to call him, was born in 1491. **JO BRAND**

Contrary to popular opinion, and when lecturing on Henry VIII, Dr David Starkey has never pointed to a portrait of Anne of Cleves, and said: "That is so not a good look.' **WILLIAM DONALDSON**

We will enter a hideous age of Puritanism. They'll close all the theatres... lace handkerchiefs for men will be illegal...and I won't be able to find a friendly face to sit on this side of Boulogne!

EDMUND BLACKADDER, *THE CAVALIER YEARS*

It was the Puritans who put an end to the practice of dancing, as well as discontinuing the tradition of kings wearing heads on their shoulders.

MIKE HARDING

History will be kind to me for I intend to write it. **WINSTON CHURCHILL**

ADVICE

The best piece of advice I ever received was: 'Don't do it again.'

LORD CUDLIPP

I have one golden rule: I ask myself what Nanny would have expected me to do. **LORD CARRINGTON**

My mother was always warning me to be careful of theatrical types and never to turn my back. **MICHAEL CRAWFORD**

Never put off till tomorrow what your wife can do today. **ANDY CAPP**

My aunt had a saying: 'Never go anywhere for the first time'. **M.K.HINES**

Don't give a woman advice: one should never give a woman anything she can't wear in the evening. **OSCAR WILDE**

There's only one motto I know of that's any good: 'Never go to law.'

HENRY CECIL

If you drink much from a bottle marked 'poison' it is almost sure to disagree with you. **LEWIS CARROLL, ALICE'S ADVENTURES IN WONDERLAND**

Never spit in a man's face unless his moustache is on fire. **HENRY ROOT**

If you have to ask if someone is male or female, don't. **PATRICK MURRAY**

Never miss an opportunity to relieve yourself; never miss a chance to sit down and rest your feet. **EDWARD VIII**

If in doubt, stick your left out. **HENRY COOPER**

Never tell a young person that anything cannot be done. God may have been waiting centuries for someone ignorant enough of the impossible to do that very thing. **G.M. TREVELYAN**

I always tell a young man not to use the word 'always'. **ROBERT WALPOLE**

It is a little embarrassing that, after 45 years of research and study, the best advice I can give to people is to be a little kinder to each other.

ALDOUS HUXLEY

Never bolt your door with a boiled carrot. **IRISH PROVERB**

Of the 36 ways of avoiding disaster, running away is the best.

LORD MOYNIHAN

If you are going through hell, keep going. **WINSTON CHURCHILL**

THE FUTURE

Only one more indispensable massacre of Capitalists or Communists or Fascists or Christians or Heretics, and there we are in the Golden Future.

ALDOUS HUXLEY

You've no idea how pleasant it is not to have any future. It's like having a totally efficient contraceptive. **ANTHONY BURGESS**

It is bad enough to know the past; it would be intolerable to know the future. **W. SOMERSET MAUGHAM**

It is wise to look ahead but foolish to look further than you can see.

WINSTON CHURCHILL

I would sum up my fear about the future in one word: boring. And that's my one fear: that everything has happened; nothing exciting or new or interesting is ever going to happen again...the future is just going to be a vast, conforming suburb of the soul. **J. G. BALLARD**

I've buried a time-capsule containing large samples of dynamite, gunpowder and nitroglycerin. It's set to go off in the year 3000. That should show people living in the future what we are really like. **ALFRED HITCHCOCK**

FOREIGNERS' EYE VIEW

THE ENGLISH LANGUAGE

Sodding, blimey, shaggin', knickers, bollocks. Oh, God, I'm turning English.

SPIKE, BUFFY THE VAMPIRE SLAYER

—Oim telling yew! Oim English!
—English women don't pump gas naked.

MADONNA AND MARGE SIMPSON, *THE SIMPSONS*

All the shop ladies called me love and most of the men called me mate. I hadn't been here twelve hours and already they loved me.   **BILL BRYSON**

All Englishmen talk as if they've got a bushel of plums stuck in their throats, and then after swallowing them get constipated from the pits.

W.C. FIELDS

When I meet an Englishman and he speaks with that funny accent, I'd never say, 'You're a liar.' But I believe that if you wake an Englishman in the middle of the night, he'll speak just like an American.   **MILT KAMEN**

If you want a linguistic adventure, go drinkin' with a Scotsman. Cause if you thought you couldn't understand him before…   **ROBIN WILLIAMS**

English is a simple yet hard language. It consists entirely of foreign words pronounced wrongly.   KURT TUCHOLSKY

When the BBC first broadcast to the USA, it took a team of translators a week to figure out that 'bangers and mash' were not some veiled British threat.   **BILL CLINTON**

It is very difficult to speak English: one writes Manchester, but says Liverpool.

RUSSIAN SAYING

English is essentially Norse as spoken by a gang of French thugs.

B. PHILIP JONSSON

There are certain things that you have to be British to appreciate: Sooty, Tony Hancock, Marmite, George Formby, HP sauce, making sandwiches from bread you've sliced yourself, really milky tea, the belief that household wiring is an interesting topic for conversation, thinking that going to choose wallpaper with your mate constitutes a reasonably good day out, seaside rock.

BILL BRYSON

MANNERS

An Englishman, even if he is alone, forms an orderly queue of one.

GEORGE MIKES

English people apparently queue up as a sort of hobby. A family man might pass a mild autumn evening by taking the wife and kids to stand in the cinema queue for a while and then leading them over for a few minutes in the sweetshop queue and then, as a special treat for the kids, saying, 'Perhaps we've time to have a look at the Number 31 bus queue before we turn in.'

CALVIN TRILLIN

To Americans, English manners are far more frightening than none at all.

RANDALL JARRELL

No one can be as calculatedly rude as the British, which amazes Americans, who do not understand studied insult and can only offer abuse as a substitute.

PAUL GALLICO

In England there is only silence or scandal.

ANDRÉ MAUROIS

Whenever I call an Englishman rude he takes it as a compliment.

GEORGE MIKES

My father, like most Englishmen, could commit assault and battery with politeness.

FLORENCE KING

The English never speak to anyone unless they have been properly introduced (except in case of shipwreck).

PIERRE DANINOS

In France it is rude to let a conversation drop; in England it is rash to keep it up. No one there will blame you for silence. When you have not opened your mouth for three years, they will think: 'This Frenchman is a nice quiet fellow.'

ANDRÉ MAUROIS

In England, the art of conversation consists in knowing when to keep silent.

PIERRE DANINOS

My father and he had one of those English friendships which begin by avoiding intimacies and eventually eliminate speech altogether.

JORGE LUIS BORGES

The Englishman, be it noted, seldom resorts to violence; when he is sufficiently goaded he simply opens up, like the oyster, and devours his adversary.

HENRY MILLER

English life, while very pleasant, is rather bland. I expected kindness and gentility and I found it, but there is such a thing as too much couth.

S.J. PERELMAN

I never was intended for a miner, and you have to go into an Englishman's brain with a pick and shovel.   **GERTRUDE ATHERTON**

If an Englishman gets run down by a truck he apologises to the truck.   **JACKIE MASON**

Curious race, the English. Once they warm up, there's no telling what they'll do for you.   **S.J. PERELMAN**

English manners are excessive. Do you notice how many times people say, 'Thank you,' when they are in a shop?   **PHILIP ROTH**

You can be broke with more dignity in London than any of the world's large cities. The British, with their beautiful manners, never ask a stranger embarrassing questions.   **ELSA MAXWELL**

CHARACTER

An Englishman is a person who does things because they have been done before. An American is a person who does things because they haven't been done before.   **MARK TWAIN**

She's English, so if you really want to hurt her you could hold her down and make her watch the American version of anything British.   **JACK MCFARLAND,** *WILL AND GRACE*

There is more than mere humorous contrast between the famous placard in the wash-room of the British Museum: 'These Basins Are For Casual Ablutions Only,' and the familiar sign at American railroad-crossings: 'Stop! Look! Listen!' Between the two lies an abyss separating two cultures, two habits of mind, two diverging tongues.   **H.L. MENCKEN**

Sot comme un Anglois. [Drunk as an Englishman.]   **FRANCOIS RABELAIS, 1534**

Britain is like Mini-Me to America's Dr Evil – helping out in all our zany schemes to take over the world. **MARGE SIMPSON,** *THE SIMPSONS*

I'm half British, half American. My passport has an eagle with a tea bag in its beak. **BOB HOPE**

I left England when I was four because I found out I could never be King. **BOB HOPE**

By his father he is English, by his mother he is American – to my mind the blend which makes the perfect man. **MARK TWAIN ON WINSTON CHURCHILL**

Americans want to believe that the average Brit wears a bowler and a school tie and maintains a stiff upper lip and has a certain dry sense of humour; they do not want to be told that a good percentage of the British population are vulgar dimwits who care about nothing but shopping, alcohol, football and Posh Spice's navel. **JOE QUEENAN**

The English think of an opinion as something which a decent person, if he has the misfortune to have one, does all he can to hide. **MARGARET HALSEY**

English culture is basically homosexual in the sense that the men only really care about other men. **GERMAINE GREER**

Even crushed against his brother in the Tube, the average Englishman pretends desperately that he is alone. **GERMAINE GREER**

—What's the difference between a Pom and a bucket of shit?
—The bucket, dickhead. **AUSTRALIAN JOKE**

No Englishman could pass for an American.   **HEYWOOD BROUN**

The Anglo-Saxon conscience doesn't stop you from sinning; it just stops you from enjoying it.   **SALVADOR DE MADARIAGA**

In England, it is bad manners to be clever, to assert something confidently. It may be your personal view that two and two make four, but you must not state it in a self-assured way, because this is a democratic country and others may be of a different opinion.   **GEORGE MIKES**

Don't forget that the Englishman's soul is like the English skies: the weather is nearly always bad, but the climate is good.   **ANDRÉ MAUROIS**

The 'paper tiger' hero, James Bond, offering the whites a triumphant image of themselves, is saying what many whites want desperately to hear reaffirmed: I am still the White Man, lord of the land, licensed to kill, and the world is still an Empire at my feet.   **ELDRIDGE CLEAVER**

GREAT BRITAIN, ENGLAND AND THE ENGLISH

Britain is the place where the ruling class does not rule, the working class does not work and the middle class is not middle.   **GEORGE MIKES**

Racial characteristics: cold-blooded queers with nasty complexions and terrible teeth who once conquered half the world but still haven't figured out central heating.   **P.J. O'ROURKE**

No McTavish
Was ever lavish.   **OGDEN NASH**

The cold of the polar regions was nothing to the chill of an English bedroom.   **FRIDJOF NANSEN, NORWEGIAN EXPLORER**

For me, England is the most exotic place in the world: the British manners, the stratification of society. You see it even in people's shoes.

HENRI CARTIER-BRESSON

Great Britain has lost an Empire and has not yet found a role. **DEAN ACHESON**

The expression 'right as rain' must have been invented by an Englishman.

WILLIAM LYON PHELPS

There's an old saw to the effect that the sun never sets on the British Empire. While we were there, it never even rose. **RING LARDNER**

Britain would be a great country if you could roof it over.

AMERICAN TOURIST IN LONDON

It's easy to understand why the most beautiful poems about England in the spring were written by poets living in Italy at the time. **PHILIP DUNNE**

For months the sky has remained a depthless grey. Sometimes it rained, but mostly it was just dull. It was like living inside Tupperware. **BILL BRYSON**

It's so easy to dress in England. You just put on warm clothing.

DIANA BARRIE, *CALIFORNIA SUITE*

The traditional English summer is always the same. Either it's rainy with sunny intervals or sunny with rainy intervals. **PAT DUPRE**

—You're a fancy dresser. Are you English?
—Oh, no, I'm gay.
—Well, it's the same thing.
—If that weren't true, I'd find it offensive. **LORRAINE AND WILL,** *WILL AND GRACE*

One brief forecast would cover every weather situation in Britain: it may rain.

WILLIAM BLACK

Englishwomen's shoes look as if they had been made by someone who had often heard shoes described, but had never actually seen any.

MARGARET HALSEY

The man who is tired of London is tired of looking for a parking space.

PAUL THEROUX

Because of the large number of suspected members of al-Qaeda who visit the capital we call it Londonistan. **UNNAMED MEMBER OF FRENCH INTELLIGENCE**

—Here we are at Piccadilly Circus!
—Wow, what a shitty circus. No animals, no clowns. What a rip-off!

WAYNE AND GARTH, *WAYNE'S WORLD 2*

Oxford Street could be in Singapore if it had less litter; Saudi Arabia if it had fewer thieves; Saskatoon if it had more things you wanted to buy.

CLIVE JAMES

The London Underground is not a political movement.

JAMIE LEE CURTIS AS WANDA, *A FISH CALLED WANDA*

Visitors to British hotels will realise *Fawlty Towers* was really a documentary. **LONELY PLANET TRAVEL GUIDE TO BRITAIN**

Dear God of England, please let me go back to America. In return I will spell 'color' with a 'u' and I will use the metric system with every cubic millilitre in my – oh, I can't do it, it's so stupid! **HOMER SIMPSON, *THE SIMPSONS***

A woman expectorated out of the window of a crowded London bus, we had tepid baths in cracked bathtubs, choked over watery Brussels sprouts, and rowed on the Thames with an ex-colonel who blamed us for both wars.
M.P. DEAN, AMERICAN TOURIST

They warm their beers and chill their baths and boil all their food, including bread.
P.J. O'ROURKE

London is the cities of cities: only Athens has more Greek sculptures; only Florence has more Italian paintings; and only India has more Indian restaurants, because only London collects everything from everywhere. London is the world in one place.
CLIVE JAMES

The English: Are They Human?
G.J. REINER, BOOK TITLE, 1931

The world still consists of two clearly divided groups; the English and the foreigners. One group consists of less than 50 million people; the other of 3,950 million people. The latter group does not really count.
GEORGE MIKES

The English are best explained in terms of tea, roast beef, and rain. A people is first of all what it eats, drinks, and gets pelted with.
PIERRE DANINOS

Try free association. Think of England and say the first ten words that come into your head. I'll give it a go: Rain...Oxford...theatre... Magna Carta, cricket, tea, vicar, Scrooge, Mad Hatter, heather...
RICHARD CRITCHFIELD

England is a Jew-owned deer park, with tea rooms.
EZRA POUND

Aspects of life here – civility, courtesy, cosiness – have always bound Britons to their country. They are part of the British myth, along with lovely countryside, dogs and horses, rose gardens, the Armada, the Battle of Britain.

R.W. APPLE JR.

Living in England, provincial England, must be like being married to a stupid but exquisitely beautiful wife.

MARGARET HALSEY

Tourists who have never read Shakespeare go to Stratford-on-Avon and hope to get the same results by bumping their heads on low beams.

MARGARET HALSEY

Is there any place in Britain where Arthur isn't buried? For someone who almost certainly never lived, King Arthur turns up in an awful lot of final resting places.

JOE QUEENAN

I wish I could bring Stonehenge to Malawi to show there was a time when Britain had a savage culture.

HASTINGS BANDA, PRESIDENT OF MALAWI

It sometimes occurs to me that the British have more heritage than is good for them.

BILL BRYSON

Some people drive out to Hampstead Heath or Richmond Park, pull up all the windows, and go to sleep…the procedure is called 'spending a lovely afternoon in the open'.

GEORGE MIKES

England is never as great as when she is alone.

ANDRÉ MALRAUX

The English possess too many agreeable traits to permit them to be as much disliked as they think and hope they are.

AGNES REPPLIER

The Englishman's telephone box is his castle. Like the London taxi, it can be entered by a gentleman in his top hat. It protects the user's privacy, keeps him warm and is large enough for a small cocktail party. **MARY BLUME**

You won't find Anglophiles in England. They live abroad. **PAUL THEROUX**

The English people are like the English beer. Froth on top, dregs at the bottom, the middle excellent. **FRANCOIS-MARIE AROUET VOLTAIRE**

Philip Larkin was so English that he didn't even care much about Britain, and he rarely mentioned it. **CLIVE JAMES**

An English gentleman is a man with a passion for horses, playing with a ball, probably one broken bone in his body and in his pocket a letter to *The Times*. **RENÉ GIMPEL**

The moment I give a fig about what you think is the day that England produces a great chef, a world-class bottle of wine, and a car that has a decent electrical system. **FRASIER CRANE,** *FRASIER*

English humour resembles the Loch Ness Monster in that both are famous but there is a strong suspicion that neither of them exists. **GEORGE MIKES**

There was a time, beginning with the Oscar Wilde era, when even the butlers were wits, and served epigrams with the cucumber sandwiches. **ROBERT BENCHLEY**

The self-complaisant British sneer. **TOM TAYLOR**

I think the Europeans are hostile toward the English because the English have some irritating habits – the habit, for instance, of ending sentences with questions that sound like reprimands: 'You say it's difficult for you to tell because you haven't read the survey? Well, you'll have to read it, then, won't you?' See how snotty that sounds?   **CALVIN TRILLIN**

The English speak French worse than the French speak English, something that it is almost impossible to do.

JOE QUEENAN

And curving a contumelious lip,
Gorgonised me from head to foot,
With a stony British stare.   **ALFRED, LORD TENNYSON**

Oh, you English are so superior, aren't you? Well, would you like to know where you'd be without us, the old US of A, to protect you? I'll tell you. The smallest fucking province in the Russian Empire.   **KEVIN KLINE AS OTTO,** *A FISH CALLED WANDA*

Once Again, London Britches Falling Down
        HEADLINE ON THE DAVID BLUNKETT AFFAIR, *WASHINGTON POST*

If it is good to have one foot in England, it is still better, or at least as good, to have the other out of it.   **HENRY JAMES**

French parents worry if their children show no signs of early intelligence; English parents worry if they do.   **PIERRE DANINOS**

Single-sex education has its CONSEQUENCES: all the English seem to think about is sexual stagnation or ambivalence (how does the race survive?)   **LUCY ELLMANN,** *MAN OR MANGO?*

The English hate children. They keep their dogs at home and send their kids off to high-class kennels, called Eton and Harrow. **KATHY LETTE**

You know, in England, if you commit a crime, the police don't have a gun and you don't have a gun. So, if you commit a crime: 'Stop! Or I'll…say stop again!' **ROBIN WILLIAMS**

I always fall for Englishmen. It's the accent. They can say stupid things and still sound clever. **NEW YORK DEBUTANTE**

English men. Charm the knickers off you with their mellow vowels and frivolous verbiage, and then, once they'd got them off, panic and run. Or stay and whinge. **MARGARET ATWOOD**

I'm married to an English guy. He's a typical English guy. He's very reserved. In fact, it wasn't until after we were married that I actually knew he wanted to go out with me. **KIT HOLLERBACH**

George Sanders: Jeeves with a hard-on. **GARY KAMIYA**

Be modest. An Englishman will say, 'I have a little house in the country'; when he invites you to stay with him you will discover that the little house is a place with 300 bedrooms. If you are a world tennis-champion, say, 'Yes, I don't play too badly.' If you have crossed the Atlantic alone in a small boat, say, 'I do a little sailing.' **ANDRÉ MAUROIS**

The Tories in England had long imagined that they were enthusiastic about the monarchy, the church and beauties of the old English Constitution, until the day of danger wrung from them the confession that they are enthusiastic only about rent. **KARL MARX**

The Englishman likes to imagine himself at sea, the German in a forest. It is impossible to express the difference of their national identity more concisely.

ELIAS CANETTI

Many may wonder how the English acquired their reputation of not working as hard as the Continentals. I am able to solve the mystery. They acquired this reputation by not working as hard.

GEORGE MIKES

Industrialisation came to England but has since left.

P.J. O'ROURKE

Most Indians think England is a Punjabi country accidentally colonised by the English.

TARUN TEJPAL

When I drove racing cars for British teams they called me 'The Tadpole' because I was too small to be a frog.

ALAIN PROST

A Frenchman without a mistress is like an Englishman without a club.

PIERRE DANINOS

My formula for success is dress British, look Irish, think Jewish.

MURRAY KOFFLER

Pass a law to give every single whingeing bloody Pommie his fare home to England. Back to the smoke and the sun shining ten days a year and shit in the streets. Yer can have it.

THOMAS KENEALLY

Don't trust any Englishman who speaks French with a correct accent.

FRENCH PROVERB

The English take their pleasures sadly, after the fashion of their country.

DUC DE SULLY

The English find ill health not only interesting but respectable, and often experience death in the effort to avoid a fuss.   **PAMELA FRANKAU**

I hire the daughters of aristocrats because aristocrats don't have any chips on their shoulders so they don't mind making coffee and licking envelopes on the floor.   **NAIM ATTALAH**

Well, Marge, if I die here in England, there's one thing I want you to remember: don't buy any videotapes in England. They won't play in our VCR.   **HOMER SIMPSON,** *THE SIMPSONS*

There'll always be an England – even if it's in Hollywood.   **BOB HOPE**

BOOKS AND AUTHORS

All Shakespeare did was to string together a lot of old well-known quotations.   **H.L. MENCKEN**

A new book says that Shakespeare was gay. In fact, his boyfriend was the first guy to do Shakespeare in the park.   **DAVID CORRADO**

Jane Austen's books, too, are absent from this library. Just that one omission alone would make a fairly good library out of a library that hadn't a book in it.   **MARK TWAIN**

What has always puzzled me is why the English, who are so profoundly honest, write the best novels about thieves, crooks and lurid murderers.   **ELSA SCHIAPARELLI**

The novels of Barbara Pym are as palatable as a feather-light sponge cake baked by a canon's widow for the dessert table at the church bazaar in one of Pym's parishes. But inside the spun-sugar consistency is a tart or bittersweet filling.   **JEAN CAFFEY LYLES**

E.M. Forster never gets any further than warming the teapot. He's a rare fine hand at that. Feel this teapot. Is it not beautifully warm? Yes, but there ain't going to be no tea. **KATHERINE MANSFIELD**

SPORT

Thank you for this award. Thank you for nominating the film.
And thank you for inventing football.
WALTER SELLES, SPEECH ON WINNING A BAFTA FOR *THE MOTORCYCLE DIARIES*

Soccer? For Americans, it's 'a strange sport played by damaged people'.
ROBIN WILLIAMS

Football is an art more central to British culture than anything the Arts Council deigns to recognise. **GERMAINE GREER**

Mortar fire is to be preferred, of course, to British sports fans. **P.J. O'ROURKE**

Cricket is quite simple. You have two sides...ours and theirs, one out in the field and one in. Each man in the side that's in, goes out, and, when he's out, he comes in and the next man goes in until he's out. Then, when they have all been in and are all out, the side that's been in the field goes in and the side that's in goes out and tries to get out those coming in. Sometimes you get men still in and not out. Then when both sides have been in and out, including not-outs, that's the end of the game...it's really very simple. **ANON**

Cricket civilises people and creates good gentlemen. I want everyone to play cricket in Zimbawbe. I want ours to be a nation of gentlemen.
PRESIDENT ROBERT MUGABE

Rugby: The women sit, getting colder and colder, on a seat, getting harder and harder, watching oafs, getting muddier and muddier. **VIRGINIA GRAHAM**

I do love cricket – it's so very English.

SARAH BERNHARDT WATCHING A GAME OF FOOTBALL

I have seen cricket, and I know it isn't true.

DANNY KAYE

I want to play cricket, it doesn't seem to matter if you win or lose.

MEAT LOAF

Rugby is not like tea, which is good only in England, with English water and English milk. On the contrary, rugby would be better, frankly, if it were made in a Twickenham pot and warmed up in a Pyrenean cauldron.

DENNIS LALANNE

Scotland is a peculiar land that is the birthplace of golf and sport salmon fishing, a fact which may explain why it is also the birthplace of whisky.

HENRY BEARD

A traditional fixture at Wimbledon is the way the BBC TV commentary box fills up with British players eliminated in the early rounds.   **CLIVE JAMES**

SEX

Continental people have sex lives; the English have hot-water bottles.

GEORGE MIKES

It's no longer true that Continental people have sex lives whereas the English have hot-water bottles – the English now have electric blankets.

GEORGE MIKES

I don't find English men sexy. They're all queer or kinky. The last Pom I went to bed with said to me, 'Let's pretend you're dead.'   **GERMAINE GREER**

The trouble with upper-class Englishmen is that they just can't drive past a perversion without pulling over.   **KATHY LETTE**

FOOD AND DRINK

The English contribution to world culture: the chip.

KEVIN KLINE AS OTTO, *A FISH CALLED WANDA*

England is merely an island of beef flesh swimming in a warm gulf stream of gravy.

KATHERINE MANSFIELD

More than any other country in Western Europe, Britain remains a country where a traveller has to think twice before indulging in the ordinary food of ordinary people.

JOSEPH LELYVELD

I was well warned about English food, so it did not surprise me, but I do wonder, sometimes, how they ever manage to prise it up long enough to get a plate under it.

MARGARET HALSEY

In England, an elevator is called a 'lift', a mile is called a 'kilometer' and botulism is called 'steak and kidney pie'.

MARGE SIMPSON, *THE SIMPSONS*

England is the only country where food is more dangerous than sex.

JACKIE MASON

On the Continent, people have good food; in England people have good table manners.

GEORGE MIKES

The English have three vegetables and two of them are cabbage. **WALTER PAGE**

Even today, well-brought up English girls are taught to boil all vegetables for at least a month and a half, just in case one of the dinner guests comes without his teeth.

CALVIN TRILLIN

British scientists have found a substance that dulls the appetite. It's called British food.   JOHNNY ROBISH

As an American, I classify *I'm a Celebrity, Get me out of Here* in the category of impenetrable British mysteries – like beans on toast. MOLLY IVINS

Next to water tea is the Englishman's proper element. All classes consume it, and if one is out on the London streets early in the morning, one may see in many places small tables set up under the open sky, round which coal-carters and workmen empty their cups of this delicious beverage.

ERIK GUSTAF GEIJER, 1810

The Englishman who visits Mount Etna will carry his tea-kettle to the top.

RALPH WALDO EMERSON

Some day an earnest young scholar in pursuit of a suitably narrow research topic may turn to the works of British writer Barbara Pym and compile an exhaustive index of the occasions when pots of tea are brewed and consumed in her eleven novels.   JEAN CAFFEY LYLES

English coffee tastes the way a longstanding family joke sounds, when you try to explain it to outsiders. MARGARET HALSEY

The soup, thin and dark and utterly savourless, tasted as if it had been drained out of the umbrella stand.   MARGARET HALSEY

Custard is a detestable substance produced by the malevolent conspiracy of the hen, the cow and the cook.   AMBROSE BIERCE

What is Shredded Wheat? Is it a television presenter?   FRENCH JUDGE

Tea to the English is really a picnic indoors.

ALICE WALKER

Every country possesses the sort of cuisine it deserves. I used to think that the English cook the way they do because, through sheer technical deficiency, they had not been able to master the art of cooking. I have discovered to my stupefaction that the English cook that way because that is the way they like it.   **WAVERLEY ROOT**

English children are still raised to enjoy a range of foodstuffs that are more or less inedible. These include such offerings as the chip butty (French fries between slices of white bread) and perplexing toppings for toast, like canned spaghetti and baked beans and Marmite, a black, salty, yeasty spread that causes gagging in foreign nationals.   **REBECCA MEAD**

ROYALTY

She was neat.   **PRESIDENT GEORGE W. BUSH ON MEETING THE QUEEN**

No sooner had I invited the Queen to join me on the dance floor than the Marine band broke into a spirited rendition of 'The Lady and the Tramp'. Only narrowly did we avert an international incident, not to mention a court martial or two.   **GERALD FORD, FORMER US PRESIDENT**

She was slightly crackers, Diana – there is no question of it – but she had a great knack of identifying with people who weren't feeling exactly 100 per cent integrated because she herself was a bit of a fruit loop.

CLIVE JAMES

If you find you are to be presented to the Queen, do not rush up to her. She will eventually be brought round to you, like a dessert trolley at a good restaurant.   *LOS ANGELES TIMES*

When royalty leaves the room it is like getting a seed out of your tooth.

NORA PHIPPS

When you look at Prince Charles, don't you think someone in the Royal Family knew someone in the Royal Family.   **ROBIN WILLIAMS**

Don't forget that upper class twits and your Royal Family are tremendous tourist draws. Carry on the way you've been going, next thing you'll be doing is burning thatched roofs and smashing Toby jugs. Will tourists pay to come see vegans in Islington?   **P.J. O'ROURKE**

This guy kept saying to me, 'Lady Di, Lady Di.' I thought, I don't look anything like the late Princess of Wales. Then I realised – he was telling me what to do. I'm so mad at my father.   **WENDY LIEBMAN**

One day there will be only five kings left, hearts, spades, diamonds, clubs and England.   **KING FAROUK OF EGYPT**

INDEX

ALSO AVAILABLE FROM EBURY PRESS

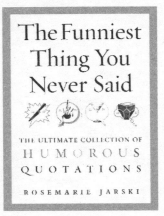

With over 6,000 quotations, from Oscar Wilde to Woody Allen, George Bernard Shaw to George W. Bush, Queen Victoria to Victoria Wood, *The Funniest Thing You Never Said* is packed full of the funniest quotes to delight and amuse anyone. With this book as your guide, you'll never again be short of a witty remark or riposte – it's the biggest and best humorous quote book there is!

You can order this book now by post:

The Funniest Thing You Never Said by Rosemarie Jarski
ISBN 0-09189-766-1   £7.99

FREE POST AND PACKING
Overseas customers allow £2.00 per paperback

- BY PHONE: 01624 677237
- BY POST: Random House Books
  C/o Bookpost, PO Box 29, Douglas, Isle of Man, IM99 1BQ
- BY FAX: 01624 670923
- BY EMAIL: bookshop@enterprise.net

Cheques (payable to Bookpost)
And credit cards accepted